ISTE's
Technology Facilitation
and
Leadership Standards

What Every K–12 Leader
Should Know and Be Able to Do

Jo Williamson and Traci Redish

International Society for Technology in Education
EUGENE, OREGON • WASHINGTON, DC

ISTE's Technology Facilitation and Leadership Standards
What Every K–12 Leader Should Know and Be Able to Do

Jo Williamson and Traci Redish

Director of Book Publishing: *Courtney Burkholder*
Acquisitions Editor: *Jeff V. Bolkan*
Production Editors: *Lynda Gansel, Lanier Brandau*
Production Coordinator: *Rachel Bannister*
Graphic Designer: *Signe Landin*
Rights and Permissions Administrator: *Lanier Brandau*
Copy Editor: *Kristin Landon*
Cover Design, Book Design and Production: *Kim McGovern*

Library of Congress Cataloging-in-Publication Data

Williamson, Jo.
   ISTE's technology facilitation and leadership standards : what every K-12 technologist should know and be able to do / Jo Williamson and Traci Redish. — 1st ed.
      p. cm.
   Includes bibliographical references.
   ISBN 978-1-56484-252-7 (pbk.)
   1. Educational technology—Study and teaching. 2. Information technology—Study and teaching. 3. Teachers—Training of. 4. Teachers—In-service training.   I. Redish, Traci. II. Title.
   LB1028.3.W554 2009
   371.33071
                                                                          2008049471

First Edition
ISBN: 978-1-56484-252-7

Printed in the United States of America

International Society for Technology in Education (ISTE)
Washington, DC, Office:
      1710 Rhode Island Ave. NW, Suite 900, Washington, DC 20036-3132
Eugene, Oregon, Office:
      180 West 8th Ave., Suite 300, Eugene, OR 97401-2916
Order Desk: 1.800.336.5191
Order Fax: 1.541.302.3778
Customer Service: orders@iste.org
Book Publishing: books@iste.org
Rights and Permissions: permissions@iste.org
Web: www.iste.org

About ISTE

The International Society for Technology in Education (ISTE) is the trusted source for professional development, knowledge generation, advocacy, and leadership for innovation. A nonprofit membership association, ISTE provides leadership and service to improve teaching, learning, and school leadership by advancing the effective use of technology in PK–12 and teacher education.

Home of the National Educational Technology Standards (NETS), the Center for Applied Research in Educational Technology (CARET), and the National Educational Computing Conference (NECC), ISTE represents more than 85,000 professionals worldwide. We support our members with information, networking opportunities, and guidance as they face the challenge of transforming education. To find out more about these and other ISTE initiatives, visit our website at **www.iste.org**.

As part of our mission, ISTE Book Publishing works with experienced educators to develop and produce practical resources for classroom teachers, teacher educators, and technology leaders. Every manuscript we select for publication is carefully peer-reviewed and professionally edited. We look for content that emphasizes the effective use of technology where it can make a difference—increasing the productivity of teachers and administrators; helping students with unique learning styles, abilities, or backgrounds; collecting and using data for decision making at the school and district levels; and creating dynamic, project-based learning environments that engage 21st-century learners. We value your feedback on this book and other ISTE products. E-mail us at **books@iste.org**.

About the Authors

Jo Williamson is an Assistant Professor in the Educational Leadership Department at Kennesaw State University (KSU). She is also the Associate Director of the KSU Educational Technology Center (ETC) for the Georgia Department of Education (GaDOE). In addition to her work at KSU, Dr. Williamson has also served as the Director of Educational Technology and Media for GaDOE, the Director of Area One Learning Technology Hub for the Illinois State Board of Education, and the Director of Technology for Public School District #60, Waukegan, IL. In these capacities, she has consulted with school systems and government agencies on various research, evaluation, professional development and strategic planning initiatives. Currently, she is designing and implementing instruction for aspiring technology leaders via new master's and doctoral programs at KSU. Her research interests include studying how technology facilitators and leaders implement successful technology programs in public schools. She holds an BA from Olivet Nazarene University, Kankakee, IL, an MA in Curriculum & Instruction from the University of Kansas, Lawrence and a PhD in Curriculum and Instruction from the University of Illinois, Urbana-Champaign.

Traci Redish is an Associate Professor in the Educational Leadership Department at Kennesaw State University (KSU). She also serves as the Director of the KSU Educational Technology Center (ETC) for the Georgia Department of Education (GaDOE). Dr. Redish is most well-known for the development of InTech-a premier technology integration professional learning program adopted in Georgia as an effective way of educating classroom teachers in technology integration. To present, over 80,000 Georgia educators have completed the InTech professional learning program. InTech has been adopted in other states and internationally. Dr. Redish is the current Chair of the Georgia Educational Technology Conference (GaETC) and the former Program Co-Chair of NECC 2007 in Atlanta, Georgia. She is the author or co-author of numerous publications on technology and education and serves in leadership roles in a variety of technology-oriented PK–12 organizations in Georgia, including the Georgia Educational Technology Consortium and the Georgia School Boards Association's advisory board for technology. Her current research interest includes the study of technology leadership in education, and her scholarship includes articles and conference presentations in the field of educational technology. Dr. Redish completed her undergraduate and graduate studies in education at Georgia State University.

Acknowledgments

We would like to thank the following people who made this book possible:

The committee who drafted the Technology Facilitation (TF) and Technology Leadership (TL) standards. These standards have helped us professionally and serve as an organizing framework for our day-to-day work with graduate students and practicing K–12 technologists.

The ISTE staff and volunteers. ISTE's work on the National Educational Technology Standards has been one of the most important catalysts for advancing K–12 learning in schools. In addition, ISTE's conferences, books, and other resources have been our main source of professional learning and renewal. We especially want to thank Lynn Nolan, Senior Director of Education Leadership, and Leslie Conery, Deputy Chief Executive Officer, for their encouragement during the early stages of this book. They have reminded us how open minds and just a few kind words can make a difference.

The ISTE publications staff, especially Jeff Bolkan, our editor for this project, and Anita McAnear, who helped us write and publish our first article on the TF/TL standards in ISTE's *Leading & Learning with Technology*.

Our colleagues, especially Mike Dishman, Hoke Wilcox, and Brent Williams, and the anonymous peer reviewers who read the first draft of this book and gave us great suggestions for improvement.

The technology facilitators and leaders who allowed us to construct case studies of their practice.

All those who helped us find case study participants from around the country, especially Christine Fox, Director of Professional Development and Research, State Education Technology Directors' Association (SETDA); Ferdi Serim, Southwest Region Director, National Network of Digital Schools (NNDS); Mike Lawrence, Executive Director, California Computer-Using Educators (CUE); and Marlene Johnson, Technology Specialist, Maryland Department of Education.

Kennesaw State University for giving us a wonderful place to pursue our work.

The K–12 technology leaders who mentored us as we learned how to do our jobs—often without the training, standards, books, and traditions that are available today. A special thanks to Bernajean Porter, whose work greatly influenced Chapter 8.

Our students for teaching us about technology and leadership as we learn together.

Our husbands and other family members, who have been very supportive of this project and our work in K–12 technology.

Contents

Chapter Three
TF/TL STANDARD III
Teaching, Learning, and the Curriculum 57

Chapter Four
TF/TL STANDARD IV
Assessment and Evaluation 77

Chapter Eight
TF/TL STANDARD VIII

Leadership and Vision

Conclusion

Appendix A
The TF Standards

Appendix B
The TL Standards

Appendix C
Technology Facilitation and Leadership Scoring Rubrics

Preface

Purpose and Overview of Book

The overarching purpose of this book is to support the growth and development of well-prepared, capable educational technology professionals who will shape the future of K–12 technology integration to enhance student achievement.

Using the ISTE/NCATE Technology Facilitation (TF) and Technology Leadership (TL) standards as a guiding framework, this book describes the knowledge and skills needed to be a successful technology facilitator at the school-building level and an effective technology leader at the district, regional, state, and national levels. This book also describes how these standards can contribute to the improved performance and professional status of technology facilitators and leaders in the field of education.

We are passionate about this topic. As we began our careers in K–12 technology, we often held jobs that had no precedent, no job descriptions, and no tradition to follow. Very few of our peers, friends, and family members understood our work. It was tremendously difficult to answer the common question, "What do you do?" at social gatherings, and the response was often a rather bewildered, "Oh, that's nice."

We also struggled to find formal preparation academic programs that prepared us for our work. Instructional technology courses taught us about technology and how it would transform education, but they didn't teach about designing and delivering professional learning, managing budgets and staff, constructing a shared vision, or leading change. We sought this knowledge through other sources, including peers, professional organizations (such as ISTE, CoSN, ASCD, and NSDC), and educational leadership programs.

Because of our experiences, we were naturally drawn to helping aspiring and practicing K–12 technology facilitators and leaders in schools and districts. We currently pursue this work in two ways. First, we direct Kennesaw State University's Educational Technology Center (KSU ETC), a partnership between KSU and the Georgia Department of Education. KSU ETC supports the inservice professional learning of technology facilitators and leaders in eleven school districts in the metropolitan Atlanta area. Second, we have designed and launched an MEd in Educational Leadership with a technology concentration and an EdS/EdD in Instructional Technology. Both of these degrees are interdisciplinary in nature and enacted as partnerships with other academic departments, such as Educational Leadership.

In the process of designing professional learning programs through the ETC and graduate programs for KSU, we found a treasure—ISTE's TF and TL standards. Reading the standards for the first time was very personal. The standards captured the complexity and interdisciplinary nature of our day-to-day tasks. Even after 15 years in the instructional technology field, the standards helped us solidify our professional identities and validate our work in a way we had not experienced before. Because the standards were approved by both ISTE and the National Council for Accreditation of Teacher Education (NCATE), we chose these standards to guide our professional learning and graduate programs. We also committed ourselves to sharing these standards with others.

We have observed that although the National Educational Technology Standards for Students (NETS•S), Teachers (NETS•T), and Administrators (NETS•A) have enjoyed broad attention, adoption, and influence on practice, ISTE's TF/TL standards are not as well known and applied in K–12 settings. In fact, many practicing K–12 educators—including aspiring and practicing technologists—do not know that these ISTE standards exist (Snelbecker & Miller, 2005; Williamson & Redish, 2007).

Therefore, as we constructed this text, we kept the needs and interests of the following readers in mind:

- Educational leaders, such as principals, directors, and superintendents, who are responsible for certifying, hiring, evaluating, and retaining technology professionals in schools

- Practicing technology professionals who want to improve and/or better understand their current facilitation and leadership roles

- Building-level technology facilitators who would like to assume broader technology leadership roles at the district, regional, state, or national level

- Teachers who aspire to be lead teachers or building-level technology facilitators charged with helping others use technology for teaching and learning

- University faculty preparing technology facilitators through degree and certification programs

- Professional development providers who support the learning of practicing K–12 technology professionals

- Graduate students in TF/TL aligned programs who are striving to show mastery of the TF/TL standards and performance indicators through practicum, portfolio, or other field-based experiences

- Employees from state and federal governments, intermediate service agencies, not-for-profit agencies, and professional organizations who build technology leadership capacity in school systems

Following this preface, an introduction to the book provides a brief overview of the history, importance, structure, and terminology associated with the standards. Within this discussion, we assert that the TF/TL standards contribute to specific objectives in ways that other national education technology standards cannot. These objectives include:

- Recruiting and training future K–12 technology facilitators and leaders

- Improving the performance of current K–12 technologists

- Validating the roles of K–12 technology professionals

- Shaping the identity of K–12 school technologists

- Building successful human resource structures, such as performance expectations, evaluation instruments, and professional learning programs for K–12 technology professionals

- Influencing research related to the unique needs of technology facilitation and leadership

Toward achieving these objectives, chapters 1–8 are designed to help readers understand the meaning, importance, and practical implications of the following eight overarching standard areas:

- Technology Operations and Concepts

- Planning and Designing Learning Environments and Experiences

- Teaching, Learning, and the Curriculum

- Assessment and Evaluation

- Productivity and Professional Practice

- Social, Legal, Ethical, and Human Issues

- Procedures, Policies, Planning, and Budgeting for Technology Environments

- Leadership and Vision

Each chapter has a similar format containing six sections:

1. **Current Context.** The first section of each chapter highlights the current context in which technology facilitators and leaders are enacting each standard. The current context synthesizes research, prevalent issues, terms, and concepts from a wide variety of sources. These sections will provide an orientation for educators unfamiliar with the issues surrounding educational technology. Experienced K–12 technologists and other educational leaders, such as principals, curriculum directors, and superintendents, will benefit from a high-level, multisource briefing on the current state of technology in schools.

2. **Implementing the Standard.** This section contains charts and descriptions of each performance standard, performance indicator, and performance task. It is designed to help readers gain an in-depth understanding of the topics addressed in the TF/TL standards. By displaying the TF and the TL performances in side-by-side charts, the section serves to illustrate both the differences and the interdependence between the work of technology facilitators and leaders.

3. **Performance Scenarios.** Performance scenarios for each standard provide hypothetical but typical situations in which technology facilitators and leaders might apply each standard. These scenarios may help those unfamiliar with the practice of technology facilitators and leaders better understand their functions in educational settings. This section may be especially useful to graduate students preparing for field experiences or deciding how to align their experiences to specific TF/TL standards in portfolios.

4. **Case Study.** Each chapter also contains a case study of a practicing technology facilitator or leader who has enacted some aspect of the TF/TL standards discussed. Case studies serve the same purpose as scenarios, but they are longer and describe real-life situations. They are designed not only to illustrate the standards in action, but also to show how practicing technologists grapple with the issues described in the current context.

5. **Discussion Questions.** Following the case studies, each chapter lists several discussion questions that are designed to stimulate ongoing conversations among both practicing professionals and aspiring technologists about the work and roles of school technologists and the contemporary issues they face.

6. **Resources.** In addition to professional works already cited in the current context sections, each chapter concludes with a list of resources for those who would like to continue building their knowledge and skills related to the TF/TL standards. At the beginning of each Resources section, a Spotlight Resource highlights a tool or source of information that will be especially helpful to enhancing performance.

The book's conclusion offers several practical suggestions for how the TF/TL standards might be used to improve the quality of technology facilitation and leadership in schools. As most readers will choose this book because they want to become familiar with the TF/TL standards and accompanying performance rubrics, these documents are provided in the appendixes.

We have designed the content of this book to encourage the high-quality technology facilitation and leadership necessary for technology advancement and improved student learning. We hope this book achieves this purpose and more.

References

Snelbecker, G., & Miller, S. (2005). ILT specialists as facilitators of technology integration: Implications for teachers and administrators. Mid-Atlantic Regional Technology in Education Consortium *EDTECH REVIEW*, *Series 4*.

Williamson, J., & Redish, T. (2007). Building technology facilitators and leaders: A standards-based approach. *Leading & Learning with Technology* 34(8), 22–26.

Introduction

Introduction to the TF/TL Standards

In fall 2001, the International Society for Technology in Education (ISTE) partnered with the National Council for Accreditation of Teacher Education (NCATE) to publish the Technology Facilitation (TF) and the Technology Leadership (TL) standards.

The TF standards are designed for lead teachers or instructional technology specialists who facilitate technology integration at the building level. The TL standards are designed for K–12 coordinators, specialists, or directors who lead technology programs at the district, regional, state, or national levels.

Many educators who fill these facilitation and leadership roles hold professional positions with the word *technology* in their titles (i.e., technology lead teacher, technology coordinator, technology specialist, or technology director). In other cases, technology facilitation and leadership functions are assigned to educators with more traditional instructional and administrative titles (McLeod, 2003). For example, when full-time technology coordinators are not assigned to a school building, other educators such as technology-savvy teachers, math/science coordinators, media specialists, literacy coaches, and instructional lead teachers often assume the unofficial roles of technology facilitators. Similarly, district-level technology leadership roles are often added on to existing roles assumed by the curriculum director or even the chief financial officer.

Regardless of what titles educators hold, these standards are designed for those who not only use technology effectively themselves, but also help other educators integrate technology into daily practice. To accomplish their work, technology facilitators and leaders provide their colleagues with high-quality professional learning. They also ensure that other essential conditions for successful technology programs are in place.

Importance of the TF/TL Standards

Like the NETS•S, NETS•T, and NETS•A, the TF/TL standards were intended to influence university preparation programs, district/state policies, and inservice professional development in the field (Conery, 2005; Roblyer, 2003; Thomas & Knezek, 2002). However, the TF/TL standards address unique objectives related to improving K–12 technology programs that other national technology standards do not. The following is a list of the most important of these objectives:

Recruiting and training future technology facilitators and leaders.

One of the primary purposes of the TF/TL standards is to enable high-quality university preparation programs for technology leaders and facilitators. Because the NETS•T standards are prerequisites to the TF/TL, most preparation programs for technology specialists occur at the graduate education level and yield add-on endorsements for master's, specialist's, or doctoral degrees. Because the TF/TL standards are approved by NCATE, they provide university faculty with the framework they need for designing curriculum, evaluating candidates/programs, and securing accreditation from NCATE. In fact, the first ISTE publication on the TF/TL standards was designed to help university staff complete these tasks (Twomey, Shamburg, & Zieger, 2006). For these reasons, university faculty and graduate students may be the most familiar of all audiences with the TF/TL standards.

Improving the performance of current technology facilitators and leaders.

Although university preparation and certification programs are important, ongoing professional learning in the field is also necessary to maintain a prepared workforce. Because technology facilitation and leadership roles are rather new in education, many practicing technology professionals have had little or no formal preparation for their roles. Even for those who are formally trained, the dynamic nature of the field amplifies the need to keep pace with emerging technological knowledge. To address these needs, the TF/TL standards provide practicing technology facilitators and leaders with a framework to reflect on their own performance and identify areas where they need professional development. The standards also provide a framework for the development and delivery of new inservice professional learning programs for technologists. The standards should be especially beneficial to district technology leaders who must provide professional learning for technology facilitators on their local teams. University outreach centers, intermediate service agencies, and not-for-profit organizations should also find the standards especially valuable as they attempt to provide comprehensive professional learning programs for practicing K–12 technologists.

Validating the role of K–12 technology professionals.

Formal positions for technology facilitators and leaders in education are relatively new when compared to other, more established educational roles, such as principals, teachers, media specialists, and curriculum directors. Although many support positions for technology have been established in schools and districts, other educators, board members, and community stakeholders may not understand the full range of what technology professionals do or why technology facilitation/leadership is a critical component to school improvement. This lack of understanding is common when new roles emerge in an organization. In these instances, educating stakeholders is an important first step to formalizing, justifying, and securing new types of positions in the local system. Increased understanding is also important to ensure that technologists are awarded professional status, credibility, and compensation equivalent to other educators with similar duties and responsibilities. As an additional strategy to formalize the role of technologists, some states have chosen to implement technology endorsement or certification programs based on the TF/TL standards. These states include Louisiana, Illinois, Pennsylvania, and North Carolina (Twomey, Shamburg, & Zieger, 2006).

Shaping the identity of school technologists.

Forming a professional identity is similar to validation, but much more personal. Constructing a coherent professional identity refers to the ways in which the school technologists perceive themselves and interpret their work. Because instructional technologists lack the history, tradition, and formal acculturation processes that more established educational positions enjoy, this construction process is more difficult. However, the standards can assist technologists in reflecting on what they do, forming a professional identity congruent to their work, and explaining their roles to others. The TF/TL standards provide a foundation on which these professional identities can emerge. Because the TF/TL documents encompass a broad set of performance standards and tasks, they are likely to stretch technologists' professional identities in new and positive ways.

Building successful human resource structures/tools for technology.

After positions are validated and formalized in an organization, there is still a great deal of human resource work to do to maintain, monitor, and enhance professional performance and capacity. For example, educational leaders must reflect on the current capacity to deliver technology leadership and facilitation in their school, district, or region. Key questions may include: Are all the TF/TL standards being implemented? Are there enough personnel to implement all the standards? Is there a good balance between leaders operating at a broader strategic level and facilitators implementing day-to-day instructional support? Are facilitation and leadership roles well defined, well articulated, and symbiotic? Are existing personnel addressing the standards? Are they currently able to do so? Why or why not?

To answer these questions and others, decision makers will need tools to guide their reflection and assessment. The TF/TL standards, as they now stand, can serve as an initial guide for assessing current conditions, but the standards have potential to structure the development of more specific, customized types of tools. These tools include more formal reflection guides, job descriptions, checklists, and other types of instruments for evaluating technology facilitators and leaders and establishing performance goals customized to local needs.

Influencing research related to the unique needs of technology facilitation and leadership.

Although some researchers have described the work of school technologists and explored their relationship to technology integration (Ausband, 2006; Davidson, 2003; Hearrington & Strudler, 2007; Lesisko, 2005; McLeod, 2003; Reinhart & Slowinski, 2004; Snelbecker & Miller, 2005; Strudler, 1995–96, 2001; Strudler, Falba, & Hearrington, 2005; Wright & Lesisko, 2007), more research is needed to learn about what technology facilitators and leaders are doing and should be doing to advance effective technology use in schools. There is also a need to better understand how they help others and which strategies are most effective and why. This practical and theoretical knowledge is critical for designing and implementing effective graduate preparation programs and professional learning opportunities for school technologists. The TF/TL standards provide a comprehensive, descriptive framework for technology facilitation and leadership that may guide new research.

Structure of the TF/TL Standards

Even though the TF/TL documents are similar, they are actually two separate sets of standards—one set for facilitators at the building level (TF) and another for leaders at the district, state, regional, and national levels (TL). Each is composed of the following components:

- Standards categories (8)
- Performance standards (8)
- Performance indicators (32)
- Performance tasks (78)

The standards categories and the performance indicators are the same for both the TF and the TL, but the performance standards and sample performance tasks for each are different. To illustrate these concepts, Figure 0.1 provides a comparison of TF and TL Standard I.A. and the components for each standard.

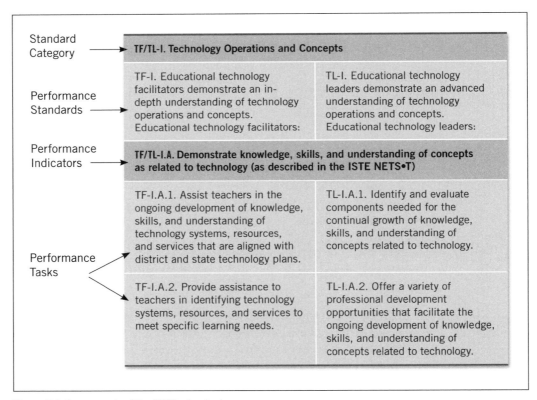

Figure 0.1 Components of the TF/TL standards

Performance Standards

Like other national education standards, the TF/TL standard categories are followed by actual performance standards. The TF/TL documents each have eight performance standards, and these standards are different for facilitators and leaders.

Because the TF standards serve as prerequisites to the TL standards, the two sets of standards are constructed as a continuum for technology professionals who begin their work in local schools as technology facilitators and then broaden their sphere of influence and increase their responsibilities over time as technology leaders. The TF and TL standards differ in the following ways:

- **Location of performance.** In many cases, technology facilitators and technology leaders engage in similar activities, but the only difference is the location of their performances. In general, facilitators perform mainly at the school level, and leaders operate at the district, state, or regional levels (see TF/TL Standard II).

- **Breadth, depth, and complexity of performance.** Facilitators are expected to have in-depth knowledge, whereas leaders are expected to have advanced knowledge (see TF/TL Standard I). Facilitators must apply, implement, assist, promote, and contribute, but leaders also design, disseminate, evaluate, and develop. Although facilitators implement the strategic directions and apply materials that others develop, leaders are often responsible for creating strategic plans, programs, and materials that meet specific needs. In many cases, technology leaders are responsible for ensuring that technology facilitators have the resources, knowledge, and skills necessary to promote effective technology use at the school level. For example, in TF/TL Standard IV, facilitators apply technology for assessment and evaluation, but leaders are expected to construct and communicate a research-based rationale for the same types of activities. These differences in breadth, depth, and complexity are also illustrated in TF/TL Standards III, V, VI, VII, and VIII.

Table 0.1 provides a side-by-side comparison of the TF/TL standards to highlight how they differ in location, breadth, depth, and complexity of performance.

TABLE 0.1 ▪ Comparison of TF/TL standards

Technology Facilitation (TF)	Technology Leadership (TL)
I. Technology Operations and Concepts	
TF-I. Educational technology facilitators demonstrate an in-depth understanding of technology operations and concepts.	TL-I. Educational technology leaders demonstrate an advanced understanding of technology operations and concepts.
II. Planning and Designing Learning Environments and Experiences	
TF-II. Educational technology facilitators plan, design, and model effective learning environments and multiple experiences supported by technology.	TL-II. Educational technology leaders assist by planning, designing, and modeling effective learning environments and experiences supported by technology at the district/state/regional level.
III. Teaching, Learning, and the Curriculum	
TF-III. Educational technology facilitators apply and implement curriculum plans that include methods and strategies for utilizing technology to maximize student learning.	TL-III. Educational technology leaders model, design, and disseminate curriculum plans that include methods and strategies for applying technology to maximize student learning.
IV. Assessment and Evaluation	
TF-IV. Educational technology facilitators apply technology to facilitate a variety of effective assessment and evaluation strategies.	TL-IV. Educational technology leaders communicate research on the use of technology to implement effective assessment and evaluation strategies.
V. Productivity and Professional Practice	
TF-V. Educational technology facilitators apply technology to enhance and improve personal productivity and professional practice.	TL-V. Educational technology leaders design, develop, evaluate, and model products created using technology resources to improve and enhance their productivity and professional practice.
VI. Social, Ethical, Legal, and Human Issues	
TF-VI. Educational technology facilitators understand the social, ethical, legal, and human issues surrounding the use of technology in PK–12 schools and assist teachers in applying that understanding in their practice.	TL-VI. Educational technology leaders understand the social, ethical, legal, and human issues surrounding the use of technology in PK–12 schools and develop programs facilitating application of that understanding in practice throughout their district/region/state.
VII. Procedures, Policies, Planning, and Budgeting for Technology Environments	
TF-VII. Educational technology facilitators promote the development and implementation of technology infrastructure, procedures, policies, plans, and budgets for PK–12 schools.	TL-VII. Educational technology leaders coordinate development and direct implementation of technology infrastructure procedures, policies, plans, and budgets for PK–12 schools.

(Continued)

Technology Facilitation (TF)	Technology Leadership (TL)
VIII. Leadership and Vision	
TF-VIII. Educational technology facilitators will contribute to the shared vision for campus integration of technology and foster an environment and culture conducive to the realization of the vision.	TL-VIII. Educational technology leaders will facilitate development of a shared vision for comprehensive integration of technology and foster an environment and culture conducive to the realization of the vision.

Performance Indicators

Performance indicators follow the TF/TL standards, just as they do in each of the NETS. At the performance indicator level, the standards are further defined. Indicators accomplish this greater level of detail by including between two and six additional elements or dimensions of performance per standard. These additional components help explain how specific types of knowledge, skills, and dispositions must be enacted to achieve the broader TF/TL standards.

For example in TF/TL Standard I, the broad performance standard suggests that K–12 technologists must have either an in-depth (TF) or an advanced (TL) understanding of technology operations and concepts. However, the performance indicators provide more information on what this understanding entails. In TF/TL Standard I, the performance indicators highlight that technologists must be able to enact technology concepts as found in the NETS•T and to stay informed about current and emerging technologies (see Figure 0.2). In this way, the performance indicators reveal the critical elements, components, or dimensions to achieving the TF/TL standards. With these performance indicators, facilitators and leaders gain a much deeper understanding of what a standard really means in practice.

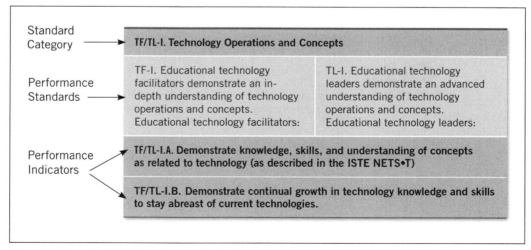

Figure 0.2 Example of TF/TL performance indicators

Performance Tasks and Rubrics

In the TF/TL standards, the performance standards and indicators are supplemented with 72 sample performance tasks. These tasks provide learners with examples of authentic tasks that facilitators and leaders should be able to perform in their daily work. Of course the list does not incorporate every type of task that K–12 technologists perform in schools, but the collection is comprehensive and representative.

In the TF/TL standards, the performance indicators are identical (32), but the performance tasks (78) are different (see Fig. 0.3). Just as represented in the performance standards, the TF and the TL indicators and tasks also vary by locale, depth of knowledge, and depth of performance.

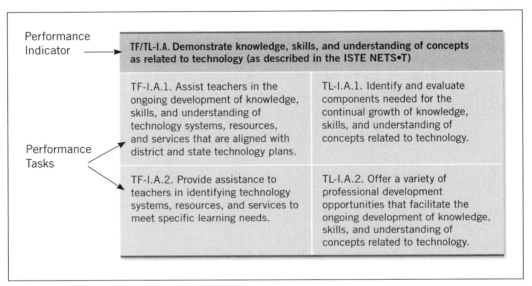

Figure 0.3 Example of TF/TL performance tasks

In addition, the TF and TL standards documents are each accompanied by a performance rubric (see Appendix C). These rubrics include the performance indicator from the actual standards document in the Meets Standard column, but the documents also provide sample performance tasks that approach and exceed each standard. With these additional performance tasks, the TF/TL performance rubrics most clearly depict the continuum of technology facilitation and technology leadership performances. Performances that exceed expectations on the facilitator rubric are identical to those that approach expectations on the leadership rubric. When considered together, the documents create a powerful tool for understanding what technology professionals must know and be able to do in K–12 education. Figure 0.4 provides an example from the TF/TL rubrics for Standard I.A. that illustrates this continuum of performance.

Technology TF/TL Standard I.A.1. Rubric

Approaches TF Standard	Meets TF Standard	Exceeds TF Standard/ Approaches TL Standard	Meets TL Standard	Exceeds TL Standard
Make appropriate choices about technology systems, resources, and services that are aligned with district and state standards.	Assist teachers in the ongoing development of knowledge, skills, and understanding of technology systems, resources, and services that are aligned with district and state technology plans.	Conduct needs assessment to determine baseline data on teachers' knowledge, skills, and understanding of concepts related to technology.	Identify and evaluate components needed for the continual growth of knowledge, skills, and understanding of concepts related to technology.	Develop and implement a professional development model that ensures continual growth in knowledge, skills, and understanding of concepts related to technology.

Figure 0.4 Example of TF/TL performance rubrics

As shown in Table 0.2, the TF/TL standards are nearly identical in structure and content to the NETS•S (2007), NETS•T (2008), and NETS•A (2002) except for the performance tasks and rubrics. As illustrated in the table, the NETS•S, NETS•T, and NETS•A do not have performance tasks attached to them. This may be one reason why the TF/TL standards are seen as being more complex than other sets of standards. However, we believe that in reality, they are simply more comprehensive and developed.

TABLE 0.2 ▪ Component comparison for NETS•S, NETS•T, NETS•A, and TF/TL standards

Component	Number of each NETS for Students (NETS•S) component	Number of each NETS for Teachers (NETS•T) component	Number of each NETS for Administrators (NETS•A) component	Number of each Technology Facilitation/ Leadership (TF/TL) standards component*
Standard Categories	6	5	6	8
Standards	6	5	6	8
Performance Indicators	14	20	31	32
Performance Tasks	0	0	0	78
Performance Rubrics	0	0	0	1

* The number of components is the same for both TF and TL standards.

These additional resources are especially useful to aspiring and practicing technologists. Graduate students can plan and complete field experiences that closely approximate the work of professionals in the field. University faculty can use TF/TL rubrics to develop authentic assignments, to assess candidate performance, and to provide evidence of student mastery of standards for program evaluation and accreditation purposes. Practicing technology facilitators and leaders can reflect on their own performance. Practicing educators can assess current levels of facilitation/leadership and identify gaps in performance in their local settings. Human resource staff and technology leaders who supervise other technologists can use rubrics in developing job performance instruments and professional learning goals and objectives.

Summary of the Standards

In this introduction we have provided a brief overview of the TF/TL standards and how they are important to the field of educational technology. As described in this introduction, these standards fulfill specific objectives that other national education technology standards cannot. The research literature refers to technology facilitators and leaders by many different names. Perhaps "technology coordinator," "specialist," and "director" are the most common, but other names are also used. Zhao, Pugh, Sheldon, and Byers (2002) use the term "translators." Nardi and O'Day (1999) refer to the presence of "gardeners." Orlikowski, Yates, Okamura, and Fujimoto (1999) note the presence of "technology use mediators." In spite of these different names, however, the research clearly touts the importance of these technologists to contextualize tools for local use and to teach others how to use new technologies. This research suggests that educators with the skills, knowledge, and dispositions represented in the TF/TL standards are critical to realizing technology's potential to support K–12 learning.

We also explained the structure and terminology associated with the TF/TL standards. This information will provide readers with a foundation for processing the content of each TF/TL standard as it is presented in subsequent chapters. In review, the following represent the most important concepts:

- The TF/TL standards have eight broad Standard Categories to help readers organize and understand the topics to be addressed in the standards.

- The TF/TL standards have eight Performance Standards. They are identified in the TF/TL documents with a Roman numeral (I–VIII).

- Each standard also has Performance Indicators. These performance indicators are represented with a letter (A–F). The performance indicators detail elements, components, or dimensions of each standard as it is enacted in day-to-day performances.

- The sample Performance Tasks are the most detailed level of the TF/TL standards. They create a portrait of how knowledge and skills are applied in the most common types of daily work. They also describe what technology professionals must be able to do to demonstrate professional competency and what other educators should be able to expect from technology professionals. These performance tasks are represented with an Arabic numeral (1–8).

These key concepts are useful in understanding what each level of the standard means and how it can be used. This Introduction also establishes a foundation for the upcoming chapters, which unpack the content associated with each performance standard, indicator, and task associated with the eight overarching categories associated with technology facilitation and leadership.

A Note on Terminology and Usage

Although the terms "performance indicator" and "performance task" are useful to distinguish between the various levels or components of standards, they are not always used in practice. In essence the performance standard, the performance indicator, and the performance task are all considered part of the TF/TL standard. In conversation, educators often refer to all the components as "standards" and use the letters and numerals to identify the level of the standard. For example, practitioners will most likely say *Standard TF-I.A.1.* instead of *Performance Task TF-I.A.1.* to refer to the following:

> Assist teachers in the ongoing development of knowledge, skills, and understanding of technology systems, resources, and services that are aligned with district and state technology plans (TF-I.A.1.).

TF/TL Standards and ISTE's Essential Conditions

ISTE's NETS are accompanied by essential conditions necessary to leverage technology for learning. Because one of the primary functions of technology facilitators and leaders is to ensure that these essential conditions are in place while constantly monitoring their status, readers are probably already seeing a tight alignment between the TF/TL standards and the essential conditions for effective technology use. To ensure that readers make this connection, Table 0.3 outlines how each of the TF/TL standards is related to ISTE's essential conditions.

Of course, the alignment shown in Table 0.3 is somewhat simplistic in some respects. The standards and the essential conditions relate to one another in a fluid and complex way. Virtually every standard and every essential condition interrelate in some way. Yet specific patterns emerge, and some standards are more closely related to each of the essential conditions areas than others. The only exception to this rule is TF/TL Standard VI. We believe that social, legal, ethical, and/or human issues are present when implementing all of the essential conditions. This Standard is pervasive, and we support our case in Chapter 6. In spite of the risk of oversimplifying, we believe the relationships presented are strong and helpful. Exploring the relationship between the TF/TL standards is one more way to help others understand the standards and to illustrate the importance of technology facilitators and leaders in establishing successful technology programs in schools.

We have chosen to use the NETS•S for our alignment because these conditions are the most recently revised and comprehensive. All essential conditions included in the NETS•S are represented in the NETS•T and NETS•A, as well.

In addition to Table 0.3, readers will find a brief essential conditions commentary in each chapter. This commentary will remind readers how each standard is related to at least one of ISTE's Essential Conditions.

TABLE 0.3 ▪ Relationship between ISTE's Essential Conditions and the TF/TL standards

ISTE's Essential Conditions (NETS•S)	Addressed in the following ISTE TF/TL standards
Shared Vision Proactive leadership in developing a shared vision for educational technology among school personnel, parents, students, and the community.	Standard VI: Social, Legal, Ethical and Human Issues Standard VIII: Leadership and Vision
Implementation Planning A systemic plan aligned with a shared vision for school effectiveness and student learning through the infusion of technology and digital learning resources.	Standard VI: Social, Legal, Ethical and Human Issues Standard VII: Procedures, Policies, Planning, and Budgeting for Technology Environments Standard VIII: Leadership and Vision
Consistent and Adequate Funding Ongoing funding to support technology infrastructure, personnel, digital resources, and staff development.	Standard VI: Social, Legal, Ethical and Human Issues Standard VII: Procedures, Policies, Planning, and Budgeting for Technology Environments Standard VIII: Leadership and Vision
Equitable Access Robust and reliable access to current and emerging technologies, digital resources, and connectivity for all students, teachers, staff, and school leaders.	Standard VI: Social, Legal, Ethical and Human Issues Standard VII: Procedures, Policies, Planning, and Budgeting for Technology Environments
Skilled Personnel Educators and support staff skilled in the use of technology appropriate for their job responsibilities.	Standard I: Technology Operations and Concepts Standard II: Planning and Designing Learning Environments and Experiences Standard V: Productivity and Professional Practice Standard VI: Social, Legal, Ethical and Human Issues

(Continued)

TABLE 0.3 ▪ *(Continued)*

ISTE's Essential Conditions (NETS•S)	Addressed in the following ISTE TF/TL standards
Ongoing Professional Learning Technology-related professional learning plans and opportunities with dedicated time to practice and share ideas.	Ongoing professional learning spans all the TF/TL standards, but it is primary in the following: Standard I: Technology Operations and Concepts Standard II: Planning and Designing Learning Environments and Experiences Standard V: Productivity and Professional Practice
Technical Support Consistent and reliable assistance for maintaining, renewing, and using technology.	Standard VI: Social, Legal, Ethical and Human Issues Standard VII: Procedures, Policies, Planning, and Budgeting for Technology Environments
Curriculum Framework Content standards and related digital curriculum resources.	Standard III: Teaching, Learning, and the Curriculum Standard VI: Social, Legal, Ethical and Human Issues
Student-Centered Learning Use of technology to facilitate engaging approaches to learning.	Standard II: Planning and Designing Learning Environments and Experiences Standard III: Teaching, Learning, and the Curriculum Standard VI: Social, Legal, Ethical and Human Issues Standard VIII: Leadership and Vision
Assessment and Evaluation Continuous assessment, both of learning and for learning, and evaluation of use of technology and digital resources.	Standard IV: Assessment and Evaluation Standard VI: Social, Legal, Ethical and Human Issues
Engaged Communities Partnerships and collaboration within the community to support and fund use of technology and digital resources.	Standard VI: Social, Legal, Ethical and Human Issues Standard VIII: Leadership and Vision
Support Policies Policies, financial plans, accountability measures, and incentive structures to support the use of technology in learning and in district and school operations.	Standard VI: Social, Legal, Ethical and Human Issues Standard VII: Procedures, Policies, Planning, and Budgeting for Technology Environments Standard VIII: Leadership and Vision
Supportive External Context Policies and initiatives at the national, regional, and local levels to support schools in the effective implementation of technology for achieving curriculum and technology standards.	Standard VI: Social, Legal, Ethical and Human Issues Standard VIII: Leadership and Vision

Discussion Questions

The distinction between technology facilitation and leadership. The TF standards are designed for lead teachers or instructional technology specialists who facilitate technology integration at the building level, and the TL standards apply to K–12 coordinators, specialists, or directors who lead technology programs at the district, regional, state, or national levels (see p. 1). Is the distinction between the roles of the facilitator and leader always clear? When does this distinction blur? Even though the line between facilitation and leadership may not always be clear, is it useful to have two sets of standards? Why or why not?

Combining technology facilitation and leadership with other job responsibilities. On page 1, the authors note that technology facilitator and leadership roles are often assumed by educators with multiple job assignments. Is the practice of combining technology facilitation and leadership with other job assignments productive? Why or why not? What are the possible positive and negative attributes of a dual-role or multiple-role structure?

The balance between technology facilitation and leadership. In this introduction, the authors imply that the technology facilitator and the technology leader both fulfill important functions in educational settings. Discuss how these two roles can work together to produce a high-quality technology program in schools. In your setting, is there a good balance between leadership and facilitation? If not, why not? If so, how is this balance achieved?

Instructional and administrative functions of technology facilitation and leadership. The TF/TL standards are aligned to both the NETS•T and the NETS•A. Do you believe that technology facilitators and leaders are more like teachers or administrators? What are the pros and cons of a technology professional being viewed as a teacher? As an administrator? Would you recommend that technology professionals be portrayed more as teachers or more as administrators, and why?

The complexity of technology facilitation and leadership. In this introduction, the authors described the TF/TL standards as "a continuum for technology professionals who begin their work in local schools as technology facilitators and, then, broaden their sphere of influence and increase their responsibilities over time as technology leaders." (see p. 5). The authors also note that the TF/TL standards sometime differ in "breadth, depth, and complexity of performance" (see p. 5). Is it correct to assume that the technology leader's job is more complex and/or difficult than the facilitator's? Why or why not? What aspect of the facilitator's job do you believe is most rewarding? Difficult? What aspect of the technology leader's job do you believe is most rewarding? Difficult? Does the facilitator or leader best suit your current career goals and why? Does the facilitator or leader best suit your long-term career goals and why?

TF/TL performance tasks and rubrics. Do you find the TF/TL performance tasks and rubrics a useful addition to the TF/TL documentation (see pp. 8–10 and Appendix B)? If so, how will you use them? Are there any negative aspects to including performance tasks and rubrics in the TF/TL documentation?

References

Ausband, L. (2006). Instructional technology specialists and curriculum work. *Journal of Research on Technology in Education, 39*(1), 1–21.

Conery, L. (2005). Standards are essential. *Leading & Learning with Technology, 33*(2), 48.

Davidson, J. (2003). A new role in facilitating school reform: The case of the educational technologist. *Teachers College Record, 105*(5), 729–752.

Hearrington, D., & Strudler, N. (2007, June). *The effects of barriers and enabling factors, homophily, and technical support on instructional support time.* Poster session presented at the annual meeting of the American Educational Research Association, Chicago, IL.

Lesisko, L. J. (2005, March). *The K–12 Technology Coordinator.* Paper presented at the annual meeting of the Eastern Educational Research Association, Sarasota, FL.

McLeod, S. (2003, February). *National district technology coordinators study: Personal and professional characteristics* (Technical Report 1). Naperville, IL: North Central Regional Educational Laboratory.

Nardi, B., & O'Day, V. (1999). *Information ecologies: Using technology with heart.* Cambridge, MA: MIT.

Orlikowski, A., Yates, J., Okamura, K., & Fujimoto, M. (1999). Communication technology and organizational form. In G. Desanctis & J. Fulk (Eds.), *Shaping organizational form: Communication, connection, and community* (pp. 71–100). Thousand Oaks, CA: Sage.

Reinhart, J., & Slowinski, J. (2004, October). *K–12 technology coordinators: Expectations and realities.* Paper presented at the Association for Educational Communications and Technology, Chicago, IL.

Roblyer, M. D. (2003). Getting our NETS worth: The role of ISTE's National Technology Standards. *Leading & Learning with Technology, 30*(8), 6–13.

Snelbecker, G., & Miller, S. (2005). ILT specialists as facilitators of technology integration: Implications for teachers and administrators. Mid-Atlantic Regional Technology in Education Consortium. *Edtech Review, Series 4.*

Strudler, N. (1995–96). The role of school-based technology coordinators as change agents in elementary school programs: A follow-up study. *Journal of Research on Computing in Education, 28*(2), 234–257.

Strudler, N. (2001, June). *The evolving role of school-based technology coordinators in elementary programs.* Paper presented at the National Education Computing Conference, Chicago, IL.

Strudler, N., Falba, C., & Hearrington, D. (2005, June). *The evolving roles, goals, and effectiveness of elementary technology coordinators.* Paper presented at the National Education Computing Conference, Philadelphia, PA.

Thomas, L., & Knezek, D. (2002). Standards for technology-supported learning environments. *The State Education Standard, 3*(3), 14–20.

Twomey, C., Shamburg, C., & Zieger, L. (2006). *Teachers as technology leaders: A guide to ISTE technology facilitation and technology leadership accreditation.* Eugene, OR: International Society for Technology in Education.

Wright, R., & Lesisko, L. J. (2007). *The preparation and role of technology leadership for the schools.* Paper presented at the annual meeting of the Eastern Educational Research Association, Clearwater, FL.

Zhao, Y., Pugh, K., Sheldon, S., & Byers, J. (2002). Conditions for classroom technology innovations. *Teachers College Record, 104,* 482–515.

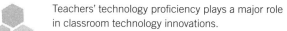

Teachers' technology proficiency plays a major role in classroom technology innovations.

— ZHAO, PUGH, SHELDON, AND BYERS, 2002

Chapter One

TF/TL STANDARD I

Technology Operations and Concepts

Terms such as competency, proficiency, literacy, and fluency are often used to describe what educators must know and be able to do to implement technology successfully. The meanings of these terms differ from source to source, and associated expectations vary from the ability to use specific types of software applications to making sophisticated pedagogical choices about technology and learning in the classroom. Despite this variation, all models of proficiency assume that effective educators in the digital age must acquire a basic set of technology-related knowledge and skills. In TF/TL Standard I: Technology Operations and Concepts, technology facilitators and leaders ensure that their colleagues possess the fundamental understanding and skills needed to operate specific technologies and understand the concepts associated with technology use.

Current Context:
Defining Technology Operations and Concepts

Technology operation and concept skills in TF/TL Standard I are distinguished from technology-related learning goals in other standard areas in that they are general, basic, and usually transferable across different hardware platforms and software applications. Examples of these basic competencies include:

- Identifying the different types of hardware devices available for use (such as computers, handhelds, mobile phones, MP3 players, scanners, printers, flash drives, and DVD/video players) and selecting them to accomplish appropriate tasks

- Identifying and using basic computer components (such as CPU, monitor, keyboard, mouse, and USB ports)

- Using the common features of computer operating systems (such as launching programs, finding files, creating folders, organizing the desktop, opening and closing windows, and toggling between windows)

- Practicing proper care and maintenance procedures for computing devices (such as starting up and shutting down systems, mounting and ejecting peripherals, charging batteries, and transporting and storing computers)

- Mastering the use of common features and functions of computer software (such as open file, save file, print, copy, cut, and paste)

- Applying basic troubleshooting techniques to solve minor problems (such as freeze, force quit, and select printer) and referencing hardware and software documentation to solve problems and complete routine maintenance

- Identifying the types of software that are available and selecting the most appropriate software tools for specific tasks

- Understanding the common features of Internet browsers, search engines, and communication tools (such as e-mail, IM, blogs, and wikis) and using these tools to find information and interact with others synchronously and asynchronously

- Understanding basic networking and infrastructure concepts enabling expanded information and communication concepts in schools (such as Internet connectivity, LAN/WAN designs, wireless versus wired infrastructure, routers, and switches)

Recent Progress in Educator Proficiency

In the mid- to late 1990s, there was a great deal of emphasis on operations and concepts because information and communication technologies were new and unfamiliar. The World Wide Web was young but gaining popularity. The personal computer and dial-up connections were becoming affordable, but home access was still not commonplace. Likewise, schools were building local and wide area networks, establishing more robust connections to the Internet, and placing new, more powerful computers in labs, class-rooms, and administrative offices, but educators had little idea how to operate them. With limited prior technical experience either at home or at school, most practicing educators depended on school technology professionals to help them acquire the knowl-edge they needed. Technology facilitators and leaders responded to this need, hoping that educators' newfound knowledge would result in effective integration practices.

Today, with the widespread proliferation of computers and connectivity, technology operations and concepts are viewed somewhat differently. Educators are more likely than ever before to acquire at least some basic technology proficiencies outside of the school environment. The Web, e-mail, and basic computing are often a part of educators' daily personal and professional lives, and, as younger teachers enter the workforce, it is increasingly likely that they will not remember a time when they did not have access to the Internet.

In addition to more exposure to technology in their personal lives, educators now have more formal opportunities to learn about technology. Responding to the ever-increasing role and promise of technology in education, schools now provide greater access to training, with many states having policies encouraging or requiring technology profi-ciency among educators. For example, in 2007, 45 states had adopted teacher technology standards containing core competencies, and 36 had similar requirements in place for administrators. In addition, 19 states required teachers seeking initial licensure to show competency in these standards through coursework or examinations; 9 had similar requirements for administrators. Slightly over half of these states also had testing or professional development requirements for teachers and administrators seeking recertification (EPE, Ed Week Technology Counts, 2007).

Data continues to suggest steady increases in teacher proficiency levels, as well. In 2003, when surveyors asked a random national sample of teachers to describe their "skill set with computers and other classroom technologies," 47% of teachers characterized their level of proficiency as "somewhat advanced" or "advanced." However, in 2006, the percentage of teachers placing themselves at these same skill levels increased to 63% (CDW-G, 2006; see Figure 1.1). Over a similar time period, the percentage of schools where teachers considered over half of their colleagues to be "beginners" in using technology dropped from 35% in 1999 to 15% in 2005 (see Figure 1.2).

Current Needs Related to Technology Operations and Concepts

Although educator proficiency has improved over the past decade, technology facilitators and leaders must continue to increase educators' knowledge of technology operations and concepts. For example, when viewed from another perspective, EdWeek's Market Data Retrieval Survey (2005) reflects that 15% of schools—roughly equaling 14,000 buildings—remain at "beginning" levels of technological proficiency, and, according to the CDW-G Teachers Talk (2006) survey, only 18% of teachers possess an "advanced" level of proficiency. Furthermore, researchers speculate that the teachers with the lowest levels of technology proficiency are likely serving some of the nation's highest-need students (Market Data Retrieval, 2004).

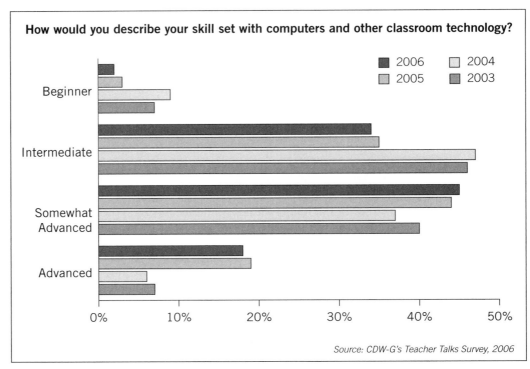

Figure 1.1 Teacher computer skills 2003–2006

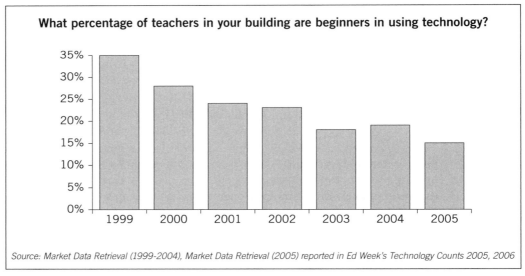

Figure 1.2 Percentage of schools where at least half of the teachers are considered "beginners" in using technology

Of course, enacting TF/TL Standard I is more complicated than closing a final gap in educator proficiency. Becoming proficient in technology operations and concepts is much more complex, interrelated, and difficult to measure than these surveys suggest. Zhao, Pugh, Sheldon, and Byers (2002) posit that even a simple classroom activity such as having students exchange writing via e-mail requires an understanding of multiple "enabling factors," such as computer operations, basic networking, and e-mail software. Some of these concepts (such as bandwidth) can be quite complicated, particularly when studied relative to and interacting with other concepts. However, pursuing this complex understanding and interrelation is important. Teachers who understand how multiple components work together to make the learning activity possible have been found to be more successful in implementing technology than teachers whose knowledge of technology operations and concepts is less evolved and more discrete (Zhao et al., 2002, pp. 489–490).

The evolving nature of technology also requires ongoing monitoring and building of educator proficiency. Technology competency is not a skill set that, once mastered, is static; rather, it is highly fluid, changing at the pace of technological innovation. Given the dynamic nature of technology, maintaining technology competency is challenging even for educators with advanced skills. Prensky (2006) reminds us that computing power may double each year, along with quantum advances in computing applications, transmission speeds, programming, and storage space. With these advances will come new technology operations and concepts that educators must master. New waves of technology—the Internet, e-mail, new operating systems, new mobile computing devices, wireless technologies, and Web 2.0 applications such as wikis, blogs, and podcasting—serve to illustrate how addressing basic technology operations and concepts is an ever-evolving task for technology facilitators, technology leaders, and the educators they serve.

Rethinking Training Methods

Finding better methods to achieve and maintain technology competency is an ongoing pursuit for technology facilitators and leaders. Critics have expressed concern that technology skills training has been overemphasized in teacher professional development, while support for integrating technology into academic content areas has been neglected (Coughlin, 1999; Sandholtz & Reilly, 2004). Data exists to support these claims. In 1999, 42% of teachers reported having six or more hours in basic skills training within the past year, whereas only 29% reported having equivalent curriculum integration training (Trotter, 1999; see also Ronnkvist, Dexter, & Anderson, 2000). Data also suggests that professional development including a curriculum integration focus is more effective in helping teachers feel prepared to integrate technology than professional development that centers solely on technology operations and concepts (Trotter, 1999).

Some training methods have been criticized for not modeling the types of instruction expected of teachers in the classroom. Experts encourage teachers to embed student technology skills in core academic content (NCREL, 2000), but some technical training models do the opposite—herding teachers and administrators into computer labs to learn skills with no apparent relationship to their daily work. Although technology skills and concepts cannot be neglected, they should be integrated into professional learning experiences emphasizing technology as a curriculum tool. Adults—like students—need to acquire basic skills and foundational knowledge, but they are more likely to understand, retain, and transfer this knowledge when it is embedded in meaningful, authentic contexts (Bransford & Cocking, 1999).

Also like their students, educators need learning environments accommodating their individual learning styles, abilities, skills, and interests. This individualization is especially important when considering that technology competency levels are more varied than they were a decade ago. Teachers at intermediate or advanced levels of understanding have needs that are different from those of novice users and cannot be expected to benefit equally from the same training experiences. In addition to the variance in initial skill levels, teachers also advance at different rates and respond to different methods of instruction. To accommodate these differences, a number of different types of professional learning approaches must be applied—providing technology facilitators and leaders an opportunity to model the types of technology-supported, differentiated instruction that they expect teachers to design and implement in the classroom.

When these concerns are coupled with the fact that technology operations and concepts comprise an ongoing, complex knowledge domain, they present significant challenges to technology facilitators and leaders as they promote educator competency in digital-age schools, including:

- Finding an appropriate level of emphasis on technology operations and concepts without neglecting other professional learning needs

- Developing learning opportunities that fit diverse needs of learners

- Developing strategies to maintain technology competency in the midst of rapid change

- Helping learners understand how technology concepts are interrelated and interdependent

In response to these challenges, skill-building approaches that are job-embedded, timely, and integrated emerge as more appropriate and effective choices. These approaches include providing online and/or video tutorials on technology topics, using individual or small-group coaching models, and integrating technology skills topics into professional learning opportunities with a broader focus on teaching, learning, and the curriculum. Not only do these methods help educators improve their knowledge and skills related to technology operations and concepts, but they also allow technologists to model the way in which teachers should seamlessly integrate technology skills into core academic areas instead of teaching technology skills in isolation.

Summary of Current Context

Recent increases in educator proficiency levels are positive developments when considering the implementation of TF/TL Standard I. These advances—most often achieved by the efforts of technology facilitators and leaders—should be celebrated. However, increasing teacher basic proficiency must not result in technology leaders and facilitators abandoning the teaching of technology operations and concepts. Ignoring the importance of this standard after experiencing initial indicators of success would be a mistake. Although TF/TL Standard I may not be accompanied by the same sense of urgency as in the past, achieving technology proficiency should remain an ongoing pursuit. Keeping pace with emerging technologies—an important component of TF/TL Standard I—is another reason why this standard will never be obsolete. In helping educators gain technical knowledge, however, technologists should avoid the mistake of teaching technology operations and concepts in isolation—a practice that was often common in the past. Instead, current best practices in technology facilitation and leadership integrate technology operations and concepts with professional development related to teaching and learning.

Implementing the Standard

This section reviews the standard, performance indicators, and performance tasks of TF/TL Standard I in order to fully understand how technology facilitators and leaders can improve educators' ability to operate and integrate available technologies. For reference, the full standard is listed on page 25.

Performance Standards

All technology leaders and facilitators must possess expertise in technology operations and concepts. They are also expected to build technical proficiency among their fellow educators. In this standard, the difference between technology facilitators and leaders is determined by skill level. Technology facilitators are expected to demonstrate an in-depth understanding of technology operations and concepts, whereas leaders are expected to perform at a more advanced level. Although the distinction between "in depth" and "advanced" is not immediately apparent from the performance standard, the performance tasks will deepen and distinguish levels of technology operations and concepts expected of technologists at each of these levels.

Performance Indicators

A review of the performance indicators associated with TF/TL Standard I suggests that technology facilitators and leaders are expected to address two distinct areas related to technology operations and concepts. The first relates to knowledge, skills, and understanding of technology operations and concepts as described in the ISTE NETS•T (TF/TL-I.A.). The second standard refers to the ability to continually extend knowledge, skills, and understanding of these concepts and to integrate knowledge of new technologies as they emerge (TF/TL-I.B.).

Performance Tasks

The performance tasks associated with TF/TL Standard I.A. and Standard I.B. illustrate the difference between in-depth knowledge expected of technology facilitators and advanced knowledge associated with leaders. As illustrated in these tasks, the difference in performance expectations between facilitators and leaders does not necessarily hinge on technical expertise. We have observed that experienced facilitators often possess greater knowledge of the intricacies of technology operations and concepts than do leaders because of their proximity to practice and the "hands-on" nature of their jobs. Leaders, on the other hand, often report deteriorating awareness of current hardware and software as the administrative demands of their positions erode their familiarity with technologies available in the classrooms. Instead, the distinction relates to the differing performance expectations and roles of facilitators and leaders in improving others' technology proficiency and the scope of influence they exert on technological operations.

Based on the performance tasks, the work of technology facilitators most likely occurs in one-to-one coaching or small group scenarios. Facilitators assist teachers in developing knowledge, skills, and understanding of technology systems, resources, and services that are aligned with district and state technology plans (TF-I.A.1.). Facilitators also assist teachers in identifying technologies to meet specific learning needs (TF-I.A.1.). As facilitators develop personal strategies to keep pace with current and emerging technologies related to education, they model these strategies to other educators who are striving to keep pace with constant change (TF-I.B.1.).

Whereas facilitators assist teachers and model strategies, leaders offer structured, systematic programs building technology capacity among groups of other educators—teachers, administrators, and technology facilitators—including identifying and evaluating components necessary to systemically build capacity for technology integration. As a necessary prerequisite to meeting TL Standard I, technology leaders must assess educators' current knowledge and skills related to technology operations. Leaders must also evaluate the effectiveness of current facilitation efforts, such as coaching and modeling (see the Exceeds TF Standards/Approaches TL Standards column for TF/TL Standard I in the Performance Continuum, in Appendix C).

Based on these assessments, technology leaders can then identify and evaluate components needed to enhance educators' knowledge (TL-I.A.1.), providing professional learning opportunities that address gaps in knowledge related to technology operations, technology concepts, and emerging technologies (TL-I.A.2., TL-I.B.1.). To meet these performance indicators, leaders are not necessarily required to develop or assess the professional learning opportunities offered to educators in their organization(s); however, leaders at more advanced levels will do so (see the Exceeds TL Standards column for TF/TL Standard I in the Performance Continuum, Appendix C). This higher level of performance may even lead to professional development programs that are adopted outside a leader's local district, region, or state.

Technology Operations and Concepts (TF/TL-I)	
Technology Facilitation Standard	**Technology Leadership Standard**
(TF-I) Educational Technology Facilitators demonstrate an in-depth understanding of technology operations and concepts.	(TL-I) Educational Technology Leaders demonstrate an advanced understanding of technology operations and concepts.
TF/TL-I.A. Demonstrate knowledge, skills, and understanding of concepts related to technology (as described in the ISTE NETS•T).	
Performance Tasks for Facilitators	**Performance Tasks for Leaders**
TF-I.A.1. Assist teachers in the ongoing development of knowledge, skills, and understanding of technology systems, resources, and services that are aligned with district and state technology plans.	TL-I.A.1. Identify and evaluate components needed for the continual growth of knowledge, skills, and understanding of concepts related to technology.
TF-I.A.2. Provide assistance to teachers in identifying technology systems, resources, and services to meet specific learning needs.	TL-I.A.2. Offer a variety of professional development opportunities that facilitate the ongoing development of knowledge, skills, and understanding of concepts related to technology.
TF/TL-I.B. Demonstrate continual growth in technology knowledge and skills to stay abreast of current and emerging technologies.	
TF-I.B.1. Model appropriate strategies essential to continued growth and development of the understanding of technology operations and concepts.	TL-I.B.1. Offer a variety of professional development opportunities that facilitate the continued growth and development of the understanding of technology operations and concepts.

ISTE's Essential Conditions and TF/TL Standard I

TF/TL Standard I: Technology Operations and Concepts ensures that schools have skilled personnel. Of course, building knowledge of technology operations and concepts requires ongoing professional learning, a responsibility assumed by technology facilitators and leaders. Skilled Personnel and Ongoing Professional Learning are two of the essential conditions necessary for achieving the NETS•S.

Performance Scenarios

School-based instructional technology facilitators notice that teachers, especially those new to the district, need a great deal of support in learning basic technology operations and concepts such as logging into the network, printing, and saving files to the district servers. In response to this need, the district technology leader suggests that the facilitators develop quick tip guides that can be posted online and accessed by teachers. The technology leader also discusses this problem with other district leaders in a cabinet meeting. The leadership team decides that new teacher induction should include a one-hour orientation to introduce basic information on the district's network and computer systems. The technology leader designs this orientation and delivers it to new teachers. She also trains facilitators to redeliver the information to existing faculty and staff in the schools on an as-needed basis.

The school district has agreed to provide each teacher with a laptop computer. The technology leader supervising the project realizes that teachers will need a basic overview of how to use and maintain the laptop. Because the device is portable, teachers will need to know how to connect to the district network and the Internet both at school and at home. Given the size of the district, the training demand will exceed the capacity of local technology staff. Therefore, the district leader provides all school-based technology facilitators with laptops and asks them to generate a list of what teachers will need to know and be able to do. The leader uses this list to specify training goals in a request for proposal (RFP) for an outside training contractor. A state-funded technology center responds to the RFP and collaborates with the local technology staff to deliver the training.

A district technology leader notices that the technology facilitators in her district are so busy helping educators in their buildings that they have little time to stay abreast of current and emerging technologies. In response to this problem, the leader establishes two strategies. First, she creates a blog to post relevant information gleaned from what she reads on a regular basis. She also encourages the facilitators to post any information they encounter. Second, she establishes a budget for facilitators to attend state and national technology conferences on a rotating basis. The blog also serves as a place to report what was learned at these conferences. As a result, the whole team benefits from sharing what they know.

While working in the schools, a technology facilitator encounters a teacher with a great interest in instructional technology. This teacher has even expressed interest in becoming a technology facilitator. To mentor this teacher, the facilitator shares several publications and websites that are useful for learning about current and emerging technologies.

case study

HELPING EDUCATORS UNDERSTAND TECHNOLOGY

Operations and Concepts by Investing in People

When Palm Beach County Technology Grant Coordinators John Long and Teresa Wing received a large Title IID award from the Florida Department of Education, they encountered the same dilemma that many technologists face every day. The grant was designed to help more than 360 teachers integrate technology more frequently and effectively into teaching, but their technology skills were incredibly uneven.

"In my opinion, we had about three groups—the advanced, with fewer people in this group than the others, and then the intermediates and the absolute beginners, with about the same number in each," explained Long.

The other problem was defining what concepts and skills the teachers needed to know. According to Wing and Long, the grant is very project-based. Teachers construct technology-supported instruction to implement in their classes. "In this type of grant, teachers are engaged in designing a wide variety of activities," explained Wing. "First, how could we know what skills each of them need for their individual projects, and second, how could we be there to help all of them when they need it? There are just two of us!"

Long explained that old models just didn't work for them. "Yes, I've spent hundreds of hours in the past teaching basic skills, but that just doesn't help integration. I could be teaching something and only one person needs to know it. It's not efficient. We have to spend our whole-group time on more important things, and the basic skills have to be taught in a just-in-time, right-when-they-need-it kind of way."

To solve the dilemmas, Long and Wing invested in people. They used their grant funds to provide stipends for 57 teacher "technology ambassadors" who could help their colleagues learn about technology. At the elementary level, these teacher technology facilitators are called the M.O.D. Squad (multimedia-on-demand), and at the secondary level, they are called SMaRT Ambassadors (science, math, reading, and technology).

Ambassadors were assigned a small group of grant participants for whom they were responsible. The ambassador answered questions and led small-group meetings for their fellow teachers. Because ambassadors might not be at the same school as those on their teams, they often used e-mail and other tele-collaborative tools to communicate. Building teachers' knowledge about technology operations and concepts was a frequent and necessary topic, but it did not assume a central role. According to Long and Wing, this method of building skills is subtle but powerful.

Both Long and Wing are pleased with the results. "Somehow, the participants' technical skills are just kind of leveling out. Sure, some of them are still more advanced than others, but everyone has come a long way! The mentors learned from mentoring. The small groups learned from each other. We learned from them. It was definitely the right strategy for us. We'd do it again. No question," Long commented.

(Continued)

case study *(Continued)*

Wing noted that having mentors close to practice is critical. "We do use the Inventory of Teacher Technology Skills (ITTS) provided by the Florida DOE to gather information, and this is a great tool, but we've found that no one assessment tool is enough. The ITTS provides us with good information that is especially powerful for program evaluation, but observing teachers in their daily practice is necessary, too. The ambassadors are able to do that in a much different way than even John and I can."

In closing, Long reflected that his perception of technology competency has changed over the course of this project. "We define competency as whatever teachers need to know to use technology in their classrooms. That could be a million things! Now we know we can provide technical support in that way. We just needed help! We just needed people!"

To visit the website for the Technology Ambassador Program, go to:
http://web.mac.com/mrdv/Tech_Ambassadors/About.html

To read more about Palm Beach County's Title IID grant project, visit:
http://web.mac.com/wing_t/Project_SMaRT/Overview.html

Discussion Questions

- Why do you believe TF/TL Standard I: Technology Operations and Concepts is important to improving technology integration in schools?

- How would you describe the technology proficiency levels of educators in your school, district, region, and/or state? How do these proficiency levels affect daily instructional and administrative practices? What factors contribute to the current proficiency levels? What would help increase proficiency levels?

- What are the best practices you have experienced for helping educators acquire basic technology skills?

- In the first paragraph of this chapter, the authors mentioned the terms computer or technology proficiency, competency, literacy, and fluency. How do these terms differ? Which terms are most appropriate when discussing technology operations and concepts as defined in this chapter?

- There are three chapters and standard areas that focus on technical skills. How do the skills described in TF/TL Standards I, V, and VII differ?

- In addition to the challenges presented in this chapter, technology facilitators and leaders also struggle with explaining complex technical topics to educators in ways that they can understand, without oversimplifying or misrepresenting the concept. What tools and strategies might be helpful for technologists grappling with this issue?

- Some critics have claimed that placing Technology Operations and Concepts as the first in a series of standards implies that learning about technology is more important than learning with technology. Perhaps this view influenced the 2007 revision of the National Educational Technology Standards for Students (NETS•S). Technology Operations and Concepts was not eliminated, but it was moved from the first standard to the last. What do you think about this revision? How do you think Technology Operation and Concepts ranks in importance to the other standards?

- The case study in this chapter illustrates the difficulty of building knowledge of technology operations and concepts when teachers have a wide variety of skill levels and individual learning needs. How can technology facilitators and leaders improve educators' technical skills, given this complex reality?

Resources

The resources identified under TF/TL Standard I pertain to technology operations and concepts. Assessment tools are provided to assist technologists in assessing the technology literacy of educators. Although these assessment tools generally evaluate technology integration, all contain a section relating specifically to technology literacy. Because an important component of technology literacy includes understanding how to navigate operating systems, links to three major operating systems are provided. Several tutorials are included to assist educators in learning basic technology operations and concepts. Finally, the National Academy of Engineering report describes the importance of mastering technology operations and concepts, helping facilitators and leaders develop and articulate a clear justification for the use of technology in schools.

Technology Literacy Assessment Tools

Taglit
www.taglit.org
> This assessment tool is designed to help principals and other school leaders gather information about how technology is used for teaching and learning. One of the skills measured involves teachers' computer skills.

LoTi
www.loticonnection.com
> The PCU component of the LoTi framework is designed to assess classroom teachers' comfort and skill level with using a personal computer.

ProfilerPRO
http://profilerpro.com
> This tool allows for the evaluation of knowledge, attitudes, and skills based on simple surveys implemented via the World Wide Web and could be used to evaluate the computer competency of educators.

Major Operating Systems

Apple

www.apple.com/support/osfamily/

> This site provides support to the Apple operating system along with free downloads, templates, and updates.

Microsoft

www.microsoft.com

> This site provides support to the Windows operating system along with free downloads, templates, and updates.

Linux

www.linux.org

> This site provides a list of links to a large number of websites discussing Linux.

Reports

Technically speaking: Why all Americans need to know more about technology. (2002). National Academy of Engineering

http://books.nap.edu/openbook.php?record_id=10250&page=R1

> This report can be read online by clicking on the right arrow circle on the Page bar.

Tutorials/Websites

Microsoft Digital Literacy Curriculum

www.microsoft.com/about/corporatecitizenship/citizenship/giving/programs/up/digitalliteracy/eng/Curriculum.mspx#ComputerBasics

> Online courses for basic computer operations and concepts.

Computer/Internet Tutorials

www.anniston.lib.al.us/computerinternettutorial.htm

> These easy-to-use tutorials address basic computer knowledge.

Fact Monster: Computers and Technology

www.factmonster.com/ipka/A0772279.html

> This free reference site includes lots of information about computers and technology.

How Laptops Work

http://communication.howstuffworks.com/laptop.htm

> This site includes information that will help you understand how your laptop works, and it is chock full of links to other computer articles as well.

How Stuff Works—Computer

http://computer.howstuffworks.com

> This site is dedicated to explaining how computer hardware, software, peripherals, and security work. It also explains how the Internet works.

Jan's Illustrated Computer Literacy

www.jegsworks.com/Lessons/lessonintro.htm

> These illustrated tutorials help users fill in the gaps in their knowledge about computers.

LearnThat.com

www.learnthat.com

> This site is one of the most popular destinations on the Web for free online courses and free tutorials on a variety of computer topics.

Microsoft XP 101: Using Windows XP Professional in the Classroom

www.microsoft.com/Education/WinXP101Tutorial.mspx

> This tutorial can be helpful as educators learn the basics of the Windows XP operating system.

 Spotlight Resource

Professional Competency Continuum (PCC)
www.mff.org/publications/publications.taf?page=280

This tool, developed by the Milken Foundation, measures current skill levels and professional practices in core technology skills, along with several other competencies relating to technology integration in schools and classrooms. These include administrative competency; classroom and instructional management; curriculum, learning, and assessment; and professional practice.

Web Teacher

www.techcorps.org/Webteacher/windows.html

> This site published by TechCorps offers a set of free tutorials to help users learn and understand nearly everything about using the Web, peripherals, utilities, multimedia, and more.

References

Bransford, J. & Cocking, P. (1999). *How people learn: Brain, mind, experience, and school.* Washington, DC: National Academies Press.

CDW-G. (2006). *Teachers Talk survey.* Retrieved August 23, 2007, from http://newsroom.cdwg.com/features/feature-06–26–06.html

Coughlin, E. (1999), as quoted in M. Zehr. (1999, September 23). Moving teachers along a competency continuum. *Education Week Special Issue: Technology Counts 1999, 19*(4), 41.

Editorial Projects in Education (EPE) Research Center. (2007). Annual state technology survey, as reported in C. Bausell & E. Klemick. (2007, March 29). Tracking U.S. Trends. *Education Week Special Issue: Technology Counts 2007, 26*(30), 42–44.

Market Data Retrieval. (2001–2004). Technology in education surveys 1999–2004, as reported in E. Fox (2005, May 5). Tracking U.S. trends. *Education Week Special Issue: Technology Counts 2005, 24*(35), 40–42.

Market Data Retrieval. (2005). Technology in education survey, as reported in Swanson, C. (2006, May 4). Tracking U.S. Trends. *Education Week Special Issue: Technology Counts 2006, 25*(35), 50–52.

North Central Regional Educational Laboratory (NCREL). (2000). *enGauge; A framework for effective technology use. Condition: Practice, Indicator: Alignment.* Retrieved August 23, 2007, from www.ncrel.org/engauge/framewk/efp/align/efpalipr.htm

Prensky, M. (2006). *Don't bother me, Mom—I'm learning.* St. Paul, MN: Paragon House.

Ronnkvist, A., Dexter, S., & Anderson, E. (2000). *Technology support: Its depth, breadth, and impact in America's schools.* Retrieved August 23, 2007, from www.crito.uci.edu/tlc/findings/technology-support/startpage.htm

Sandholtz, J. & Reilly, B. (2004). Teachers, not technicians: Rethinking technical expectations for teachers. *Teachers College Record, 106,* 487–512.

Trotter, A. (1999, September 23). Training Matters: Preparing teachers for the digital age. *Education Week Special Issue: Technology Counts 1999, 19*(4), 37–43.

Zhao, Y., Pugh, K., Sheldon, S., & Byers, J. (2002). Conditions for classroom technology innovations. *Teachers College Record, 104,* 482–515.

Fundamental change is more likely to occur by a process of shifting . . . a series of small sustainable steps rather than a rapid conversion to a new order. Each shift acknowledges the local context and sets the foundation for a new shift. Each shift interacts with and modifies the prevailing web of forces in a way that permits the next shift to occur. Over an extended period of time, this accumulation of shifts translates into a profound educational transformation.

— ROGERS, 1995

Chapter Two

TF/TL STANDARD II

Planning and Designing Learning Environments and Experiences

Technologies such as personal computing, productivity software, and the Internet offer new tools and opportunities for learning. Using technology tools to solve problems or create original products can aid students in constructing meaning and demonstrating their learning—often in ways similar to practicing professionals in the field. The Internet provides students with access to information, tools to collaborate with others, and new places to publish their work. The connected classroom even affords students opportunities to contribute knowledge to a disciplinary field and to participate in civic action.

However, realizing this potential is not easy. Integrating technology into classroom practice requires teachers to engage in sophisticated planning and design processes, but there is no guarantee that teachers will have the support they need to accomplish their tasks successfully. This is why enacting TF/TL Standard II plays a key role in the advancement of instructional technologies in K–12 education. TF/TL Standard II provides a comprehensive description of how technology facilitators and leaders can support teachers during critical instructional planning and design phases.

Current Context: The Need to Help Teachers Plan and Design Learning Experiences

Despite technology's potential to augment and transform instruction, teachers generally have not implemented technology as frequently as hoped. A 2005 survey of 1,000 randomly selected teachers revealed that although 85% of teachers used technology for administrative tasks (such as taking and reporting attendance), less than 50% ever used technology to support instruction (CDW-G, 2005). In another random national survey in 2006, only slightly more than half (54%) of teachers reported that technology had significantly changed the way they teach. In the same study, only 37% responded that they integrate technology on a daily basis, and only 26% felt "highly competent" in integrating technology into instruction. Only 7% of educational leaders ranked teachers in their system as "very good" or better at integrating technology into the learning experience (Consortium for School Networking, 2005).

Frequency rates drop even further when measuring the use of technology to support constructivist practices. In repeated and ongoing analyses of classroom practice using the Level of Technology Implementation (LoTi) framework (see Table 2.1), researchers consistently find that the most common technology uses in classroom are not aligned to research-based best practices (Moersch, 2002). In the aggregate results from national LoTi project schools in 2005, nearly half (48%) of technology-supported practices are best described at Levels 0–2, ranging from no use at all to uses supporting lower-order cognitive goals. Less than 11% occur at the three highest levels (4B and above), which are characterized by higher-order thinking, authentic tasks, collaboration, student-directed learning, and performance-based assessment (Moersch, 2001; see Figure 2.1). Although instruction at all LoTi Levels is valid under certain conditions, this data suggests a lack of balance and a virtual absence of the technology-supported instructional strategies most likely to support student understanding, retention, and transfer of knowledge.

TABLE 2.1 ■ Levels of technology implementation (LoTi) framework

LEVEL	DESCRIPTION
0 **Non-use**	Technology is not used for instructional purposes.
1 **Awareness**	The use of technology-based tools is (1) one step removed from the classroom teacher (e.g., integrated learning system labs, special computer-based pull-out programs, computer literacy classes, central word processing labs), (2) used almost exclusively by the classroom teacher for classroom and/or curriculum management tasks (e.g., taking attendance, using grade book programs, accessing e-mail, retrieving lesson plans from a curriculum management system or the Internet), and/or (3) used to embellish or enhance teacher-directed lessons or lectures (e.g., multimedia presentations).
2 **Exploration**	Technology-based tools supplement the existing instruction at the knowledge/comprehension level. The electronic technology is employed as extension activities, enrichment exercises, or technology-based tools and generally reinforces lower cognitive skill development relating to the content under study.
3 **Infusion**	Technology-based, complement-selected instructional events at the analysis, synthesis, and evaluation levels. Though the learning activity may or may not be perceived as authentic by the student, emphasis is, nonetheless, placed on higher levels of cognitive processing and in-depth treatment of the content using a variety of thinking skill strategies (e.g., problem-solving, decision-making, reflective thinking, experimentation, scientific inquiry).
4A **Integration** **(mechanical)**	Technology-based tools are integrated in a mechanical manner that provides rich context for students' understanding of the pertinent concepts, themes, and processes. Heavy reliance is placed on prepackaged materials and/or outside resources (e.g., assistance from other colleagues), and/or interventions (e.g., professional development workshops) that aid the teacher in the daily management of their operational curriculum. Technology is perceived as a tool to identify and solve authentic problems as perceived by the students relating to an overall theme or concept. Emphasis is placed on student action and on issues resolution that requires higher levels of student cognitive processing and in-depth examination of the content.
4B **Integration** **(routine)**	Technology-based tools are integrated in a routine manner that provides rich context for students' understanding of the pertinent concepts, themes, and processes. At this level, teachers can readily design and implement learning experiences that empower students to identify and solve authentic problems relating to an overall theme or concept using the available technology with little or no outside assistance. Emphasis is again placed on student action and on issues resolution that requires higher levels of student cognitive processing and in-depth examination of the content.

(Continued)

TABLE 2.1   ⊠   *(Continued)*

LEVEL	DESCRIPTION
5 **Expansion**	Technology access is extended beyond the classroom. Classroom teachers actively elicit technology applications and networking from other schools, business enterprises, governmental agencies (e.g., contacting NASA to establish a link to an orbiting space shuttle through the Internet), research institutions, and universities to expand student experiences directed at problem-solving, issues resolution, and student activism surrounding a major theme or concept. The complexity and sophistication of the technology-based tools used in the learning environment are now commensurate with (1) the diversity, inventiveness, and spontaneity of the teacher's experiential-based approach to teaching and learning and (2) the students' level of complex thinking (e.g., analysis, synthesis, evaluation) and in-depth understanding of the content experienced in the classroom.
6 **Refinement**	Technology is perceived as a process, product (e.g., invention, patent, new software design), and/or tool for students to find solutions related to a "real-world" problem or issue of significance to them. At this level, there is no longer a division between instruction and technology use in the classroom. Technology provides a seamless medium for information queries, problem solving, and/or product development. Students have ready access to and a complete understanding of a vast array of technology-based tools to accomplish any particular task at school. The instructional curriculum is entirely learner-based. The content emerges based on the needs of the learner according to his/her interests, needs, and/or aspirations and is supported by unlimited access to the most current computer applications and infrastructure available.

Adapted from Moersch, C. (2002). Beyond hardware: Using existing technology to promote higher-level thinking *(pp. 47–49). Eugene, OR: ISTE.*

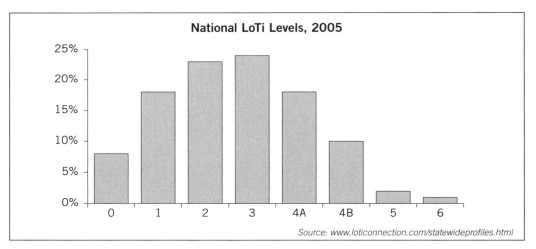

Figure 2.1 National LoTi Levels, 2005

Challenges to Providing High-Quality Support

The infrequent and unbalanced nature of current technology implementations in America's schools highlights the need for professional learning programs focusing on instructional planning and design. Technology facilitators and leaders must be prepared for the challenges inherent in providing teachers with this type of support.

Researchers and practitioners agree that planning technology-integrated instruction is challenging for teachers (Mishra & Koehler, 2006; Pierson, 2001). Even without the integration of technology, the instructional design process requires teachers to consider multiple factors such as what to teach (content), how best to teach it (pedagogy), what resources to use (instructional materials), how to manage students and resources throughout the learning process (classroom management), and how to monitor student learning (assessment). As teachers plan, they filter their instructional design decisions through a unique set of socially constructed beliefs about what constitutes knowledge in their content area, how people learn best, and what is the right approach for the specific students in their class (Schulman, 1987).

The climate in today's schools frequently complicates the planning process even further. In the quest for school improvement, teachers are currently faced with new sets of learning standards, higher student performance goals, and pressure to implement more innovative teaching methods. At the same time, professional learning opportunities, necessary instructional materials, and time for instructional planning are often limited. Under these conditions, even experienced, exemplary teachers often struggle to create meaningful, rigorous learning experiences that help students understand content deeply and transfer knowledge to new situations (Fullan, 1999).

Asking teachers to integrate technology into their instructional designs invariably adds new layers of complexity to the planning process. Teachers may know how to operate technology (TF/TL Standard I), but they are not sure how to implement technology in the classroom to support student learning. Although teachers frequently select textbooks, maps, and other types of traditional instructional resources to teach specific content, using technology tools is less familiar to them. Because the use of technology in classrooms is a relatively new practice and technology-related professional development is often focused on technology skills instead of integration, teachers do not have many examples of effective technology use for learning. As a result, technology use is often relegated to the peripheries of the learning process. Using technology as a reward when students' "real" work is done and teaching technology skills in isolation from other content areas are two frequently cited examples (Moersch, 2002).

In the planning process, teachers must also consider how students will acquire technical skills needed to complete learning tasks. Though many feel that student technology literacy outpaces the knowledge and skills of educators, implementing technology in the classroom still requires training students how to use technologies for specific learning purposes. Many teachers remain uncertain as to how to embed technical training into instruction and are uncomfortable assuming the role of technical trainer in their classrooms. Because they lack strategies to integrate student computer skills efficiently and seamlessly into instruction, teachers are also concerned that training students to use technology will drastically reduce the amount of time dedicated to achieving mandated content standards.

Teachers must develop new ways to manage resources and students in technology-rich classrooms. Using technology in the classroom affects the learning environment and culture. The mere presence of technology alters space arrangements and the flow of activities. New technologies foster new social practices for teachers and students. Even when technology-related changes are positive and promising, they can raise questions for teachers. How do I manage student access to computers? How do I manage student safety on the Internet? How can technology be used to implement differentiated instruction and to accommodate students with special learning needs? How do I know the students are learning when they use computers? Answering these questions requires the formation of new practices, policies, procedures, and norms of behavior in the classroom.

The Challenge of Facilitating and Leading Instructional Change

Although the challenges previously mentioned are formidable, they pale in comparison with facilitating and leading instructional change. Theory and research suggest that technologies with a high degree of alignment to current practice have a greater chance of being adopted and used by practitioners (Fishman, 2005). Yet many new educational technologies are not designed to reinforce traditional practice—especially because scholars and educational leaders are calling for a shift away from those practices to more student-centered, inquiry-based instructional models in classrooms. The work of school technology professionals is therefore more complex than simply helping teachers support traditional, teacher-centered instruction with new technologies. Instead, technology facilitators and leaders are likely to find themselves in the most difficult type of change initiative—one that challenges teachers' long-standing beliefs about teaching and learning.

From the onset of large-scale instructional technology programs, scholars have cautioned educators about the complexity of their tasks. Means (1993) clearly categorizes technology integration efforts as systemic change initiatives aspiring to shift instruction from a conventional to a reformed paradigm (see Table 2.2).

TABLE 2.2 ■ Comparison of conventional and reformed approaches to instruction

CONVENTIONAL INSTRUCTION	REFORMED INSTRUCTION
Teacher directs	Students explore
Instruction is didactic	Instruction is interactive
Students receive short blocks of instruction on a single subject	Students perform extended blocks of authentic and multidisciplinary work
Students work individually	Students work collaboratively
Teacher is knowledge dispenser	Teacher is facilitator
Students grouped by ability	Students grouped heterogeneously
Students who have demonstrated mastery of the basics work on advanced skills	All students practice advanced skills
Students assessed on fact knowledge and discrete skills	Students assessed on performance

Source: Means, B. (1993). Introduction: Using technology to advance educational goals. In B. Means (Ed.), Technology and school reform: The reality behind the promise (pp. 1–22). San Francisco: Jossey-Bass.

In a similar way, Jones, Valdez, Nowakowski, and Rasmussen (1995) warn educators that, in order for technology to have the greatest impact on student learning, it must be embedded in effective learning environments. To help educators understand the characteristics of these effective environments, these researchers synthesized information on effective instruction and generated a list of descriptors (referred to as the indicators of engaged learning; see Table 2.3) to guide technology integration efforts. Like Means' (1993) descriptors of reformed instruction, these indicators stand in sharp contrast with current instructional practices and illustrate the substantial cultural and pedagogical shifts that school technologists must encourage and support.

TABLE 2.3 ▪ Indicators of engaged learning

VARIABLE	INDICATOR	INDICATOR DEFINITION
Vision of Learning	Responsible for learning Strategic Energized by learning Collaborative	Learner involved in setting goals, choosing tasks, developing assessments and standards for the tasks; has big picture of learning and next steps in mind; Learner actively develops repertoire of thinking/learning strategies; Learner is not dependent on rewards from others; has a passion for learning; Learner develops new ideas and understanding in conversations and work with others.
Tasks	Authentic Challenging Multidisciplinary	Pertains to real world, may be addressed to personal interest; Difficult enough to be interesting but not totally frustrating, usually sustained; Involves integrating disciplines to solve problems and address issues.
Assessment	Performance-based Generative Seamless and ongoing Equitable	Involving a performance or demonstration, usually for a real audience and useful purpose; Assessments having meaning for learner, maybe produce information, product, service; Assessment is part of instruction and vice versa—students learn during assessment; Assessment is culture fair.
Instructional Model	Interactive Generative	Teacher or technology program responsive to student needs, requests (e.g., menu driven); Instruction oriented to constructing meaning, providing meaningful activities/experiences.
Learning Context	Collaborative Knowledge-building Empathetic	Instruction conceptualizes students as part of learning community; Activities are collaborative; Learning experiences set up to bring multiple perspectives to solve problems so that each perspective contributes to shared understanding for all, goes beyond brainstorming; Learning environment and experiences set up for valuing diversity, multiple perspectives, strengths.

(Continued)

TABLE 2.3 ■ *(Continued)*

VARIABLE	INDICATOR	INDICATOR DEFINITION
Grouping	Heterogeneous Equitable Flexible	Small groups with persons from different ability levels and backgrounds; Small groups organized so that over time all students have challenging tasks/experiences; Different groups organized for different instructional purposes so each person is a member of different work groups, works with different people.
Teacher Roles	Facilitator Guide Co-learner/ co-investigator	Engages in negotiation, stimulates and monitors discussion and project work but does not control; Helps students to construct their own meaning by modeling, mediating, explaining when needed, redirecting focus, providing options; Teacher considers self as learner, willing to take risks to explore areas outside his or her expertise, collaborates with other teachers and practicing professionals.
Student Roles	Explorer Cognitive Apprentice Teacher Producer	Students have opportunities to explore new ideas/tools, push the envelope in ideas and research; Learning is situated in relationship with mentor who coaches students to develop ideas and skills that simulate the role of practicing professionals (i.e., engage in real research); Students encouraged to teach others in formal and informal contexts; Students develop products of real use to themselves and others.

Source: Jones, B., Valdez, G., Nowakowski, J., & Rasmussen, C. (1995). Plugging in: Choosing and using educational technology *(p. 9). Oakbrook, IL: North Central Regional Educational Laboratory.*

Responding to the Challenge

Although these challenges represent the context in which school technologists must enact TF/TL Standard II, their tasks—including facilitating and leading change—are not impossible. Researchers have documented how technology facilitators and leaders have successfully navigated teachers toward successful technology integration in the past, and these cases provide a path for the future.

The following briefly summarizes some of the most important lessons learned from these experiences. They should serve as guiding principles for facilitators and leaders as they implement TF/TL Standard II.

Specify what types of learning experiences teachers should design. In the planning process, teachers will benefit from a clear description of what types of learning experiences they should be designing. Providing teachers with a descriptive framework, such as the indicators of engaged learning, is especially important to support change. If no criteria are provided, teachers will continue to plan and design the same types of learning experiences that they have implemented in the past (see Creighton, 2003, pp. 67–75).

Provide teachers with models of the types of technology uses desired in classrooms. In spite of their importance, descriptive frameworks, such as the indicators of engaged learning, are usually not enough to change instruction. Frameworks are most effective when they are accompanied by multiple models of exemplary practice. School technologists must model effective technology use while facilitating professional learning for teachers. Furthermore, scenarios, sample lesson plans, or videos of teachers using technology to engage learners in authentic experiences will help educators envision how technology can improve teaching and learning. Researchers consistently find that these types of models are critical in helping teachers use technology effectively in the classroom— which usually requires a transformation in the way they teach. Without these models, teachers often misinterpret or oversimplify instructional frameworks. Most people require models to understand the framework completely and apply it to practice.

Immerse teachers in professional learning experiences similar to the learning experiences they are expected to design. Often teachers do not have a different vision for learning because they have not experienced this type of learning environment themselves. Therefore, technologists must engage teachers in the types of interactive, complex, inquiry-based learning scenarios that they expect teachers to enact in their classrooms. In these learning contexts, teachers should work collaboratively to solve real problems related to integrating technology into instructional practices, and technologists should serve as facilitators and guides. By designing professional learning in this manner, the technologist provides one of the strongest types of models for change—a model that is based in personal experience (Zepeda, 1999).

Provide teachers with a process for designing. Although a descriptive framework is useful, it does not provide teachers with a process to accomplish their tasks. Even though rigid step-by-step process approaches are usually considered inappropriate for complex, loosely-structured creative tasks such as instructional design, teachers will benefit from a planning model to structure their efforts (Grabe & Grabe, 2007; Roblyer, 2006; Wiggins & McTighe, 2006).

Communicate a research-based rationale for why these types of learning experiences support student learning. Brief but powerful research-based rationales facilitate the change process and provide credibility to planning efforts. Because most educators lack the time to process large numbers of individual research studies, most facilitators and leaders lean on the work of credible scholars who synthesize a body of knowledge, summarize the evidence, and present it in an accessible format for practitioners. A few select readings and a carefully constructed bibliography of additional resources often serve to help educators know they are doing the right thing for their students (Bransford & Cocking, 1999).

Link technology efforts to other curriculum and instruction initiatives. Because successful technology integration has as much—or more—to do with effective pedagogical practices than with technology (Pierson, 2001), TF/TL Standard II highlights the curricular aspects of the technologist's job responsibilities. Because these responsibilities probably overlap with those of other personnel in the organization, Ausband (2006) suggests coordinating efforts with other curriculum and instructional staff and programs focused on school improvement. Such coordination can prevent conflicts among educators with similar purposes, add credibility to educational technology initiatives because they are focused on learning, conserve resources, and reduce the risk of teacher overload from participating in multiple change initiatives (Ausband, 2006; Fullan, 1999).

Understand the change process and build in support for conceptual change. Some researchers describe technology integration, planning, and design as a process that evolves over time. Understanding the stages that teachers may experience during this transformation helps technologists understand their own work better and prepares them to support teachers as they plan and design learning experiences differently (Fullan, 2001; Hall & Hord, 2005; Matzen & Edmunds, 2007; Rogers, 1995).

View the planning as ongoing and cyclical. Collaborative planning and reflection are ongoing cycles in effective schools, but many times professional learning programs do not dedicate resources to this phase of planning, thus truncating teachers' ability to design high-quality lessons and navigate change. When implementing new technologies and instructional designs, teachers benefit from piloting learning experiences, reflecting with peers, and revising plans for future implementation. Teachers also benefit from observing peers and providing feedback (Zepeda, 1999).

Be patient and realistic. Everyone won't change. There are many barriers to instructional change and technology adoption—including school cultures of autonomy and academic freedom that rightfully allow teachers a great deal of latitude in their individual classrooms. Because of this, technology facilitators and leaders can only build social forces toward change over time. The work is slow, tedious, and indispensable.

Summary of Current Context

It is obvious why TF/TL Standard II plays a central role in the advancement of instructional technologies in K–12 education—if technology is going to be fully implemented in classrooms, teachers must plan how they will embed these new tools into student learning and must be supported in implementing technology-integrated instruction. Given the complexities of instructional design generally and the specific challenges of planning for technology use, it is easy to see why teachers need a great deal of support from technology facilitators and leaders. In order to help teachers with these complexities, technology facilitators and leaders need an extensive repertoire of knowledge, skills, and dispositions firmly grounded in theories and research on effective instruction, classroom management, adult learning, and conceptual change. TF/TL Standard II provides a comprehensive description of what this support looks like and how to deliver it.

Implementing the Standard

This section reviews the standard, performance indicators, and performance tasks of TF/TL Standard II, which can be found in the standards table on pages 44–45.

Performance Standards

Although there is a formidable list of challenges that teachers face when designing technology-supported instruction, TF/TL Standard II provides technology facilitators and leaders with a road map to systematically address each one of these barriers in coordinated but unique ways. In Standard II, the difference between the performance standards for facilitators and leaders hinges on locale. Because technology facilitators are located in school buildings, the facilitators' proximity to practice affords them greater opportunities to plan and design technology-supported learning environments and experiences with teachers. Facilitators may even have the opportunity to model innovative technology-supported instruction in classrooms. By contrast, technology leaders are more distanced from schools and daily instructional practices. Therefore, they generally operate on a broader scale to assist in the planning, designing, and modeling process at the district, state, and regional levels.

Performance Indicators

The performance indicators that technology facilitators and leaders share for TF/TL II are targeted and strategic. They are designed to alleviate the greatest challenges that teachers face when planning for technology use in the classroom. When enacting this standard, facilitators and leaders introduce teachers to high-quality instructional technology tools that are well designed, developmentally appropriate for their students, and tied to content standards. Technologists also provide teachers with models of how other educators have integrated technology into instruction. Supporting teachers as they actually plan technology-rich learning experiences, these suggestions and examples help teachers envision how technology can enrich learning in their own classrooms (TF-II.A., C., F.).

Technology facilitators and leaders also help teachers overcome their questions about teaching technology skills to students, preserving instructional time for content standards in core academic areas, organizing and managing instruction in a technology-rich environment, and meeting the individual needs of all learners. To do this, facilitators and leaders provide teachers with strategies, options, and best-practice examples for managing technology resources and student learning in the classroom (TF-II.D., E.).

Current research on teaching, learning, and technology integration must anchor the work of teachers and technologists as they plan and design technology-supported learning experiences (TF-II.B., F.). Research helps technologists infuse credibility into their work, building teachers' confidence that they are planning the right kinds of experiences for their students. Having a strong research-based rationale for action is especially important for teachers who are attempting pedagogical change. Long-standing beliefs about teaching and learning are deeply ingrained into teachers' practices and identity. Change requires a convincing argument and emotional support. Research can play an important role in providing a rationale and a catalyst for action.

Performance Tasks

In TF/TL Standard II, facilitators assume the key role of directly supporting teachers. Facilitators accomplish this support function by providing options, strategies, resources, and feedback in the planning process. They model strategies, consult with teachers, assist teachers, and support teachers during instructional design. At advanced stages of performance, facilitators may provide formal professional learning programs for teachers, but most often they serve as coaches, consultants, and advisers to teachers when implementing this standard.

Leaders provide that critical "outside-in" collaboration that many experts cite as important for local change initiatives to be successful (Fullan, 1999). While local facilitators work with teachers, leaders scan best practice examples and the professional literature to identify, research, locate, and evaluate information that would be helpful to their building-based colleagues. In advanced stages, leaders also develop products and models to assist other educators in designing learning. Once critical information is located or created, leaders develop mechanisms to disseminate this knowledge, which includes designing and implementing formal, ongoing professional development programs. In these ways, leaders not only provide critical support to teachers and facilitators in schools, they also establish directions, frameworks, and quality control for planning.

Planning and Designing Learning Environments and Experiences (TF/TL-II)

Technology Facilitation Standard	Technology Leadership Standard
(TF-II) Educational Technology Facilitators plan, design, and model effective learning environments and multiple experiences supported by technology.	(TL-II) Educational Technology Leaders assist by planning, designing, and modeling effective learning environments and experiences at the district, state, and regional levels.

TF/TL-II.A. Design developmentally appropriate learning opportunities that apply technology-enhanced instructional strategies to support the diverse needs of learners.

Performance Tasks for Facilitators	Performance Tasks for Leaders
TF-II.A.1. Provide resources and feedback to teachers as they create developmentally appropriate curriculum units that use technology.	TL-II.A.1. Research and disseminate project-based instructional units modeling appropriate uses of technology to support learning.
TF-II.A.2. Consult with teachers as they design methods and strategies for teaching computer/technology concepts and skills within the context of classroom learning.	TL-II.A.2. Identify and evaluate methods and strategies for teaching computer/technology concepts and skills within the context of classroom learning and coordinate dissemination of best practices at the district/state/regional levels.
TF-II.A.3. Assist teachers as they use technology resources and strategies to support the diverse needs of learners including adaptive and assistive technologies.	TL-II.A.3. Stay abreast of current technology resources and strategies to support the diverse needs of learners including adaptive and assistive technologies and disseminate information to teachers.

TF/TL-II.B. Apply current research on teaching and learning with technology when planning learning environments and experiences.

TF-II.B.1. Assist teachers as they apply current research on teaching and learning with technology when planning learning environments and experiences.	TL-II.B.1. Locate and evaluate current research on teaching and learning with technology when planning learning environments and experiences.

TF/TL-II.C. Identify and locate technology resources and evaluate them for accuracy and suitability.

TF-II.C.1. Assist teachers as they identify and locate technology resources and evaluate them for accuracy and suitability based on district and state standards.	TL-II.C.1. Identify technology resources and evaluate them for accuracy and suitability based on the content standards.
TF-II.C.2. Model technology integration using resources that reflect content standards.	TL-II.C.2. Provide ongoing appropriate professional development to disseminate the use of technology resources that reflect content standards.

TF/TL-II.D. Plan for the management of technology resources within the context of learning activities.

TF-II.D.1. Provide teachers with options for the management of technology resources within the context of learning activities.	TL-II.D.1. Identify and evaluate options for the management of technology resources within the context of learning activities.

TF/TL-II.E. Plan strategies to manage student learning in a technology-enhanced environment.

TF-II.E.1. Provide teachers with a variety of strategies to use to manage student learning in a technology-enhanced environment and support them as they implement the strategies.	TL-II.E.1. Continually evaluate a variety of strategies to manage student learning in a technology-enhanced environment and disseminate through professional development activities.

TF/TL-II.F. Identify and apply instructional design principles associated with the development of technology resources.

TF-II.F.1. Assist teachers as they identify and apply instructional design principles associated with the development of technology resources.	TL-II.F.1. Identify and evaluate instructional design principles associated with the development of technology resources.

ISTE's Essential Conditions and TF/TL Standard II

When implementing TF/TL Standard II: Planning and Designing Learning Environments and Experiences, technology facilitators and leaders help teachers understand and implement *Student-Centered Learning*, an important essential condition for achieving ISTE's NETS•S. In helping teachers shift from teacher-centered to student-centered learning, technology facilitators and leaders assume the role of professional learning coaches as they help teachers learn how to integrate technology to support engaging approaches to learning. Therefore, TF/TL Standard II technologies also strengthen two other essential conditions—*Ongoing Professional Learning* and *Skilled Personnel*.

Performance Scenarios

At a faculty meeting, the school's technology facilitator introduces himself and offers to provide assistance to teachers who want to use technology for instruction. After the meeting, the fourth-grade team asks the facilitator to help them infuse technology into one of their favorite units on immigration. The technology facilitator gathers relevant videos from the Internet and locates an online project where students share their family immigration stories with other students from all over the world. The teachers preview these items and integrate them into their unit. Because the teachers have not participated in an online project before, the technology facilitator agrees to be in class to support the teachers as they introduce the project and teach the students how to use the website.

A district technology leader attends a seminar on adaptive and assistive technologies offered at the local university and realizes that schools already have many tools that can support the needs of diverse learners, such as concept mapping and text-to-speech functions in word processors. After the seminar, the leader shares this information with technology facilitators, who are able to assist teachers in deploying these tools in the classroom.

Although classroom technology use is becoming more frequent, a district technology leader is concerned that teachers are not maximizing the use of technology to support student-centered learning and higher-order thinking—central goals of the district's strategic plan. To encourage different types of uses, the leader gathers models of preferred types of technology uses and presents them to technology facilitators. The models help facilitators understand what types of technology uses best support the district's goals, and they encourage teachers to shift their practices when planning learning environments and experiences.

In a current research journal, the technology leader reads an article on the effective uses of technology to support student learning in math. The leader shares this study with the math curriculum director and the facilitators in the district. The article creates an understanding of why technology should be used to support student-centered learning and higher-order thinking, and the facilitators apply this knowledge as they help teachers plan and design math instruction in the local schools.

case study

SHAPING HOW TEACHERS USE TECHNOLOGY

Authentic Training for Teachers

The Cherokee County School District, located approximately 35 miles north of Atlanta, is committed to transforming its schools into 21st-century learning environments through Teach21, a comprehensive reform effort to help teachers use technology for learning.

The program provides an interactive whiteboard, a student response system, a mounted LCD projector, a teacher laptop, and five new student computers in each classroom. More importantly, under the direction of Instructional Technology Supervisor Debbie Childress, the program also provides extensive support for teachers as they learn about these new technologies and plan for their use.

Teach21 is the brainchild of Superintendent Frank Petruzielo, who knew that without proper training and support the teachers would not be able to take full advantage of the tools they were being given. The superintendent challenged Childress to draft a professional development plan and sample district policies to support the initiative. To complete her task, Childress drew on her professional learning and teaching experience, her colleagues, local university faculty, and a review of professional literature.

The plan immerses teachers in the same type of engaging, authentic learning experiences that Childress hopes teachers will implement with students. In return for receiving equipment in their classrooms, Teach21 teachers commit to spending 100 hours to complete various technology integration projects throughout the first year and a more extended capstone project at the end of the first program year. The teachers are allowed to request additional technology to complete their projects. Mobile laptop labs, digital video cameras, and microphones for creating podcasts are the most requested equipment for the Teach21 classrooms. The capstone project is defined as an action research project or a standard-based instructional unit designed to engage students. These projects are completed collaboratively by teams and published in online portfolios.

"The portfolios accomplish three things," said Childress. "First, they allow us to share ideas and learn from one another. Second, they show the teacher's growth over time. Third, the public forum raises the bar for high-quality work. If there is an authentic audience, learners will look at their work differently."

To ensure that teachers are designing high-quality integration projects, Childress has published criteria and evaluation rubrics for these projects. These criteria are grounded in NCREL's engaged learning indicators and Moersch's Level of Technology Implementation (LoTi) framework. Teachers use the rubrics to reflect on their own work, and others use the rubrics to provide collegial feedback for improvement.

"Without criteria that challenge teachers to do different things, we might have experienced technology use that overemphasized direct instruction and lower-order cognitive skills. The framework stretched all of our thinking," noted Childress.

(Continued)

case study (Continued)

Childress believes that focusing the professional learning component around planning and designing learning experiences is powerful. "This design addresses what students and teachers have to do. They have this equipment. They want this equipment. Now they have to figure out how to use it for instruction. This is the authentic question on all of the teachers' minds. Why not help them answer it?"

This authentic question puts teachers in the driver's seat, and Childress and the eight technology integration specialists who serve on her team assume the roles of mentors and coaches. "The task we have established for the teachers is challenging, so we have to have a comprehensive program to support them," commented Childress.

The comprehensive support for planning includes a required orientation to the program, which includes an overview of engaged learning, models of effective technology integration, and a discussion on the changing needs of 21st-century learners. In addition to this required orientation, teachers are also required to choose from a menu of professional learning options offered by the instructional technology supervisors (ITSs). These training requirements comprise another 100 hours of professional learning in addition to the 100 hours of more informal, collaborative work to design and publish learning experiences.

However, this project requires the Cherokee tech team to do much more than teach technology classes. The ITSs also support Teach21 teachers in four or five schools. According to Childress, this type of in-class coaching, one-on-one support, and small-group consultation is critical during instructional change. "During planning, teachers need a more experienced facilitator to help them solve problems, provide responses, add ideas to the mix, and help them visualize what the learning experience will be like," explained Childress.

Worried that the ITSs wouldn't be able to meet all the demands for local support during change initiatives, the district also budgeted for one tech mentor at each school. Tech mentors are teachers who retain their teaching duties but receive an extra-duty stipend to provide technical support for participants, and serve as liaisons between the local school and the district technology staff. Other roles of the tech mentors include easing the technical demands on the ITSs during the term of the project and serving as points of contact when the ITS isn't in the building.

"It is a commitment for us and for the teachers, but this is what it takes to plan and design high-quality, technology-supported learning experiences," acknowledges Childress. "There are no shortcuts, but at least Teach21 provides some support and incentives for the hard work that needs to be done."

Teachers receive their equipment at the beginning of their two-year commitment, but once they complete the capstone, they also earn a technology endorsement from the district and a $400 stipend. "I was worried that we weren't offering enough money for teachers to go through all that planning," Childress reflected, "but I've learned it's not about the money. Teachers want to have the technology and they want to plan new learning experiences that are meaningful and exciting to students. They just need the structured time and support—and the challenge—to do so."

To visit Cherokee Counties Teach21 website, go to: http://webtech.cherokee.k12.ga.us/tech/endorsement/

Discussion Questions

- Describe how technology is currently used in your school, district, region, or state. How frequently do students use technology for learning? How do they use technology? Are you pleased with the frequency and context of technology use? What other uses of technology would you like to see and why?

- What challenges do teachers face as they integrate technology into learning experiences for students? How can technology facilitators and leaders help them overcome these challenges?

- The LoTi framework or the engaged learning indicators emphasize the importance of student-centered, inquiry-based learning models that support higher-order thinking. What types of technology use and tools are best suited to supporting these instructional goals? How often do you see technology being used in these ways?

- Do you believe technology implementations are skewed toward lower-order cognitive skills and didactic learning environments? If so, why do you think teachers most often implement technology in this way?

- As teachers plan technology-supported learning experiences, what questions do they have about managing the technology in their classrooms? What strategies have they implemented to manage technology effectively in their classrooms?

Resources

The resources identified under TF/TL Standard II pertain to planning and designing learning environments and experiences. Journals are included providing current ideas for using technology in the teaching and learning process. Software review sites help inform technology facilitators and leaders when selecting software titles. Current texts provide current thinking on how technology can be used to support meaningful learning. Numerous websites are included to keep technology facilitators and leaders informed on a range of topics, including assistive technology, best practices, differentiated instruction, instructional design, online collaborations, 21st-century skills, and innovative learning models.

Periodicals

From Now On
www.fno.org
> This site by Jamie McKenzie is an online educational technology journal promoting engaged learning and educational technology literacy.

Learning & Leading with Technology
www.iste.org/LL

> ISTE's flagship periodical provides practical ideas for improving educational outcomes with technology.

Technology & Learning
www.techlearning.com

> This magazine provides K–12 educators with essential resources for managing, teaching, and training with technology.

Software Reviews

California Learning Resource Network
www.clrn.org/home/

> This site is a searchable database with hundreds of learning resource reviews.

Educational Software Preview Center
www.temple.edu/martec/onlinetools/preview.html

> This site by MAR*TEC is a searchable database of educational products and software. Reviews on usability and accessibility are available for some titles.

EvaluTech
www.evalutech.sreb.org

> This site by the Southern Regional Education Board (SREB) includes more than 10,000 reviews of software and print resources.

SuperKids
http://superkids.com

> This site provides software reviews for teachers published as part of a resource site for teachers and parents.

Books

Ashburn, E., & Floden, R. (Eds.) (2006). *Meaningful learning using technology: What educators need to know and do.* New York: Teachers College.

Boss, S., & Krauss, J. (2007). *Reinventing project-based learning: Your field guide to real-world projects in the digital age.* Eugene, OR: ISTE.

Grabe, M., & Grabe, C. (2007). *Integrating technology for meaningful learning* (5th ed). Boston: Houghton-Mifflin.

Marzano, R., & Kendall, J. (2007). *The new taxonomy of educational objectives.* Thousand Oaks, CA: Corwin.

Roblyer, M. D. (2006). *Integrating technology into teaching* (4th ed.). Upper Saddle River, NJ: Pearson.

Solomon, G., & Schrum, L. (2007). *Web 2.0: New tools, new schools.* Eugene, OR: ISTE.

Wiggins, G., & McTighe, J. (2006). *Understanding by design* (2nd ed.). Upper Saddle River, NJ: Pearson.

Websites

Apple Education
www.apple.com/education/k12/
> This site provides information and resources for K–12 educators who use Apple products.

Apple Learning Interchange
http://edcommunity.apple.com/ali/
> This site is sponsored by Apple and serves as a social network for educators with a wealth of content and resources available.

Assistive Technology Resources
www.onlineconferencingsystems.com/at.htm
> This site serves as a one-stop for free assistive technology resources.

Assistive Technology and Special Needs Resources
www.Internet4classrooms.com/assistive_tech.htm
> This site provides links to assistive technology resources for educators.

Assistive Technology
www.4teachers.org/profdev/index.php?profdevid=at
> This site provides numerous links to assistive technology centers, assistive technology organizations, and funding opportunities for educators.

Center for Applied Research in Educational Technology (CARET)
http://caret.iste.org
> This site evaluates the research on educational technology to improve overall technology decisions.

CyberBee
www.cyberbee.com
> This site provides fresh ideas on how to use technology and integrate it into the curriculum.

Differentiated Instruction
www.Internet4classrooms.com/di.htm
> This site offers a list of resources on learning styles, instructional theory, practical tips for the classroom, and sample units and lessons.

Education World
www.educationworld.com
> This site offers a wide variety of resources for educators, including lesson plans, practical information for educators, information on how to integrate technology into the classroom, articles written by education experts, site reviews, and more.

Eduscapes

http://eduscapes.com/tap/topic84.htm

> This site is designed to help educators effectively integrate technology into teaching and learning environments.

Edutopia

www.edutopia.org

> Edutopia documents and disseminates exemplary programs in K–12 schools. It has a video library of classroom uses of technology that are especially useful as models in professional development. The site allows educators to order custom DVDs of their favorite clips. To engender change, technology facilitators and leaders will be particularly interested in reviewing videos categorized as project-based learning.

Encyclopedia of Educational Technology

http://coe.sdsu.edu/eet/

> This site is a collection of short multimedia articles on a variety of topics related to the fields of instructional design and education and training.

Gateway to 21st Century Skills

www.thegateway.org

> This site provides access to thousands of learning resources, teaching tools, and assessments.

Global Schoolhouse

www.globalschoolnet.org/GSH/

> This site is dedicated to online collaborations for educators, parents, students, and the community.

Harnessing the Web

www.gsn.org/web/

> This site is a tutorial that helps teachers implement collaborative, project-based learning on the Internet.

IBM Education

www-03.ibm.com/industries/education/

> This site offers IBM solutions that can help educators utilize technology to enhance teaching and learning, streamline administrative processes, and build a strong infrastructure.

Indicators of Engaged Learning

www.ncrtec.org/capacity/profile/profwww.htm

> This profile tool helps compare current instructional practices with a set of indicators for engaged learning and high-performance technology.

Intel Education

www.intel.com/education/

> This site provides free tools and resources to support collaborative student-centered learning through the use of technology. It also provides information about Intel's global programs to help improve math, science, and technology education.

Kathy Schrock's Guide for Educators

http://school.discovery.com/schrockguide/

> This site contains a categorized list of sites useful for enhancing curriculum and professional growth.

Let Your Mentors Do the Coaching

www.techlearning.com/story/showArticle.php?articleID=164302277

> This article provides insights on how to create a successful coaching and mentoring program.

Spotlight Resource

LoTi

www.loticonnection.com

One of the significant problems in technology implementation has been—and remains—a lack of a clear standard by which teachers can measure their proficiency in integrating technology into instruction. This has resulted in a number of teachers believing that they are quite technologically proficient, yet seldom integrating technology for higher-order thinking and problem-solving. LoTi is a tool for assisting technologists in both assessing the current level of technology implementation in schools and providing teachers with a standard for technology implementation against which they can measure themselves. By providing and categorizing specific indicators of technology use, educators obtain a clear understanding of their current level of technology implementation as well as indicators of more sophisticated technology use.

Microsoft Education

www.microsoft.com/education/

> This site includes Microsoft's technology, tools, programs, and solutions to help address education challenges while improving teaching and learning opportunities.

Partnership for 21st Century Skills

www.21stcenturyskills.org

> This site provides a framework for 21st-century knowledge and skills needed to succeed as effective citizens, workers, and leaders.

TeachersFirst

www.teachersfirst.com

> This site offers an extraordinary collection of lessons, units, and Web resources for teachers.

Teachnology

www.teach-nology.com

> This site provides thousands of free and easy-to-use resources, such as lesson plans and rubrics for teachers.

Understanding by Design Exchange

www.ubdexchange.org

> The UbD exchange contains tools and resources to help teachers design curriculum, assessments, and instruction that "leads students to deep understanding of content."

U.S. Department of Education Office of Educational Technology

www.ed.gov/about/offices/list/os/technology/

> This government website provides information and resources on the department's educational technology policies, research projects, and national technology summits.

References

Ausband, L. (2006). Instructional technology specialists and curriculum work. *Journal of Research on Technology in Education, 39*(1), 1–21.

Bransford, J., & Cocking, R. (Eds.). (1999). *How people learn: Brain, mind, experience, and school.* Washington, DC: National Academies Press.

CDW-G. (2005). *Teachers Talk Technology survey.* Retrieved August 23, 2007, from http://newsroom.cdwg.com/features/feature-08–29–05.htm

Creighton, T. (2003). *The principal as technology leader.* Thousand Oaks, CA: Corwin.

Consortium for School Networking. (2005). *Digital leadership divide.* Available from www.cosn.org/resources/grunwald/digital_leadership_divide.pdf

Fishman, B. (2005). Adapting innovations to particular contexts of use. In C. Dede, J. Honan, & L. Peters (Eds.), *Scaling up success: Lessons from technology-based educational improvement.* San Francisco: Jossey-Bass.

Fullan, M. (1999). *Change forces: The sequel.* London: Falmer.

Fullan, M. (2001). *Leading in a culture of change.* San Francisco: Jossey-Bass.

Grabe, M., & Grabe, C. (2007). *Integrating technology into meaningful learning* (5th ed.). New York: Houghton Mifflin.

Hall, G., & Hord, S. (2005). *Implementing change: Patterns, principles, and potholes* (2nd ed.). Boston: Allyn & Bacon.

Jones, B., Valdez, G., Nowakowski, J., & Rasmussen, C. (1995). *Plugging in: Choosing and using educational technology.* Oakbrook, IL: North Central Regional Educational Laboratory.

Matzen, N., & Edmunds, J. (2007). Technology as a catalyst for change: The role of professional development. *Journal of Research on Technology in Education, 39*(4), 417–433.

Means, B. (1993). Introduction: Using technology to advance educational goals. In B. Means (Ed.), *Technology and school reform: The reality behind the promise* (pp. 1–22). San Francisco: Jossey-Bass.

Mishra, P., & Koehler, M. (2006). Technological pedagogical content knowledge: A framework for teacher knowledge. *Teachers College Record, 108*(6), 1017–1054.

Moersch, C. (2001). Next steps: Using LoTi as a research tool. *Learning and Leading with Technology, 29*(3), 22–27.

Moersch, C. (2002). *Beyond hardware: Using existing technology to promote higher-order thinking.* Eugene, OR: ISTE.

Pierson, M. (2001). Technology integration practice as a function of pedagogical expertise. *Journal of Research on Computing in Education, 33*(4), 413–430.

Roblyer, M. D. (2006). *Integrating technology into teaching* (4th ed.). Upper Saddle River, NJ: Pearson.

Rogers, E. (1995). *Diffusion of innovations* (4th ed.). New York: Free Press.

Schulman, L. (1987). Knowledge and teaching: Foundations of the new reform. *Harvard Educational Review, 57*(1), 1–22.

Wiggins, G., & McTighe, J. (2006). *Understanding by design* (2nd ed.). Upper Saddle River, NJ: Pearson.

Zepeda, S. (1999). *Staff development: Practices that promote leadership in learning communities.* Larchmont, NY: Eye On Education.

Because of the pervasiveness of technology, an understanding of what technology is, how it works, how it is created, how it shapes society, and how society influences technological development is critical to informed citizenship. Technological choices influence our health and economic well-being, the types of jobs and recreation available, even our means of self-expression. How well citizens are prepared to make those choices depends in large part on their level of technological literacy.

— NATIONAL ACADEMY OF ENGINEERING & NATIONAL RESEARCH COUNCIL, 2006, P. 1

Chapter Three

TF/TL STANDARD III

Teaching, Learning, and the Curriculum

TF/TL Standard II describes how technology facilitators and leaders assist teachers in planning learning experiences for students, and TF/TL Standard III outlines how school technologists influence teaching and learning from another strategic direction—the curriculum.

In an era when the needs of students are rapidly changing, schools are not providing digital-age learners with the types of environments that parallel the connectivity and social interaction patterns that they are accustomed to outside of school. This disparity threatens to alienate youth further and encourage the already growing student perceptions that schools are outdated and irrelevant to their interests and goals.

In a similar vein, current instructional practices and academic curricula are not producing students who have the knowledge, skills, and dispositions needed for digital-age work and citizenship. Although students may be skilled in using technology to pursue their own social and entertainment purposes outside of school, they are still unprepared to use technology to pursue postsecondary studies, daily work in various professional and technical fields, lifelong learning, and civic engagement.

By infusing student technology standards into state and local curricula and developing accompanying curriculum resources, technology facilitators and leaders create both a mandate for technology integration and the structural support teachers need to implement that mandate. Pursuing this strategic direction is especially important as educators respond to the evolving needs of K–12 students and other community stakeholders.

Current Context: Educating the Net Generation

As technology facilitators and leaders implement TF/TL III, they will find a strong disconnect between the ways technology is used for teaching and learning and the ways students use technology in their own personal lives. Because technology permeates how students think, communicate, and process information, accommodating the positive attributes of their media-rich learning styles can help educators update teaching, learning, and the curriculum.

Recent studies portray the current K–12 student as increasingly immersed in media-rich environments beyond the school day. A recent report from the Pew Foundation claims that 87% of youth between the ages 12 and 17 use the Internet—a 45% increase since the last national survey of students five years earlier. Seventy-five percent (75%) of these Internet-using youth also relied on instant messaging for discussing homework assignments and engaging in personal interactions with friends (Hitlin & Rainie, 2005).

A study sponsored by the Kaiser Foundation (2005) reports that 13% of youth (ages 8–18) own a handheld device that connects to the Internet. More than eight in ten (86%) have a computer at home, three in four (74%) have Internet access at home, and one in three (31%) has a high-speed connection. Nearly one-third (31%) have a computer in their bedroom, and one in five (20%) has an Internet connection to that computer. The Kaiser Report also reveals that America's youth average 44.5 hours a week (or 6.35 hours a day) using media. Twenty-six percent (26%) of this time, students are involved in using more than one medium simultaneously. Table 3.1 represents the average amount of time that youth use different types of technologies in a typical day.

TABLE 3.1 ■ Average daily time spent using media

TYPE OF MEDIA	NUMBER OF HOURS:MINUTES
Watching TV (live TV, videos, DVDs, pre-recorded shows)	3:51
Listening to music (radio, CDs, tapes, MP3s)	1:44
Using a computer (online or offline)	1:02
Playing video games (console or handheld)	0:49
Reading (books, magazines, newspapers)	0:43
Watching movies	0:25

Note: Amount of time cannot be summed due to overlapping media use.
Source: Kaiser Foundation. (2005). Generation M: Media and the lives of 8–18-year olds. *Retrieved August 20, 2007, from www.kff.org/entmedia/upload/Generation-M-Media-in-the-Lives-of-8–18-year-olds.pdf*

This data suggests that today's students not only desire but need engaging, media-rich learning experiences to maximize their learning potential. Students seem to support Prensky's twofold plea for technology-enhanced and student-centered instruction. When asked what types of school settings they prefer, students called for one-to-one, ubiquitous computing environments that are simple, fast, interactive, and wireless (NetDay, 2006). In such environments, students claim they could learn better and more deeply by constructing products, accessing online learning opportunities, finding information tailored to specific learning goals, and connecting with teachers, beyond-school mentors, and peers for purposes of learning. They also hoped for learning contexts that were challenging, meaningful, interesting, and relevant to their future (Gates Foundation, 2006).

Yet schools seem to be falling short of meeting the learning needs of digital-age learners. Results from the Pew and Kaiser studies indicate that students use the Internet more frequently outside of school than in school. Nearly one-third of teens report that they do not use the Internet at school at all (Hitlin & Rainie, 2005). Sixty-five percent (65%) of students reported that they access the Internet most often at home, whereas only 14% claimed school as their primary access site (Kaiser Foundation, 2005).

Although the relationship between the lack of high-quality technology use in classrooms and students' motivation to learn is not entirely clear, policy makers and the general public are concerned about students' lack of access to challenging, relevant, technology-rich learning environments, high dropout rates, and failing schools.

Ketelhut, McCloskey, Dede, Breit, and Whitehouse (2005) provide a useful summary of the gap between school and beyond-school technology uses and the probable consequences of this inconsistency. These scholars also note that even when technology is used in schools, the tools and contexts are probably not as engaging and interactive as students' out-of-school experiences with media:

Rapid technological advances are reconstituting our temporal understanding of a "generation." Based on experiences with new interactive media, students today likely have significantly different lifestyles than their peers even five years earlier. Many children are comfortable using and working with multiple information and communication technologies, including Web browsers and search engines, multimedia applications, instant messaging, and wireless mobile devices with image and video capabilities (such as cell phones and portable game consoles)—often simultaneously. For those who have come of age using sophisticated gaming devices such as Xbox and other immersive, collaborative, entertaining experiences in their lives outside of school, the relatively simplistic interfaces and content of many learning technologies leave them uninspired; furthermore, exposure to emerging interactive media is altering student learning strategies and styles, yet schools frequently wall off students from their strengths and interests by "unplugging" them when in classrooms. (p. 239)

Student Technology Literacy

Although meeting the new learning styles and preferences of digital-age students is important, other social pressures to rethink current teaching, learning, and curricula also make TF/TL Standard III relevant in today's schools. Business community members, parents, government officials, and educators are concerned that schools are not preparing students for life, work, and learning after high school.

In spite of the central role technology plays in modern life, the Partnership for 21st Century Skills maintains that there is a gap between what students learn in school and the knowledge and skills they need for their future careers (Partnership for 21st Century Skills, 2006). Business partners and educational technology advocates frequently assert that mastering core academic content as defined in the past is not sufficient to prepare students for meaningful participation in today's global economy. Higher education administrators and faculty members are also concerned that students lack the technological knowledge necessary for postsecondary academic study and technical training. In addition to foundational academic knowledge, students must be able to use technologies in ethical, accurate, and insightful ways to support the demands of economics and citizenship in modern society (Honey, Fasca, Gersick, Mandinach, & Sinha, 2005).

Although very little empirical data exists to support these assumptions, a recent pilot of Educational Testing Services' iSkills test found that less than half of college students participating were able to narrow a search or adapt Web-based material for a different audience. This illustrates that although teens may be able to use technology in their own personal lives, educators may have neglected to teach them how to use technology for learning and work (Educational Testing Service, 2006). In statewide 2005–06 assessment of fifth and eighth-graders' technology literacy, the Arizona Department of Education found that only 27% of fifth-grade students and 37% of eighth-grade students met state standards (Arizona Department of Education, 2006).

Curriculum Successes

In many ways, recent trends in curriculum theory and development are addressing the needs of learners and business and helping technology facilitators and leaders promote technology use in the classroom. K–12 curricula in core academic areas at the national, state, and local levels are shifting away from discrete, fact-based learning objectives toward performance standards designed to elicit higher-order thinking, creativity, problem-solving, and deeper understanding of content. Because constructivist technology instruction is generally seen as integral to achieving these types of learning goals, these curricular shifts are conducive to technology integration even though technology may not be directly addressed.

Other curricular changes, however, explicitly require learning with and learning about technology. The National Educational Technology Standards for Students (NETS•S) also draw attention for the need to integrate technology into learning. After ISTE released the first set of NETS•S in 1998, the standards rapidly gained popularity. The NETS•S were updated in 2007. Today, the NETS•S are adopted, adapted, or referenced in at least 48 state curricula, with the remaining states developing their own sets of standards for students largely replicating NETS•S. Student technology standards have been in place since 2001 for approximately 70% of states, and the percentages climbed to 95% by 2005 (see Figure 3.1).

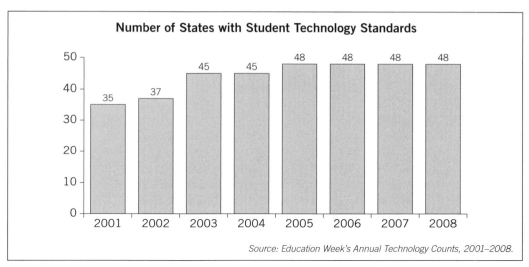

Figure 3.1 States with student technology standards (including District of Columbia)

The release of the new NETS•S in July 2007 refocused attention on the need for student technology literacy, resulting in states and districts updating their local standards. These new standards focus more on what students must be able to do with technology rather than on the tools themselves—a revision that should facilitate the integration of student technology standards into core academic areas. The NETS•S are accompanied by a set of profiles, or common examples of learning activities, that students might be expected to complete at certain grade levels. They also contain publications explaining the standards, exemplary learning experiences that implement the standards, and various professional learning opportunities to help educators understand the standards, such as ISTE's annual conference. The NETS•S (www.iste.org/nets/) are listed on the following page.

1. **Creativity and Innovation**

   Students demonstrate creative thinking, construct knowledge, and develop innovative products and processes using technology.

2. **Communication and Collaboration**

   Students use digital media and environments to communicate and work collaboratively, including at a distance, to support individual learning and contribute to the learning of others.

3. **Research and Information Fluency**

   Students apply digital tools to gather, evaluate, and use information.

4. **Critical Thinking, Problem Solving, and Decision Making**

   Students use critical thinking skills to plan and conduct research, manage projects, solve problems, and make informed decisions using appropriate digital tools and resources.

5. **Digital Citizenship**

   Students understand human, cultural, and societal issues related to technology and practice legal and ethical behavior.

6. **Technology Operations and Concepts**

   Students demonstrate a sound understanding of technology concepts, systems, and operations.

Curriculum Gaps

The national support for student technology standards and the proliferation of these standards among states present a promising portrait for improving technology literacy. However, it is unclear to what extent the adopted standards have been developed into implementable curricula at the classroom level. The NETS•S establish a sound curricular foundation for implementing student technology standards in teaching and learning; however, this is, at best, a good first step. Without meaningful implementation, the NETS•S will remain an aspiration.

For technology to be effectively integrated into the curriculum—and ultimately the classroom—local school boards, administrators, teachers, and parents must know about the student technology standards in the state curricula, and school districts must fully implement them. To integrate technology into the curriculum effectively, local school districts must align student technology standards to standards in other core academic curricular areas and develop grade-specific benchmarks. Then, mechanisms to assess both core curricula and technology components must be established and implemented. Without curricular alignment, grade-specific benchmarks, and assessment practices, teachers may be unwilling or unable to integrate technology into instruction.

Although national professional organizations (such as ISTE) provide examples of how technology standards can be integrated with other learning standards in core academic areas, states and local systems must ensure technology and curriculum alignment across their entire local curriculum. This integration is necessary to ensure that technology skills are taught and appropriately integrated into subject area instruction.

Implementing curriculum requires instructional resources. In well-established curricular areas, teachers have resources to implement the curriculum—a science class will contain textbooks, scientific instrumentation tools, and other supplies for experiments. For student technology literacy programs, this step of evaluating and securing resources seems to be neglected. Owing perhaps to educators' unfamiliarity with technology generally and subject-specific technology particularly, they may be unaware of the resources needed. However, implementing student technology standards and integrating instruction requires more than a modern, Internet-connected computer. Depending upon the particular learning objectives, software, online subscriptions, and other types of devices such as global positioning systems, graphing calculators, and probeware may be needed.

Once the student technology standards are aligned to the local curriculum, resources have been selected, and grade-level benchmarks developed, a curriculum guide for student technology standards can be published for students and parents. Such a guide will help teachers understand teaching and learning and place student technology standards on par with other curricular areas with a rich history and support for disciplinary knowledge construction.

Even with better curriculum resources and documentation, educators will need ongoing professional learning opportunities providing instruction in best practices in implementing student technology standards. Locating and disseminating multiple models of exemplary practice and in-class coaching are two promising methods for helping teachers implement a new curriculum.

Without the implementation of these important strategies, the NETS•S cannot be transformed into a useable, local curriculum for classroom teachers. Although there is little information about their current stage of development at the state and local levels, it seems that many of these strategies are still not being addressed at those levels. As a result, technology standards are not receiving the same type of curriculum development and support as standards in other content areas. Table 3.2 summarizes curricular strategies important to implementing the standards and assigns primary responsibility for implementation. The darker shaded areas highlight strategies where progress is currently unknown and possibly weak—thus identifying the need for technology facilitation and leadership.

TABLE 3.2 ■ Curriculum strategies to support technology integration and student technology literacy

CURRICULUM STRATEGIES	RESPONSIBILITY FOR IMPLEMENTATION		
	National Professional Organizations	State Education Agencies	Local School Districts/ Schools
Establish National Educational Technology Standards for Students (ISTE, 1998, 2007)	X		
Promote and monitor state adoption of these educational technology standards	X		
Adopt student technology standards as part of the mandated state curricula		X	
Inform the local school board of state requirements to implement student technology standards			X
Publish the state's student technology standards as part of local curricula and inform teachers that they are responsible for integrating these standards into teaching and learning			X
Align student technology standards to standards in other core academic curricular areas		X	X
Develop grade-specific performance benchmarks or profiles of student technology standards to help educators understand what students should know and be able to do at each developmental level	X	X	X
Evaluate curriculum standards to determine what instructional resources are necessary to implement them and secure those resources for use by students and teachers		X	X
Develop, locate, and disseminate multiple models of exemplary instruction at all grade levels and content areas that address the technology standards and core academic standards in an integrated manner	X	X	X

(Continued)

TABLE 3.2 ▪ *(Continued)*

CURRICULUM STRATEGIES	RESPONSIBILITY FOR IMPLEMENTATION		
	National Professional Organizations	State Education Agencies	Local School Districts/ Schools
Provide teachers with a detailed curriculum guide that includes suggested learning experiences and available resources to teach the standards		X	X
Implement professional learning opportunities to make educators and policy makers aware of student technology standards and how to implement them	X	X	X

 Darker shaded areas: areas where progress is unknown

Summary of Current Context

There is currently a great need to transform teaching, learning, and curricula as described in TF/TL-III. Student technology learning standards likely have been adopted in state and local curricula for years; however, they still are not making a wide-scale impact on teaching and learning. As a result, students' learning styles and preferences are not being addressed in the classroom, and students are technologically ill prepared for work and postsecondary learning programs. Technology facilitation and leadership are necessary to implement the new NETS•S in the classroom. TF/TL Standard III provides specific performances to support this task.

Implementing the Standard

This section reviews the standard, performance indicators, and performance tasks of TF/TL Standard III, which can be found in the standards table on pages 67–68.

Performance Standards

To distinguish TF/TL-III from TF/TL-II, school technologists must remember that Standard III focuses on supporting teaching and learning through curriculum development. To emphasize this distinction, the standards focus technologists' activities on curriculum plans—the key elements supporting the implementation of the NETS•S. Curriculum plans include resource and material development, permitting educators to integrate the NETS•S into teaching and learning. TF/TL-III also emphasizes the importance of methods and strategies, the details of the curriculum plan that are frequently neglected. These methods and strategies are especially important in a curriculum area unfamiliar to most teachers.

Although technology facilitators and leaders both focus on curriculum planning, leaders design the plan. To do so, leaders must create the types of documentation and resources that teachers will need to implement the NETS•S. Once leaders create usable products to implement the plan, they must disseminate it to others and explain how to use it. This will include modeling strategies and methods for technology facilitators, who will, in turn, model best practices for teachers. Facilitators may help leaders create the plan, but their primary functions are to apply and implement the plan.

Performance Indicators

The performance indicators provide insights into the topics to which technology facilitators and leaders must attend as they develop the curriculum. In TF/TL-III.A., technologists are reminded of the importance of addressing technology and content standards to ensure an integrated approach. TF/TL-III.B. and C. focus on learner-centered instruction that promotes higher-order thinking and creativity—themes reflected in most core-content areas and in the new NETS•S. Because any curricula must be accessible to all learners, TF/TL-III.B. includes a focus on diverse needs of students. TF/TL-III.D. and E. draw attention, once again, to the details necessary for a good curriculum plan. To implement these standards, teachers will need to know how to manage technology in the classroom and to build research-based units and lessons of instruction. Examples and guidance in these areas are crucial components for completing the curriculum plan.

Performance Tasks

In harmony with the performance standards for TF/TL-III, the leaders' tasks mostly focus on designing models and strategies so that others can see how the student technology standards can become a reality in the classrooms. Leaders also model these strategies to others and disseminate information.

Facilitators, on the other hand, use and apply the products and processes that leaders design and disseminate. Unlike TF/TL Standard II, for which teachers were the primary actors and facilitators supported the teachers' activities, the facilitator assumes the more active role in TF/TL-III. Often, teachers are unable to implement student technology standards until they see sample lessons, strategies, and methods. To alleviate this problem, facilitators must model best practices for teachers when they deliver professional learning opportunities or when they teach students in classrooms.

Because TF/TL-III is related to curriculum, most of the performance tasks are linked to moving the NETS•S from a set of global standards for students to a detailed curriculum plan that can be implemented in schools (TF/TL-III.A.1.–7.). Technologists' performance tasks will also focus on the use of assistive technology when addressing the needs of diverse learners (TF/TL-III.B.1.). In an effort to model exemplary practices, the performance tasks include modeling research-based strategies that integrate technology with other content areas and promote student-centered learning, higher-order thinking, and problem solving (TF/TL-III.A.4., B.1., C.1., E.1., E.2.). Because there is little time for modeling the strategies that leaders design and facilitators use and apply, each example must be carefully crafted. Leaders and facilitators must always model these characteristics.

Teaching, Learning, and the Curriculum (TF/TL-III)

Technology Facilitation Standard	Technology Leadership Standard
(TF-III) Educational technology facilitators apply and implement curriculum plans that include methods and strategies for utilizing technology to maximize student learning.	(TL-III) Educational technology leaders model, design, and disseminate curriculum plans that include methods and strategies for applying technology to maximize student learning.

TF/TL-III.A. Facilitate technology-enhanced experiences that address content standards and student technology standards.

Performance Tasks for Facilitators	Performance Tasks for Leaders
TF-III.A.1. Use methods and strategies for teaching concepts and skills that support integration of technology productivity tools (refer to NETS for Students).	TL-III.A.1. Design methods and strategies for teaching concepts and skills that support integration of technology productivity tools (refer to NETS for Students).
TF-III.A.2. Use and apply major research findings related to the use of technology in education to support the integration of communication tools through the curriculum (refer to NETS for Students).	TL-III.A.2. Design methods for teaching concepts and skills that support the integration of communication tools (refer to NETS for Students).
TF-III.A.3. Use methods and strategies for teaching concepts and skills that support integration of research tools (refer to NETS for Students).	TL-III.A.3. Design methods and strategies for teaching concepts and skills that support integration of research tools (refer to NETS for Students).
TF-III.A.4. Use methods and strategies for teaching concepts and skills that support integration of problem-solving/decision-making tools (refer to NETS for Students).	TL-III.A.4. Design methods and model strategies for teaching concepts and skills that support integration of problem-solving/decision-making tools (refer to NETS for Students).
TF-III.A.5. Use methods and strategies for teaching concepts and skills that support use of media-based tools such as television, audio, print, media, and graphics (refer to NETS for Students).	TL-III.A.5. Design methods and model strategies for teaching concepts and skills that support use of media-based tools such as television, audio, print media, and graphics (refer to NETS for Students).
TF-III.A.6. Use and describe methods and strategies for teaching concepts and skills that support use of distance learning systems appropriate in a school environment (refer to NETS for Students).	TL-III.A.6. Evaluate methods and strategies for teaching concepts and skills that support use of distance learning systems appropriate in a school environment (refer to NETS for Students).
TF-III.A.7. Use methods for teaching concepts and skills that support use of Web-based authoring tools in a school environment (refer to NETS for Students).	TL-III.A.7. Design methods and model strategies for teaching concepts and skills that support use of Web-based and non-Web-based authoring tools in a school environment (refer to NETS for Students).

TF/TL-III.B. Use technology to support learner-centered strategies that address the diverse needs of students.

TF-III.B.1. Use methods and strategies for integrating technology resources that support the needs of diverse learners, including adaptive and assistive technology.	TL-III.B.1. Design methods and strategies for integrating technology resources that support the needs of diverse learners, including adaptive and assistive technology.

TF/TL-III.C. Apply technology to demonstrate students' higher-order skills and creativity.

TF-III.C.1. Use methods and strategies for teaching problem-solving skills using technology resources.	TL-III.C.1. Design methods and model strategies for teaching problem-solving skills using technology resources.

TF/TL-III.D. Manage student learning activities in a technology-enhanced environment.

TF-III.D.1 Use methods and classroom management strategies for teaching technology concepts and skills in individual, small group, classroom, and/or lab settings.	TL-III.D.1 Design methods and model classroom management strategies for teaching technology concepts and skills used in PK–12 environments.

TF/TL-III.E. Use current research and district/region/state/national content standards to build lessons and units of instruction.

TF-III.E.1. Describe and identify curricular methods and strategies that are aligned with district/region/state/national content and technology standards.	TL-III.E.1. Disseminate curricular methods and strategies that are aligned with district/region/state/national content and technology standards.
TF-III.E.2. Use major research findings and trends related to the use of technology in education to support integration throughout the curriculum.	TL-III.E.2. Investigate major research findings and trends related to the use of technology in education to support integration throughout the curriculum.

ISTE's Essential Conditions and TF/TL Standard III

When implementing TF/TL Standard III: Teaching, Learning, and the Curriculum, technology facilitators and leaders help establish a Curriculum Framework, an ISTE essential condition that refers to content standards and related digital curriculum resources. This curriculum framework could reinforce traditional teacher-centered modes of teaching, but TF/TL Standard III calls for technology leaders and facilitators to support a pedagogical shift. To meet the performance tasks, they must align the curriculum framework and expectations for teaching and learning to the needs and interests of digital-age learners. Therefore, in implementing TF/TL Standard III, technology facilitators and leaders also strengthen ISTE's essential condition for Student-Centered Learning.

Performance Scenarios

A state has recently adopted the new NET•S as the student technology standards in the state curriculum. The state technology leader calls for district technology leaders and facilitators throughout the state to provide examples of how teachers are implementing these standards in the classroom. The best examples are posted on the state curriculum website to provide models for educators implementing the standards in local schools. School-level facilitators use the examples on the website to help teachers understand how to implement the NETS•S.

District technology leaders prepare a presentation on the NETS•S for the local board of education, explaining why they are important to address in the curriculum. They use the state's website to illustrate how the NETS•S must be integrated into the content areas and taught across the curriculum.

The district high school social studies curriculum includes a unit in which students must pose a solution to a problem facing the local community. To test the public reaction to their solution, students must poll community members and report the results. The district technology leader and the curriculum director target this unit to integrate problem-solving and decision-making tools (NETS•S). They purchase a subscription to an online survey tool allowing students to create and administer surveys and to analyze results electronically. In the high school, the technology facilitators show teachers and students how to use the tool and spreadsheet software to complete their unit of study.

To implement the NET•S, the school district purchases two wireless laptop labs in mobile carts for each of the elementary schools. Knowing that teachers will need support in managing the new technologies, the district technology leader creates protocols for using the equipment with students. The first time that teachers use the laptops for instruction, facilitators model these protocols for students and teachers in the classroom. The teachers are anxious to use the laptop carts, but find that having students remove laptops from the cart, set them up, and return them is chaotic. They are unsure of how to manage the new technology available for their classroom. Knowing that teachers will need support in managing the new technologies, the technology facilitator in the school and the district technology director create protocols for using the equipment with students. The first time that teachers use the laptops for instruction, facilitators model these protocols for students and teachers in the classroom so that the new technology does not create a classroom management issue.

ESTABLISHING A CURRICULUM FRAMEWORK

Building Technology Literacy in Maryland

As the project manager of Maryland's TL8 consortium since 2003, Kalani Smith is dedicated to helping his state develop a curriculum framework for student technology literacy.

"We need to address technology standards in school," he explains. "Technology literacy levels the playing field in the 21st century. We have students who have the technology at home, and these students have a high-level of technology skills. Then there are other students who do not have these opportunities outside of school. When these students without technology skills enter the job market, they are not going to be as competitive. As educators, we need to ensure that all students have the same access and learn the same skills. It is just like learning to read! If students don't have technology skills because of poverty and we don't address this, we are just going to recreate that poverty cycle."

The TL8 consortium, made up of all 24 school districts in the state of Maryland, was formed in response to the NCLB goal that all students will be technology literate by the end of eighth grade. Funded by NCLB Title IID competitive grants from the Maryland State Department of Education (MSDE), the group has defined technology literacy, drafted student technology standards, and explored ways to assess student progress toward the standards. To ensure high-quality implementation, the consortium has also aligned the technology standards to Maryland's voluntary curriculum and developed high-quality professional development modules for teachers.

The group started with the ISTE NETS•S as a foundation for their work but decided that they had to extend them. Explains Smith, "In Maryland, we needed more. We wanted grade-level benchmarks, not just a grade range, for example. We also wanted to develop all the supporting materials teachers would need to implement the standards in the classroom." In retrospect, Smith believes the decision to construct and not just adopt standards was the best decision for their group. The process enabled Maryland educators to reflect on the ISTE standards, understand what they mean, and think about how best to accomplish them. According to Smith, the result has been a great deal of ownership and pride in the standards—an outcome he believes could not have happened without the collaborative work of the consortium members.

Smith finds his job with the consortium exciting, but very different from his previous job as an instructional trainer for a school district. As an instructional trainer, Smith modeled lessons, trained teachers on new technologies, and helped teachers plan instruction. However, his job with the consortium is much more administrative.

"I do a lot of planning, organizing, and communicating," responds Smith. "It is rather difficult to explain. The goals and objectives of the consortium were established when I took the job, and most of the actual work comes from the consortium members. My job title is accurate. I really do manage the project. I keep things going."

(Continued)

case study (Continued)

Some of his regular tasks include planning agendas for monthly consortium meetings. He also facilitates those meetings, takes notes, and distributes minutes. At these meetings, he helps consortium members discuss tasks and develop plans to complete work. As the work is completed, Smith often reviews, synthesizes, and edits documents. Then, he cycles the drafts back to consortium members for review and response. "It is a long process to build consensus, but that is the way we operate. We all must be able to live with a decision and support it back in our school system," he explains.

To stay close to the needs of the consortium, Smith has also traveled to most of the districts in the consortium and met with designated representatives one-on-one. "This was a way for me to connect with each of the consortium members and hear their individual needs," he reflects. "I think that this step was vitally important in getting feedback and ensuring that their individual needs were being heard."

In addition to managing the day-to-day work of the consortium, Smith collaborates with those outside the consortium, as well. For example, Smith has regular meetings with the TL8 advisory board composed of various stakeholders, including classroom teachers, school-based administrators, institutions of higher education, the business community, parents, school district leaders, and various departments from MSDE. When the standards were being drafted, Smith organized open feedback sessions with a broad group of stakeholders, including business partners, parents, teachers, administrators, and students—even elementary students, who Smith believes are frequently overlooked in community processes because of their age.

After a draft of standards was completed, the consortium contracted with external consultants to review the standards. The reviewers compared Maryland's standards to the national standards and other state standards. They also checked the consortium's alignment of the technology standards to Maryland's voluntary curriculum.

"They made some very important suggestions," comments Smith. "The consortium accepted most but not all of them. It was my role to help consortium members understand the report and address each recommendation. We either accepted the advice of the consultants or we said, 'No, that's not what we want to do.' If we didn't accept the advice, we documented it. I would record notes, point-by-point, as we worked through the document."

Smith's most sustained outside collaboration is with staff from MSDE. For example, Smith meets regularly with Nancy Carey, who oversees the grant that funds TL8, but Carey does more than just grant monitoring. Carey also helped the consortium obtain feedback from MSDE content experts and navigate the process for bringing the consortium's technology literacy standards to Maryland's State Board of Education for approval, which was granted in February 2007.

In addition to organizing, planning, and communicating, Smith also recalls one final category of work—one he jokingly refers to as "paperwork." For example, he recalls the process to create an RFP for the external review of the curriculum and to award that contract. Of course, this is just one example. Receiving or spending any funds for the grant requires proper paperwork and documentation. Because the TL8 is funded

(Continued)

by federal funds, Smith files progress reports twice a year to receive funds. To sustain funding, the consortium must reapply for funding annually, and Smith completes this application process as well. Because the grant calls for partner districts to submit professional development plans for approval before they receive funding from the TL8 grant, reviewing plans and approving them for funding is yet one more example of what Smith calls a paperwork task.

Smith feels that what prepared him most for this job was his experience in the classroom as a teacher. "I could never understand curriculum and standards in the way that I do without having taught. Classroom experience is absolutely critical for all educators," he states.

However, he also reflects on a time when his district switched from Integrated Learning Systems (ILS) to software-based solutions. "I was put in charge of visiting schools that were using the ILS, meeting with their principals and other staff to determine how they were using their ILS and then recommending software that would replace that functionality. We then set up demos of the various pieces of software, and the teachers came to review them and determine which products they wanted. Then, we ordered software for them and delivered training. So, I did have some experience with project management before," he comments.

When asked about the most difficult parts of his job, he cites two examples. First, he notes that he has learned a lot about accounting practices and financial procedures. "I didn't know much about that," he smiled. "But, our accounting department walks me through it and teaches me. I think I understand it pretty well now! I know how an invoice should look and I know what it takes to pay out money from the grant."

However, the most uncomfortable part of his job to date has been reviewing and approving the professional development plans from consortium districts. "In the professional development plans, districts have to outline how they are going to use the professional development funds that the grant provides to train teachers on the technology literacy standards," he relates. "It's my job to review them and make sure they meet the state's criteria for high-quality professional learning. At first, it was very awkward to tell peers that their work needed to be modified. I had told kids what to do before, and I had helped other educators, but I never had to assume that monitoring role before. Nancy Carey, who is in charge of professional learning for MSDE, helped me learn how to provide that type of feedback in a constructive way."

When asked what he will do after the grant comes to a close and the TL8 consortium's work is over, Smith finds it hard see past the work that needs to be done. "We have come a long way, but there is still more to do. We have addressed only the core academic areas, but not math, art, foreign language, physical education. . . . We still are struggling with the assessment issue. We have not realized our goals of implementing these standards in the classroom. As long as there is grant funding to continue this work, the consortium will want to keep pressing forward. The process we have gone through is equally as important as the products we've produced."

Discussion Questions

- To what extent are the NETS•S or another set of state technology standards being implemented in your school, district, state, or region?

- Review Table 3.2. What strategies have been implemented to support the NETS•S in your local setting? What other action is needed to realize a full implementation of the NETS•S?

- Compare and contrast the 2007 NETS•S to the 1998 NETS•S. How do you think the NETS•S revision will affect classroom practice?

- Review the NETS•S and generate examples of how these standards could be integrated into the core content areas at different grade levels.

- This chapter implies that schools should accommodate students' preferences for technology-rich, interactive learning environments. However, is there a danger of being too plugged in? What strategies can educators use to ensure that students maintain a healthy balance of face-to-face and online learning activities?

Resources

As technology facilitators and leaders implement TF/TL Standard III, they may benefit from several types of resources that either assist technologists by deepening their understanding of concepts discussed in the chapter or provide tools technologists may share with other educators. Although all the resources are valuable, we have identified one "Spotlight Resource" in each chapter that has particular utility to technologists.

The resources identified under TF/TL Standard III pertain to teaching, learning, and the curriculum. A series of articles by Marc Prensky (creator of the terms "digital natives" and "digital immigrants") are included. These articles provide technology facilitators and leaders with an understanding of digital-age century learners, their expectations, and their needs. An e-book is listed that discusses the Net Generation and implications for teaching and learning. An e-newsletter highlights youth, education, and technology news, tools, and resources. Reports are included that provide research on the use of technology having the greatest impact on learning. A series of links to the ISTE standards are included as quick references for technology facilitators and leaders. Finally, a few websites are listed that focus on teaching and learning in modern schools.

Articles

Prensky, M. (2005). *Engage Me or Enrage Me.*
www.educause.edu/ir/library/pdf/ERM0553.pdf

Prensky, M. (2005). *Listen to the Natives.*
www.ascd.org/authors/ed_lead/el200512_prensky.html

Prensky, M. (2001). *Digital Natives.*
www.marcprensky.com/writing/Prensky–Digital Natives, Digital Immigrants–Part1.pdf

Prensky, M. (2001). *Do They Really Think Differently?*
www.marcprensky.com/writing/Prensky–Digital Natives, Digital Immigrants–Part2.pdf

E-Book

Educating the Net Generation (2005)
www.educause.edu/educatingthenetgen/
> This e-book is downloadable for no charge from the Educause website. It is a collection of 15 articles by American authors who explore the Net Gen and the implications for teaching, learning, and the curriculum.

E-Newsletter

YouthLearn
www.youthlearn.org/resources/newsletter
> The YouthLearn Initiative led by the Education Development Center offers educators comprehensive services and resources for using technology including an excellent newsletter with great resources. Click on Issue 100 for "100 Big Things in Youth, Education and Technology."

Reports

CEO Forum on Education and Technology (2001)
www.ceoforum.org/downloads/report4.pdf
> Key Building Blocks for Student Achievement in the 21st Century. Contains recommendations for effective uses of technology to enhance student achievement.

The Learning Return on Our Educational Technology Investment (2002)
www.wested.org/cs/we/view/rs/619
> This report by WestEd addresses research findings, focusing on policy and pedagogical issues regarding whether the current level of spending on technology makes a difference in student learning.

Standards

Spotlight Resource

ISTE NETS for Students (2007)
www.iste.org/nets/

ISTE released the next generation of the NETS•S in 2007. As technology, resources, practices, and assessments change over time, it becomes necessary to review and refresh the standards. These new standards represent the work of educators all across the nation plus input from 22 other countries.

Websites

Partnership for 21st Century Skills

www.21stcenturyskills.org

The Partnership for 21st Century Skills has emerged as a leading advocacy organization focused on infusing 21st-century skills into education. This website includes numerous resources including a framework for learning in the 21st century, 21st-century standards, ICT Literacy Maps for different content areas, various reports, state initiatives, and more.

NetDay

www.netday.org/speakup/

A national effort to collect and share the views and feedback from young people, teachers, parents, and other stakeholders on how best to harness the power of technology.

References

Arizona Department of Education. (2006). *2005–06 student technology literacy assessment.* Retrieved August 25, 2007, from www.ade.az.gov/technology/

Educational Testing Service. (2006). *ICT literacy assessment: Preliminary findings.* Retrieved August 27, 2007, from www.ets.org/Media/Products/ICT_Literacy/pdf/2006_Preliminary_Findings.pdf

Gates Foundation. (2006). *Why do kids drop out?* Retrieved August 25, 2007, from www.gatesfoundation.org/nr/downloads/ed/TheSilentEpidemic3–06FINAL.pdf

Hitlin, P., & Rainie, L. (2005). *Teens, technology, and school.* Retrieved August 20, 2007, from www.pewInternet.org/pdfs/PIP_Internet_and_schools_05.pdf

Honey, M., Fasca, C., Gersick, A., Mandinach, E., & Sinha, S. (2005). *Assessment of 21st century skills: The current landscape.* Retrieved June 11, 2007, from www.21stcenturyskills.org/images/stories/otherdocs/Assessment_Landscape.pdf

Kaiser Foundation. (2005). *Generation M: Media in the lives of 8–18-year-olds.* Retrieved August 20, 2007, from www.kff.org/entmedia/upload/Generation-M-Media-in-the-Lives-of-8–18-Year-olds.pdf

Ketelhut, D., McCloskey, E., Dede, C., Breit, L., & Whitehouse, P. (2005). Core tensions in the evolution of online teacher professional development. In C. Dede (Ed.), *Online professional development for teachers.* Cambridge, MA: Harvard.

National Academy of Engineering & National Research Council (NAE & NRC). (2006). *Tech tally: Approaches to assessing technological Literacy.* Washington, DC: National Academies Press.

NetDay. (2006). *Speak up.* Retrieved August 27, 2007, from www.tomorrow.org/speakup/index.html

Partnership for 21st Century Skills. (2006). Are they really ready to work: Employers' perspectives on the basic knowledge and applied skills of new entrants to the 21st century U.S. workforce. Retrieved August 24, 2007, from www.21stcenturyskills.org/documents/FINAL_REPORT_PDF09–29–06.pdf

We have opportunities to put new technologies to use in assessment, to create new kinds of tasks, to bring them to life, to interact with examinees. . . .

— MISLEVY, STEINBERG, ALMOND, HAERTEL, AND PENUEL, 2003

Given the level of spending of precious dollars and hours on technology-based activities, we have an obligation to learn as much as we can about how to do it right. We need to know not just which technology uses make us feel good, but which have real, long-term payoffs for our students and the adults who work with them in schools and how to maximize their benefits.

— MEANS AND HAERTEL, 2004

Chapter Four

TF/TL STANDARD IV

Assessment and Evaluation

In the current age of accountability, educational leaders are required to be more skilled in assessment and evaluation than their predecessors were. Technology facilitators and leaders are no exception. TF/TL Standard IV highlights the unique and critical roles that instructional technologists must assume in this area. The following list includes some of the current topics technology facilitators and leaders are likely to address in their schools, districts, states, and regions:

- Using technology to assess student learning of core academic content and to differentiate instruction based on students' individual learning needs

- Assessing student technology literacy

- Using technology to collect, analyze, interpret, and report all types of data, including student achievement data, for the purposes of school improvement

- Evaluating the implementation of technology programs, including the impact of technology on student learning, for the purposes of accountability and program improvement

Current Context: Using Technology to Assess Student Learning in Core Academic Areas

Although the terms "assessment," "evaluation," and "accountability" apply to a wide range of issues in education, none receives more attention than the assessment of student learning in core academic areas. For many years, leading researchers and practitioners have argued that the most successful school improvement efforts are structured as ongoing, collaborative inquiry around student assessment data (DuFour & Eaker, 1998; Joyce, Calhoun, & Hopkins, 1999). Accountability also has become the centerpiece of federal educational policy. The 2001 reauthorization of the Elementary and Secondary Education Act of 1965 (ESEA), popularly titled No Child Left Behind (NCLB), requires states to establish specific goals for student achievement and to publish annual Adequate Yearly Progress (AYP) reports. Although the AYP concept is not without controversy, its impact on the educational community is indisputable, effecting a seismic change in American public education. Even if the requirements for future education legislation shift in years to come, regular, systematic student assessment and public reporting will likely remain a fixture of federal educational policy. These current conditions increase the demand for educational technologists to demonstrate how technology can improve assessment of student learning in the classroom, district-level benchmarking throughout the school year, and annual administrations of high-stakes, standardized testing.

Computer-based testing (CBT) is emerging as one of the most promising technologies to address these current needs. CBT permits educators to quickly and efficiently identify and map student content areas to be assessed on tests, to create multiple forms of tests, to grade tests, and to analyze results. CBT technologies also provide teachers, students, and parents with frequent and immediate feedback on student performance—a quality that has been linked to improved student learning (Hammond & Yeshanew, 2007; Hattie & Timperley, 2007). When implemented properly, these features of CBT reduce teacher administrative work to prepare assessments and provide educators with the student assessment data needed to modify and differentiate instruction.

Some of the most engaging and efficient CBT products include handheld student response systems, adaptive testing, and online standardized test administration. In classrooms, handheld student response systems allow individual students to answer multiple choice or true/false questions displayed to the class. Immediately after students provide their answers, aggregate, anonymous results—including the percentage of correct and incorrect responses—can be displayed to the group in a variety of graphical formats. Teachers can also view responses by individual students. Teachers can use student response data to assess student mastery of content, stimulate class discussion, and identify common misconceptions. Teachers can also save the assessment results electronically in order to track and evaluate student progress over time.

Adaptive computer-based testing is another promising innovation emerging from the CBT tradition. Adaptive testing automatically adjusts questions to the individual test-taker's level of performance—increasing rigor for students who consistently demonstrate mastery and identifying specific areas of weakness for others. Adaptive testing may be especially useful for formative classroom assessment and district-level benchmark testing. Although schools and districts wish to avoid overtesting, educators need to collect and analyze intermediate student assessment data between annual high-stakes exams. By analyzing this interim data for trends and gaps in student achievement, local educators are better able to identify individual student learning needs and differentiate instruction before state and federally mandated exams occur. With the capability to adjust items to the performance of the learner, adaptive testing has the potential to assess student learning more quickly, thus shortening the intrusion of testing on instruction.

The most high-profile—and high-promise—CBT application relates to the annual "high-stakes" exams themselves. Computer-based standardized testing, also referred to as online standardized testing, offers educators and students the opportunity to take state and federally mandated examinations electronically, using the Internet to transfer data between schools and testing companies securely. This emerging practice promises to address one of the most frequent criticisms of standardized assessment—the delay between administering high-stakes testing and receiving the results. This delay, which can occasionally be months, hinders educators from making timely curriculum and instruction decisions to improve performance. If standardized tests could be administered online, results could be obtained more quickly or perhaps even immediately, in some cases.

Because CBT is grounded in traditional assessment theory, it is not without critics. As Mislevy et al. (2003) point out, "While familiar practices of assessment and test theory originated in trait and behaviorist psychology, contemporary views of learning and cognition fit more comfortably into the headings of cognitive and situative psychology" (p. 168). Although CBT is playing a role in current assessment practices, technologists must be reflective about matching assessment practices to desired learning outcomes and watch the horizon for new developments in technology-supported assessment.

In addition to CBT, computers and networked environments may significantly contribute to alternative assessment methods outside traditional testing models. Now that performance-based learning standards and constructivist practices are valued, technology provides a way for students to create authentic, original products—such as short-answer questions, essays, performance assessments, oral presentations, demonstrations, exhibitions, and portfolios— representing what they have learned (North Central Regional Educational Laboratory, 2004). Word processors, spreadsheets, desktop publishers, blogs, wikis, podcasts, video production, and computer-assisted design systems are a few of the tools helping students demonstrate learning through products similar to those employed by professionals in their fields. When appropriate criteria for acceptable performances are in place, these student artifacts and reflections can yield insight into learning in different and often deeper ways than multiple choice, true-false, and matching items on traditional tests.

Technology not only helps students create products for alternative assessment; by its readily archived and recalled nature, technology aids teachers in the assessment process as well. Electronic tools, such as online electronic rubric makers and database software, assist teachers in creating alternative assessment instruments. Once created, these instruments can be loaded on handheld computers, permitting teachers to circulate among students and document student performance. E-portfolio systems gather and store performance data electronically, allowing teachers to upload records and analyze historic results and trends for individual students, subgroups, or entire student populations easily.

Over time, the variety of technology-supported alternative assessments will continue to expand and evolve. New types of performance assessments may take the form of simulations and games (Honey, Fasca, Gersick, Mandinach, & Sinha, 2005; National Academy of Engineering & National Research Council, 2006). Applets embedded in traditional test items may allow students to launch tools with a mouse or keystroke, permitting students to complete their computations on spreadsheets or graphing calculators. In the future, these expanded practices should allow standardized test developers to measure creativity, innovation, problem solving, and higher-order thinking in new ways—thus blurring the distinction between computer-based testing and alternative assessments.

In spite of these promising contributions, neither CBT nor electronic tools for alternative assessment are well integrated into current instructional practices. In most classrooms, technology-supported assessment strategies are partially implemented or not used at all. Occasionally, the lack of implementation stems from the unavailability of hardware or a lack of professional development in its application. For example, although student response systems are gaining in popularity, they are not widely available and educators are only beginning to understand their full potential. In other situations, limited integration results from educators' reluctance to change historical testing methods or their limited understanding of the capabilities of the technology placed in the classroom. Teachers commonly use electronic assessments bundled with textbooks or use quiz or test makers to generate items and exams, but these tests often are administered and graded in traditional ways. Because educators generally lean toward traditional assessment methods, technology-supported alternative assessments are even less common. Although some teachers may use online tools to create checklists and rubrics to assess student work, technology-rich student projects and e-portfolio systems are still not commonly used in classrooms.

Technology-supported assessment practices at the district, state, and federal levels are in similar stages of development. In spite of the potential to offer immediate feedback and targeted instruction, few districts have coordinated assessment programs to measure interim student progress between standardized tests. Even fewer have technology-supported benchmark testing. Similarly, online standardized testing is diffusing slowly. Recent national data suggests that only 9 states offer computer-based tests to all students and 14 states offer computer-based assessments to some students, but over half (28 states) still do not offer computerized testing options to students at all (Bausell & Klemick, 2007). Although there is certainly an increased recognition of technology's potential role in the new era of accountability, a substantial gap between promise and implementation remains.

Assessing Student Technology Literacy

In addition to maximizing the use of technology in assessing student progress in core academic areas, technology facilitators and leaders also play a central role in determining how to assess students' technology literacy. Business partners and educational technology advocates frequently assert that mastering core academic content as defined in the past is not sufficient to prepare students for meaningful participation in today's global economy (Honey et al., 2005; NAE & NRC, 2006). In addition to foundational academic knowledge, students must be able to use technologies in ethical, accurate, and insightful ways to support the demands of economics and citizenship in modern society.

Recognizing this need, Title II, Part D: Enhancing Education Through Technology, of NCLB (2001) requires all students to be technologically literate by the end of eighth grade. Although this goal was welcomed as a positive step toward student technology literacy, legislators and educators have struggled to assess progress toward the goal. Recent survey results indicate that 48 states have either adopted ISTE's National Technology Standards for Students (NETS•S) or developed their own. However, only five states responded that they implemented a statewide test for student technology literacy during the 2007–08 school year (Bausell & Klemick, 2008). A majority of states are asking school districts to implement their own assessment strategies and report results annually. Local assessment programs are acceptable under NCLB guidelines, but these "home-grown" efforts often do not produce high-quality assessment results that are comparable across school districts.

Although current technology literacy assessment practices remain relatively weak, this is not completely indicative of a lack of commitment. There are logical explanations for the inadequacies, and there is evidence of progress in the field.

Limited availability of high-quality assessment tools. Most researchers and practicing technologists claim that the greatest barrier to assessing technology literacy is the lack of high-quality instruments and/or assessment processes available to schools. Although several technology literacy assessments are available, the authors of a recent publication co-sponsored by the National Academy of Engineering and the National Research Council (2006) conclude that "none of these instruments is completely adequate to the task of assessing technological literacy." According to Garmire and Pearson, currently available assessments do not cover the full spectrum of technology and primarily emphasize knowledge domains. Few reviewed instruments addressed critical thinking and decision making in context. However, a few emerging models and trends are promising (Honey et al., 2005; NAE & NRC, 2006). Great Britain is already implementing a national test on technology literacy for K–12 students (National Assessment Agency, 2007). In the United States, the Educational Testing Service developed and piloted a technology literacy test for college-age students (Educational Testing Service, 2007). Whereas most current efforts focus on creating stand-alone technology assessments, other models, such as the Programme for International Student Assessment (Organisation for Economic Co-operation and Development, 2007), embed a technology literacy component into content-area testing.

Developing environments appropriate for technology literacy assessment is expensive. Designing and testing any new, high-stakes assessment is a costly pursuit. Whereas core content areas have a long assessment history, measuring technology literacy is much less developed. Educators are only beginning to define technology literacy, and few assessment frameworks are available to guide the work. In addition to these typical design challenges, experts note that technology literacy assessments require technology-rich testing environments (Honey et al., 2005). Although technology literacy can be assessed with pencil-and-paper tests, many believe that electronic assessments with performance-based components, despite their high cost, would be more appropriate to the knowledge domain.

Limited financial resources. Financial resources for developing and purchasing student technology literacy assessments are scarce. Funding for developing technology literacy assessments has not been a high-priority issue in the past, and these development costs cannot be shouldered by the individual school systems. Even school districts receiving significant federal assistance for technology may find themselves torn among high priorities, such as updating aging computers, implementing technology-supported instructional and assessment programs, and providing much-needed professional development for teachers.

Stronger federal emphasis on core content areas. NCLB represents a historic shift in federal accountability requirements. Responding to these shifts requires states and school districts to engage in deep, systemic change. Some of these changes include establishing new data collection and reporting systems, revising instructional plans to raise low performance, and charting student progress over time. The difficulty of these tasks coupled with the high-stakes consequences of failing to move forward presents an all-consuming challenge for the educational community. Although Title II, Part D of NCLB succeeded in placing a new emphasis on technology literacy, educators were left with little energy to tackle the issue. The current context requires that achievement in core academic content areas must receive top priority.

Lack of federal requirements for technology literacy assessment and reporting. The eighth-grade literacy requirement in Title II, Part D of NCLB is stated as a goal, but the legislation lacks the specificity about reporting and accountability that is present for assessment in other core academic areas. With most states allowing school districts to determine their own method of assessment with few resources to do so, measurement will be inconsistent. The requirement may help local districts think about technology literacy in new ways and gather local data that is meaningful. It may even result in uncovering promising practices for the future. However, it will be virtually impossible for most states to compare data across districts or for the U.S. Department of Education to draw any conclusions about technology literacy at the national level. Given the barriers surrounding the assessment of technology literacy, the softer language of Title II, Part D may represent an understanding that—although a noble goal—the large-scale assessment of technology literacy was simply impossible when NCLB was released and would have placed an onerous burden on states and school districts at that particular point in history. This slower, gentler implementation may have been an appropriate strategy for the time, but many believe that future policies should be strong enough to command attention of those outside the educational technology community and to stimulate more meaningful technology literacy assessment practices.

Although high-quality, large-scale assessments of technology literacy seem to be limited by funding, expectations, and the availability of appropriate instruments, there are several current movements to address these issues for the future. First, there are already calls to direct federal research and development funding toward technology literacy assessments (Honey et al., 2005; NAE & NRC, 2006). Second, professional organizations representing technology facilitators and leaders, such as ISTE, the State Education Technology Directors Association (SETDA), and the Consortium for School Networking (CoSN), are encouraging lawmakers to strengthen student technology literacy components in future iterations of the ESEA (see www.setda.org). Third, organizations such as the Partnership for 21st Century Skills continue to monitor the development of new tools and disseminate this information to practitioners (see www.21stcenturyskills.org).

In addition to these wide-scale efforts on the national level, local technology facilitators and leaders monitor progress in available tools and implement technology literacy assessments in their own schools, districts, states, and regions. Even though current availability of high-quality products is limited, there are a growing number of solutions available to schools, and new developments are emerging rapidly. Because some of these products are excellent intermediate steps, technologists should educate themselves regarding what types of technology literacy assessments are available, who is using them, how they are being implemented, and what results they are producing. By reviewing these current and emerging tools and practices, school technology professionals not only help their school districts select the best possible products for the short term, but also position themselves to shape future development.

It is unclear what path technology literacy assessments will take in the future. Some forecast that full-scale implementation of rigorous technology literacy assessments—whether stand-alone or integrated into current high-stakes exams in other content areas—may be almost a decade from full-scale implementation (NAE & NRC, 2006). Until then, it will be the role of technology facilitators and leaders to sustain and propel the work until meaningful, high-quality solutions are readily available. As discussed more fully below, technology literacy assessment is a key component for the advancement of technology-supported education.

To make a case for raising the level of technology literacy, one must be able to show that the present level is low, which is difficult to do without a good measure of technological literacy. Until technology literacy is assessed in a rigorous, systematic way, it is not likely to be considered a priority by policy makers, educators, or average citizens (NAE & NRC, 2006, p. 4).

Data Collection and Analysis

Collecting student assessment data and other information related to the management and operations of schools is an essential component of school improvement; however, it is only a preliminary step. Technology—in the form of sophisticated, secure database applications at the school, district, state, and national levels—must also be used to store, manage, analyze, and report this data for the purposes of decision making. Fueled by research on school improvement and federal reporting policy, technology facilitators and leaders create, implement, sustain, and improve practices designed to holistically integrate technology-driven data collection and use in school improvement. As described in the National Educational Technology Plan (U.S. Department of Education, 2004), their tasks are systemic and transformational in nature.

> On average, there is little aggregation of student data in today's school systems. Information is siloed, redundant, and difficult to share. The technologies used—if any—are aging and frequently incompatible. An ideal state has complete aggregation and alignment. It is easier to ensure that students meet challenging standards, teachers target instruction, parents know teachers are helping their children, school districts know how to allocate resources effectively, and the government know exactly how schools are doing (U.S. Department of Education, 2004, p. 25).

In moving toward integrated data management systems, states and school districts have acquired a variety of student information systems, primarily from for-profit vendors. Most of these systems are designed to store and manage a variety of data, including:

- Student assessment data, including special education documentation

- Transcripts

- Attendance records

- Health information

- Disciplinary actions

- Student contact and demographic information

- Scheduling and room assignments

These student information systems often are implemented simultaneously with a host of other local databases containing information related to finance, human resources, transportation, nutrition, and other administrative and support functions.

Although educators have used technology to manage most of this information for many years, these newer information systems are more comprehensive and powerful. They expand reporting capability and may be Web-enabled so that a wider variety of users, including teachers and parents, can have access to customized views and functions. For example, with Web interfaces, teachers are able to enter information, such as grades, from their classroom or home computers, and parents can check their children's academic progress online. Updated student information systems also facilitate the electronic transfer of required information between district- and state-level data collection systems.

Because student information systems tend to focus on current school-year data, states and some school districts are also interested in establishing data warehouses integrating electronic information from disparate sources and storing it over longer periods of time. These data warehouses create a technical environment conducive to complex analysis of data to determine results not easily computed by other means. Examples of these analyses include a review of multiyear data to determine trends over time; the correlation of disparate data, such as expenditures and student achievement, to determine possible relationships; and the comparison of student performance data from various subgroups and different settings. With increased computing power and advanced software applications, decision makers and researchers may draw conclusions that previously would have taken years to construct. Embedded visualization tools also represent data in more meaningful ways—especially for non-educators, such as board of education members, elected officials, parents, business partners, and the general public. These emerging practices are analogous to business intelligence applications and data mining practices familiar in corporate environments, and they promise to be effective for planning and research for schools, as well (Petrides & Guiney, 2002).

Research on the current state of school-level data collection and analysis is rare, but several sources track developments on state-level progress. For example, the Data Quality Campaign and the National Center for Educational Accountability administered surveys to state education agencies concerning their PK–12 data collection practices. Similar surveys administered in the past provide points of comparison. On one hand, these survey results suggest steady growth in the capacity of states to collect, manage, analyze, and report data. For example, in 1999, only 8 states possessed a way to uniquely identify students over time and across setting, but, four years later, the number of states with this capability had nearly tripled. In the most recent survey (in 2006), 43 states had achieved this goal. On the other hand, the results also indicate that technology-driven data collection and analysis is in its infancy. Of the ten basic elements crucial to PK–12 longitudinal data systems at the state level identified by surveyors, only one state (Florida) possessed all of the elements, with 20 states having only five or fewer (Data Quality Campaign & National Center for Educational Assessment, 2006).

This data, the recent technological advances in information management, and the heightened need for data collection and reporting suggest new and demanding roles for technology facilitators and leaders. Given the current climate, practicing school technologists are immersed in purchasing decisions, upgrades, and customized training for specific and diverse groups of users, including teachers, parents, support staff, and administrators. Because of the highly technical nature of the current work in this area, many school districts and states have created new technical positions or contracted with outside specialists to complete this work. Although much of the current workload for school technology professionals is related to establishing a new infrastructure for data management, data-related work demands are not likely to diminish in the near future. Even after basic technological components stabilize, skilled staff will still be needed to maintain these new technologies and train educators in how to maximize their use effectively. In many ways, the situation parallels work patterns in the mid- to late 1990s when schools were establishing LANs, WANs, and connectivity to the Internet.

Evaluating Educational Technology

Although calls for improvement and accountability have permeated every aspect of public education in the past decade, some scholars and journalists have been especially critical of educational technology programs (Cuban, 2001; Healy, 1998; Oppenheimer, 2003). Their most prevalent criticisms include the following:

- Available technologies remain underused in schools

- Teaching practices remain largely unchanged

- Evidence suggesting that technology use improves student learning is weak

- Technology-supported learning methods are less successful than traditional methods for young children learning to read

- The recurring, high costs of technology programs are unwarranted given the lack of positive outcomes produced

- Technology programs drain funds from other worthy causes, such as athletics and the arts

Although many of these criticisms could and should be debated, they are not wholly without merit. Even technology advocates recognize that although technology can and does improve learning, both the complexity of technology integration and the time involved have been frequently underestimated. Even when desirable technology-related outcomes are met, educators often have failed "to document the effect on student learning, teacher practices, and system efficiencies" (Metiri Group & Cisco Systems, 2006, p. 2).

To improve performance, to answer current critics, and to protect future initiatives from similar attacks, it is important for technology facilitators and leaders to implement high-quality programs and to critically evaluate technology's impact on educational practice and student learning. To reach these goals, technology facilitators and leaders need to be skilled and knowledgeable in evaluation principles to design, implement, defend, and improve programs effectively.

There are great challenges to producing evaluations that are rigorous and defensible while remaining accessible and attractive to policy makers. In the introduction to *Using Technology Evaluation to Enhance Student Learning* (2004), editors Barbara Means and Geneva Haertel outline the following challenges to meeting the specification for scientifically based evaluations required by NCLB:

- Defining "technology" for the purposes of evaluation is difficult because there are thousands of different types of technologies available in schools. Although the study can be narrowed, narrowing limits the interest of policy makers desiring highly synthesized, broad conclusions about the overall impact of technology.

- The context of implementation affects the types of outcomes produced; consequently, context must be considered in the evaluation design. For example, two teachers probably use the same technologies in very different ways, and different students approach technologies from different perspectives. For these reasons, it is very difficult to conduct controlled studies ensuring all conditions remain constant except the technologies being used. This is especially difficult because, as Means & Haertel note, "many learning technology developers set their goal as providing learning experiences that would be impossible without the technology" (p. 3).

- Because technology is so pervasive in modern culture, it is difficult to contain technological access between experimental and control groups outside of the study. Technologies are readily available at home or in other classes, so the evaluators often have no way of knowing whether the control group used technology tools similar to those used by their experimental counterparts.

- The readily available measures of learning (such as standardized tests) may not be well suited to the learning goals of technology-supported learning environments, which often focus on creativity and higher-order thinking that cannot readily be measured on standardized, multiple-choice examinations. Such a significant disconnection between instruction and assessment, according to Means and Haertel, "can easily mask real impacts on learning" (p. 4).

These complexities are not unique to evaluating educational technology. Effective evaluation is generally complex and time-consuming. Although technology facilitators and leaders are not expected to become research-design experts, they must be able to design simple evaluation plans demonstrating program results. They must also be capable of meaningful collaboration with educational evaluators trained to grapple with more sophisticated designs—especially those attempting to show links to improved student achievement. Above all, technology facilitators and leaders must accept that high-quality program evaluation is both a possible and necessary part of modern education. As Means & Haertel (2004) conclude:

> As a nation, we are making a tremendous investment in technology for schools. We are asking prospective and practicing teachers to learn technology skills and techniques for using technology in their instruction. We are giving our kids time with software and the Internet in an environment where everyone feels there is not enough time for them to learn everything they need to prepare them for further schooling and adulthood. Given the level of spending of precious dollars and hours on technology-based activities, we have an obligation to learn as much as we can about how to do it right. We need to know not just which technology uses make us feel good, but which have real, long-term payoffs for our students and the adults who work with them in schools and how to implement those technologies to maximize benefits (p. 5).

Summary of Current Context

To implement TF/TL Standard IV in today's current context, technology facilitators and leaders need an understanding of how technology can help assess student learning in core academic areas. In accomplishing these tasks, technologists must be sensitive to "overtesting" and be careful to balance traditional computer-based testing and electronic tools for alternative assessment. Technologists must be prepared to shape new strategies to assess student technology literacy. Standard IV also addresses the need to conduct high-quality program evaluations related to technology. Although conducting these evaluations is challenging, they are necessary to provide stakeholders with information about how their investments in technology are translating into improved learning opportunities for students.

Implementing the Standard

This section reviews the standard, performance indicators, and performance tasks of TF/TL Standard IV, which can be found in the standards table on page 90.

Performance Standards

In implementing Standard IV, technology leaders assume strategic and visionary roles related to assessment and evaluation. In this new and growing field, they forecast the potential impact of emerging technologies on educational practice, read relevant professional literature, and study best-practice examples of technology-supported assessment and evaluation. Through these activities, they build a research-based rationale for what types of practices are most appropriate for their district, state, or region. They also communicate this knowledge to other educators.

While technology leaders influence the strategic direction of technology-related assessment and evaluation initiatives, technology facilitators integrate these initiatives into daily practice in schools. They apply technology for the purposes of assessment and evaluation, and in so doing, demonstrate how technology can automate and enhance existing strategies as well as enable new ones. They move the vision for technology-supported assessment and evaluation into practice and help others do the same.

Performance Indicators

The performance indicators for this standard outline three broad categories of technology-related assessment and evaluation tasks that technology facilitators and leaders are expected to perform.

1. **Assessing student learning (TF/TL-IV.A.).** Technology has the potential to improve the frequency and quality of teacher-generated assessments in classrooms and enable broader-scale benchmark testing and wide-scale administrations of high-stakes, standardized testing. However, without effective technology facilitators and leaders, this potential will never be realized. When enacting this performance indicator, technology facilitators must address student learning of both core academic content standards and state and national technology standards. Because assessment in core content areas has a rich history and well-developed practices, many educators are unaware that technology literacy is also a core knowledge domain requiring regular and rigorous assessment.

2. **Collecting, analyzing, and reporting data (TF/TL-IV.B.).** Technology-supported assessment practices will generate a large amount of electronic information on student achievement. This information will be added to other data critical to school improvement efforts, including information on student attendance, teacher qualifications, disciplinary incidents, and crime statistics. The data can become overwhelming and useless if it is not organized properly and analyzed for strengths and weaknesses. In this performance area, technology facilitators and leaders assist educators in implementing information technologies for collecting, storing, analyzing, and reporting data for school improvement.

3. **Evaluating technologies for effective use (TF/TL-IV.C.).** In the age of accountability, technology facilitators must constantly evaluate technology for educational efficacy, determining effectiveness through a variety of methods. Before purchasing technology, they must evaluate its potential impact on learning and determine specific goals for its use. They also must apply formative evaluation measures to ensure that implementation is leading to desired results. Finally, they must be able to report to what extent the technology-related program achieved established goals.

Performance Tasks

In TF/TL-IV.A., the performance tasks are related to student assessment, whereas those in TF/TL-IV.B. focus on data collection, analysis, and reporting. In both of these performance areas, the technology leaders' and facilitators' performance tasks differ in locale and scope.

At the district, state, or regional levels, technology leaders are concerned with identifying, procuring, or providing technological resources; assisting educators with student assessment; data collection and analysis; and reporting (TL-IV.A.2.; TL-IV.B.1.). Simply making technologies available will not necessarily change practice; consequently, leaders are expected to establish desirable uses or best practices for these new tools. They can do this by developing techniques themselves or facilitating this development by others (TL-IV.A.1.).

Unlike leaders, facilitators are not expected to acquire technologies or to establish expectations for implementation, but they are expected to model the established vision of how new technologies should be used at the building level (TF-IV.A.1). As always, facilitators have a special charge to assist and guide teachers in using new technologies. In this performance area, they focus on student assessment, data collection, and analysis tools to improve instruction (TF-IV.A.2.; TF-IV.B.1.).

Other key terms in TF/TL-IV.A.1. and 2. include variety of techniques, data, and artifacts. These terms suggest that technology facilitators and leaders understand that no single data source or method of assessment provides a complete picture of student learning. Effective assessment programs, including those supported by technology, include multiple measures of student learning and both traditional and alternative methods of assessments. In TF-IV.B.1., the words "improve instructional practice" and "maximize student learning" remind technology leaders and facilitators that school improvement and enhanced student achievement are the ultimate goals of technology-supported assessment, data collection, and analysis.

In TF/TL-IV.C., the emphasis shifts to evaluation. As described in these performance tasks, technology facilitators and leaders have shared responsibility, but differing roles, for ongoing evaluation. Leaders must be able to design strategies and methods for evaluating the effectiveness of technology (TL-IV.C.1.) and conduct research evaluating specific technologies in PK–12 settings (TL-IV.C.2.). Facilitators enact the results of leaders' evaluation activities. They assist teachers in using recommendations from district, state or regional evaluations and examine and apply results of evaluations to their own work (TF-IV.C.1.; C.2.).

Assessment and Evaluation (TF/TL-IV)

Technology Facilitation Standard	Technology Leadership Standard
(TF-IV) Educational technology facilitators apply technology to facilitate a variety of effective assessment and evaluation strategies	(TL-IV) Educational technology leaders communicate research on the use of technology to implement effective assessment and evaluation strategies.

TF/TL-IV.A. Apply technology in assessing student learning of subject matter using a variety of assessment techniques

Performance Tasks for Facilitators	Performance Tasks for Leaders
TF-IV.A.1. Model the use of technology tools to assess student learning of subject matter using a variety of assessment techniques.	TL-IV.A.1. Facilitate the development of a variety of techniques to use technology to assess student learning of subject matter.
TF-IV.A.2. Assist teachers in using technology to improve learning and instruction through the evaluation and assessment of artifacts and data.	TL-IV.A.2. Provide technology resources for assessment and evaluation of artifacts and data.

TF/TL-IV.B. Use technology resources to collect and analyze data, interpret results, and communicate findings to improve instructional practice and maximize student learning.

TF-IV.B.1. Guide teachers as they use technology resources to collect and analyze data, interpret results, and communicate findings to improve instructional practice and maximize student learning.	TL-IV.B.1. Identify and procure technology resources to aid in analysis and interpretation of data.

TF/TL-IV.C. Apply multiple methods of evaluation to determine students' appropriate use of technology resources for learning, communication, and productivity.

TF-IV.C.1. Assist teachers in using recommended evaluation strategies for improving students' use of technology resources for learning, communication, and productivity.	TL-IV.C.1. Design strategies and methods for evaluating the effectiveness of technology resources for learning, communication, and productivity
TF-IV.C.2. Examine and apply the results of a research project that includes evaluating the use of a specific technology in a PK–12 environment	TL-IV.C.2. Conduct a research project that includes evaluating the use of a specific technology in a PK–12 environment.

ISTE's Essential Conditions and TF/TL Standard IV

TF/TL Standard IV: Assessment and Evaluation directly correlates with an ISTE essential condition also titled *Assessment and Evaluation*. ISTE defines this essential condition as "continuous assessment, both of learning and for learning, and evaluation of the use of technology and digital resources." This definition closely aligns to the performance tasks that technology facilitators and leaders enact in TF/TL Standard IV.

Performance Scenarios

To support the recent acquisition of student response systems for each grade level in elementary schools and each content team in secondary schools, the district technology leader collected a variety of examples showing how the systems could be used to assess student learning and created a website to highlight these examples. Facilitators in the schools directed the teachers to the website and modeled these examples for teachers in the schools. Facilitators also posted innovative uses of the student response systems as they emerged.

School district leaders were concerned that standardized test results were the only common assessment data available to track students' academic progress. Because these were administered annually, there were no mechanisms in place to gauge intermediate progress in a coordinated way. The group was also concerned that educators had no way to track student achievement over time—even on standardized tests. The superintendent charged the district technology leader to research the availability and costs for electronic assessment systems to solve these two problems and help teachers improve their instruction based on data. The district leader reviewed websites, talked to vendors in conference exhibit halls, and visited school districts using different types of systems. Through this process, the technology leader identified several features that were important for assessment systems, including the ability to include short answers, writing samples, and assessments for capstone projects. The technology leader reported results to the leadership team, and the district eventually acquired an assessment system that allowed teachers to construct and align benchmark assessments to the state standards. The system also allowed teachers to analyze data to make instructional decisions. The technology leader involved teachers and technology facilitators in the research and decision-making processes along the way. Technology facilitators played a key role in guiding teachers' use of the assessment system once it was in place.

A school district had been struggling to meet AYP because of is poor reading scores. In an effort to increase reading achievement, the district agreed to pilot an online reading program claiming to improve reading skills dramatically within one school year. The district technology leader partnered with local university faculty to conduct a program evaluation to determine its effectiveness. This evaluation included establishing a matched comparison group who used the currently available software and an experimental group using the new software. Both groups completed a pre and post assessment of reading comprehension. School facilitators monitored the implementation of the program to ensure that teachers were, in fact, using the software as recommended. When the school year was over, the technology leader analyzed the data and found that student achievement was no different between classrooms using the old and new reading software. Furthermore, the evaluation determined that teachers found the new program more difficult to use and that students preferred the old software as well.

To implement a performance-based writing assessment strategy, the English/language arts director collaborated with teachers and the district technology leader to procure an electronic portfolio system. The district technology facilitators trained teachers in how to upload student work samples, construct rubrics to assess student work, and analyze student progress.

Prompted by mandates to measure and report student technology literacy levels, technology leaders from the state, regional, and district levels formed a group to study the strengths and weaknesses of available assessment options. District technology leaders shared what they learned with local technology facilitators and invited them to participate in the discussion. Technology leaders also prepared technology facilitators on how to inform teachers of the importance of the national goals for technology literacy and assessments to gauge progress, so that teachers would have the necessary background to understand local assessments when implemented.

case study

REALIZING THE POTENTIAL
OF TECHNOLOGY-BASED ASSESSMENT PROGRAMS

Since Antwon Lincoln became the district technology coordinator in Chula Vista Elementary Schools in Southern California in September 2006, he has helped many of the district's 44 schools implement a variety of student assessment programs.

Led by a charge from the current superintendent years ago and fueled by the learning goals of NCLB, school leaders in this site-based district have been researching and investing in software packages and Web-based tools that can identify student's individual learning needs, promote differentiated instruction, and improve student learning—especially for students who are not achieving academic standards.

"The computer-based assessment programs have a lot of promise," comments Lincoln. "Approximately 50% or 12,000 of our students are performing at basic or below basic levels. Six of our schools are in program improvement, but all of our schools have target populations that should be performing better. For these reasons, I understand the allure of computer-based programs that can provide educators with tools to frequently assess student learning, diagnose problems early, and create customized interventions for individual students. We now have several schools in our district where technology-based assessment programs have become a key component for school improvement. This is a great thing!"

However, Lincoln cautions that it is not the software that makes a difference—it is the successful implementation of the software. "Although we have experienced successes with technology-based assessment tools, people should know that it takes time and effort to reach a mature level of implementation where schools can realize success. Some schools in our district are still striving to implement the tools in recommended ways. It is one thing to purchase technology. It is another thing to use it well. This is my job—to help educators improve the implementation of technology they believe will make a difference in student learning."

When asked how he accomplishes his goal, Lincoln says he approaches the challenge with the same individual, differentiated approach expected of teachers in the classroom.

"Each school has a story—an implementation story. I begin helping them by listening to that story and deciding what to do from there," states Lincoln.

When visiting a school, Lincoln gleans perspectives on implementation from the site administrators. Next, he sits by students using the program and asks them questions such as "What are you doing?" "How are you doing?" "What is your score?"

He also asks teachers and members of the instructional leadership team (ILT) some of the following: "Are your students on task when they use the assessment tool?" "How do you know?" "How well is your target group performing?" "What is your average achievement level?" Lincoln maintains that his observations and questions help him determine the current implementation level fairly quickly.

(Continued)

case study (Continued)

"If educators can't tell you how well students are performing based on data from the program and how they are using that data to diagnose and individualize a students' instruction, then the program isn't being used effectively. It is very clear when the data generated by the assessment system is being understood and used by students, teachers, and administrators. By assessing this quality of use—and not just the frequency of how often the program is being used—I know where to begin helping."

In best cases, Lincoln finds school communities that understand the purpose of the programs. In these mature implementations, Lincoln reports that teachers have mastered the tool. They use it for specific purposes, analyze the data, and design individual learning plans for the students. Administrators and ILTs also track student progress at grade and school levels. In these settings, Lincoln can show teachers more advanced program features and reporting functions they can use.

On the other end of the continuum, some schools are only scratching the surface of the software's capability. "In these cases, students can't articulate their scores or their progress. Teachers are not controlling the tool for specific purposes. Every student is just sent to use the technology and somehow—magically—the technology is supposed to improve learning. Well, it won't. Teachers have to look at the data produced from the software program to identify if a student needs frequent assessment with a specific math concept, or a student needs to work on comprehension skills that focus on interference, for example. The use of these tools will produce this information. The technology is only effective if the educators know how to maximize its use."

When Lincoln finds a school that is struggling with the implementation of the assessment program, he often asks them to scale back the use to a small group of target students—usually those who need the most assistance. Lincoln feels that scaling back helps teachers learn how to use the software well without being overwhelmed. As teachers gain confidence and skill, they can increase the number of students using the program until all students have access.

Of course, this individualized coaching model is challenging given that Lincoln is the only technology coordinator in the 44-school district, but his strategy is to "build capacity" in local school personnel. "I find someone or the principal suggests someone who can become the local champion of the assessment program. Then, if I receive new information or training from the vendor, I communicate with the local experts. Although I am not in a specific school all the time, the champions are there every day. Often the champions are computer lab teachers, reading specialists, ILT members, or sometimes even teachers who are exemplary users."

Lincoln has found that building this network of experts is the best way to promote effective use of assessment systems in his district. "Assessment systems can be very powerful if used correctly. However, they are complex tools, and teachers must have time to learn to use them effectively. The implementation has to be monitored and nurtured over time. Without coaching and tweaking, it is unlikely that an assessment system will really make a difference in student achievement, and we might as well just turn it off. On the other hand, in mature, teacher-led implementations, it is a wonderful tool for improving achievement."

Discussion Questions

- How is technology used to assess student learning in core academic content areas in your local setting? What other types of electronic assessment strategies would you like to see implemented and why? What must technology facilitators and leaders do to realize these assessment practices?

- Do you fear that electronic assessment tools will contribute to overtesting in schools? Why or why not? How can technology facilitators and leaders protect schools from assessment overload?

- What barriers, if any, prevent online standardized testing in your school, district, state, or region? How difficult would it be to overcome these barriers in order to administer all standardized testing online? Do you support online standardized testing? Why or why not?

- How do you currently assess student technology literacy in your school, district, or state? What do you believe is the best way to assess student technology literacy? What barriers, if any, prevent K–12 schools from assessing technology literacy in this way?

- To what extent are teachers currently using technology resources to collect and analyze data, interpret results, and use findings to improve instructional practice (see TF-IV.B.1.)? How would technology leaders and facilitators encourage these data practices at the classroom level?

- How are technologies currently evaluated in your local setting? What evaluations would you like to conduct and why? How would you design and implement this evaluation? What challenges would you encounter during the evaluation process?

Resources

As technology facilitators and leaders implement TF/TL Standard IV, they may benefit from several types of resources that either assist technologists by deepening their understanding of concepts discussed in the chapter, or provide tools technologists may share with other educators. Although all the resources are valuable, we have identified one "Spotlight Resource" in each chapter that has particular utility to technologists.

The resources identified under TF/TL Standard IV pertain to assessment and evaluation. A report is included that provides software titles that technology facilitators and leaders may use for data collection. Several tools are listed to facilitate the rubric development process. Numerous websites are provided focusing on program evaluation, project assessment, and data collection.

Report

Software Enabling School Improvement Through Analysis of Student Data
www.csos.jhu.edu/crespar/techReports/Report67.pdf
> This technical report reviews some of the software available to support data collection in schools and is useful as a model of how to compare products and what critical issues to consider.

Books

Boudett, K. P., City, E., & Murnane, R. (2005). *Data wise: A step-by-step guide to using assessment results to improve teaching and learning.* Cambridge, MA: Harvard.

Lyman, H. (1998). *Test scores and what they mean.* Boston: Allyn & Bacon.

Popham, W. J. (2006). *Assessment for educational leaders.* Boston: Pearson.

Tools

Observation Protocol for Technology Integration in the Classroom (OPTIC)
www.netc.org/assessing/home/integration.php
> This tool by the Northwest Educational Technology Consortium (NETC) is intended to assist school leaders in assessing the degree of technology integration in classrooms and schools.

Rubistar
http://rubistar.4teachers.org
> This site contains a free tool to help teachers create high-quality rubrics to assess student learning.

Rubrics at Teach-nology
http://teach-nology.com/web_tools/rubrics/
> This site offers a tool that walks teachers step-by-step through the rubric development process.

QuizStar
http://quizstar.4teachers.org
> QuizStar is a low-cost Web-based quiz maker that enables you to create, administer, and automatically grade your quizzes online!

Websites

4Teachers.Org
www.4teachers.org/profdev/
> This site offers links to a variety of free resources for authentic assessment, rubric development, electronic portfolios and more.

Capacity for Applying Project Evaluation (CAPE)

www.serve.org/Evaluation/Capacity/

> This SEIR*TEC site offers a suite of resources, tools, and professional development activities technology facilitators and leaders could use for program evaluation including a School Technology Needs Assessment (STNA) and the Looking for Technology Integration (LoFTI) observation protocol.

Collaborative Evaluation Led by Local Educators:
A Practical, Print- and Web-Based Guide

www.neirtec.org/evaluation/

> This guide by NEIR*TEC provides a process and framework for practical, focused evaluation of improvement efforts in a school context.

CoSN Data-Driven Decision Making Initiative: Vision to Know and Do

www.3d2know.org

> This site offers up-to-date, unbiased information for educators on collecting, understanding and using data effectively.

Edutopia—Assessment Overview

www.edutopia.org/assessment

> This section of the Edutopia website focuses on assessment practices and includes articles, video clips, and media.

Helen Barrett's Electronic Portfolios

http://electronicportfolios.com

> This site, by one of the foremost experts on electronic portfolios, contains a variety of information and resources on portfolios as an assessment tool.

Intel Education: Assessing Projects

www.intel.com/education/assessingprojects/

> This site provides access to a free online application to develop assessments, along with access to hundreds of high-quality, ready-made assessments. The site also contains research and theory behind effective assessment as well as strategies to make assessment an integral part of the teaching and learning process.

Spotlight Resource

ISTE's Classroom Observation Tool
http://icot.iste.org

ISTE's Classroom Observation Tool is a free, online tool that helps observers examine and record data on key components of effective technology integration. The website provides educators with different ideas or "use scenarios" depending on the specific purposes of the observations. Training resources are also provided.

Kathy Schrock's Guide for Educators—Assessment and Rubric Information
http://school.discovery.com/schrockguide/assess.html
> This site contains a collection of rubrics, graphic organizers, articles, and other resources encouraging the use of both formative and summative assessments.

Schools Interoperability Framework Association
www.sifinfo.org
> SIF is a not-for-profit organization promoting a common set of rules and definitions permitting school systems to share data across platforms and products from different vendors. This framework represents a critical step forward in creating integrated data systems with which technology facilitators and leaders should be familiar.

Teacher Tap Electronic Portfolios
http://eduscapes.com/tap/topic82.htm
> This site offers a multitude of links to assessment resources including articles and sample portfolios.

References

Bausell, C. V., & Klemick, E. (2007). Tracking U.S. trends. *Education Week: Technology Counts 2007*, pp. 42–44.

Bausell, C. V., & Klemick, E. (2008). Tracking U.S. trends. *Education Week: Technology Counts 2008*, pp. 39–42.

Cuban, L. (2001). *Oversold and underused*. Boston: Harvard.

Data Quality Campaign & National Center for Educational Assessment. (2006). Retrieved August 2, 2007, from www.dataqualitycampaign.org/survey_results/

DuFour, R., & Eaker, R. (1998). *Professional learning communities at work: Best practices for enhancing student achievement*. Bloomington, IN: National Educational Service.

Educational Testing Service. (2007). *iSkills assessment*. Retrieved August 2, 2007, from www.ets.org

Hammond, P., & Yeshanew, T. (2007). The impact of feedback on school performance. *Educational Studies, 33*(2), 99–113.

Hattie, J., & Timperley, H. (2007). The power of feedback. *Review of Educational Research, 77*(1), 81–112.

Healy, J. (1998). *Failure to connect: How computers affect our children's minds—for better and worse*. New York: Simon and Schuster.

Honey, M., Fasca, C., Gersick, A., Mandinach, E., & Sinha, S. (2005). *Assessment of 21st century skills: The current landscape*. Retrieved June 11, 2007, from www.21stcenturyskills.org/images/stories/otherdocs/Assessment_Landscape.pdf

Joyce, B., Calhoun, E., & Hopkins, D. (1999). *The new structure of school improvement: Inquiring schools and achieving students*. Philadelphia: Open University.

Means, B., & Haertel, G. (2004). Introduction. In B. Means & G. Haertel (Eds.), *Using technology evaluation to enhance student learning* (pp. 1–8). New York: Teachers College.

Mislevy, R, Steinberg, L., Almond, R., Haertel, G., & Penuel, W. (2003). Improving educational assessments. In Haertel, G. & Means, B. (Eds.). *Evaluating educational technology: Effective research designs for improving learning*. New York: Teachers College.

Metiri Group & Cisco Systems. (2006). *Technology in schools: What the research says*. Retrieved August 2, 2007, from www.cisco.com/Web/strategy/docs/education/TechnologyinSchoolsReport.pdf

National Assessment Agency. (2007). *Key Stage 3 ICT Test*. Retrieved August 2, 2007, from www.naa.org.uk/naaks3/default.asp

National Academy of Engineering & National Research Council (NAE & NRC). (2006). *Tech tally: Approaches to assessing technological Literacy*. Washington, DC: National Academies Press.

North Central Regional Educational Laboratory. (2004). *Pathways to school improvement: Alternative assessment*. Retrieved May 15, 2007, from www.ncrel.org/sdrs/areas/issues/methods/assment/as8lk30.htm

Oppenheimer, T. (2003). *The flickering mind: The false promise of technology in the classroom and how learning can be saved*. New York: Random House.

Organisation for Economic Co-operation and Development. (2007). *Programme for International Student Assessment (PISA)*. Retrieved August 2, 2007, from www.pisa.oecd.org

Petrides, L., & Guiney, S. Z. (2002). Knowledge management for school leaders: An ecological framework. *Teachers College Record, 104*(8), 1702–1717.

State Education Technology Directors Association. (2005). National Trends Report. Retrieved August 2, 2007, from www.sedta.org

U.S. Department of Education. (2004). *National Educational Technology Plan*. Retrieved August 2, 2007, from www.ed.gov/about/offices/list/os/technology/plan/

Sophisticated application of advances in information technology has dramatically altered the nature of work in many sectors of society, resulting in greater effectiveness and productivity. Education is intrinsically a human-centered enterprise, so the primary contribution of computers and telecommunications is not to automate what people do, but instead to empower teachers in their own learning and in helping students learn.

— KETELHUT, MCCLOSKEY, DEDE, BREIT, & WHITEHOUSE, 2006

Chapter Five

TF/TL STANDARD V

Productivity and Professional Practice

When illustrating the importance of technology in schools, advocates often provide examples of how students use technology to learn. However, it is important to remember that technology can make valuable contributions to education even when one step removed from the classroom. In other words, students also benefit indirectly when educators use technology to enhance their own productivity and professional practice.

Although student technology use may always take center stage—and appropriately so—educators also need modern technologies in professional practice and enhancing professional learning. As this chapter illustrates, technology plays a vital role in transforming schools into professional learning communities. Helping others to use technology to enhance productivity and professional practice establishes additional responsibilities for technology facilitators and leaders.

Current Context:
New Ways of Working and Learning

Products classified as productivity tools comprise the largest portion of the technology software market. Though all technologies could be considered productivity tools, the term is usually reserved for handheld computing devices and software designed to help users complete specific tasks. Telecommunication tools are designed to facilitate communication and collaboration across space and time, and are a specialized subset of productivity tools. As illustrated in Figure 5.1, there many different types of productivity and telecommunication tools available to schools.

- Word processing
- Desktop publishing
- Spreadsheets
- Databases
- Presentation
- Drawing
- Graphics/photo editing
- Video editing
- Sound editing/composing
- Concept mapping
- Computer-assisted design
- Modeling/visualization
- Virtual reality/3-D rendering
- Animation
- Calendar
- Project management
- Puzzle makers
- Test/Survey makers

- Rubric makers
- Web authoring
- Web browsers/search engines
- Telecommunication Tools:
  - E-mail
  - Instant messaging/chat
  - Video conferencing
  - Voice-over-IP (VoIP)
  - Discussion forums
  - Blogs
  - Learning management systems
  - Collaborative meeting spaces
  - Online document sharing
  - Wikis and other types of collaborative writing spaces
  - Podcasting
    - RSS

Figure 5.1 Productivity software in schools

Many technologies help educators address their professional tasks faster and better. These technologies enable new types of practices that were previously impossible or impractical. These include:

- Software programs helping teachers reduce time spent on grading, leaving more time for designing instruction and working individually with students

- Spreadsheets and e-mail assisting administrators in creating budgets and communicating with others

- Databases facilitating organization, access, and analysis of student achievement data

- Internet access providing educators with immediate access to a seemingly limitless collection of instructional resources and professional learning materials

However, many educator experiences run counter to these examples. Although most schools usually purchase and install many types of these tools, educators complain that they do not have time to learn how to apply them to educational purposes.

Unlike some other software applications, the most commonly available productivity tools—word processors, databases, and spreadsheets—have broad applicability across disciplines and can be used in a wide variety of ways. To realize a tool's potential, users must envision how it can be used to meet their needs and purposes. For example, spreadsheets can be used for recording and calculating grades, but educators may not think of this application without help from others. This example illustrates how it is sometimes difficult for educators to imagine how productivity tools can facilitate work in their specific contexts. Contextualization, or applying a general productivity tool to a specific academic content area or task, is complicated by the fact that most productivity tools are designed for corporate purposes, not educational ones. Though this technology unquestionably has applicability for schools, limited examples of educational uses slow the adaptation and adoption process.

Another barrier to realizing higher levels of productivity from technology in schools is the extended amount of time required to master use of a productivity tool. Productivity tools are generally developed to support the cognitive processes and complex tasks of expert practitioners. For these reasons, the tools have many robust features and often are very difficult to learn. Many educators are using available productivity tools in rudimentary ways, but not maximizing the available features of the software.

The fact that different productivity tools are designed to integrate with one another in complex ways also complicates the learning process. For example, advanced users should be able to integrate the use of databases, spreadsheets, and word processors to complete a mail merge. They should also be able to use these same productivity tools with an e-mail client to send out individualized letters electronically. However, these uses require a great deal of knowledge about several different productivity tools and how to integrate them.

The term "learning curve" is often used to convey the relationship between experience and efficiency. The more difficult the learning curve, the longer it takes users to realize the benefits of the technology. According to this principle, contextualization and complexity often make it difficult for educators applying productivity tools to specific instructional tasks and environments.

This learning curve may result in frustration for educators who are attempting and policy makers promoting educational advancement through technology. However, education is hardly unique in experiencing delayed productivity during the implementation phase of new technology. This is a common phenomenon in industry. Businesses often use the term "productivity dip" to describe a decline in performance during the initial stages of complex technology implementations. However, in successful implementations, these dips are typically followed by enhanced productivity.

High learning curves and the need to contextualize the software can explain why productivity tools are both widely available and greatly underused. To bolster use, technology facilitators and leaders can contextualize the tool for educators. Contextualization activities include constructing a database so that educators only need to input information, providing educators with templates and examples of how a tool might be used, or purchasing productivity tools that are already contextualized for educational purposes, for example, grade books, contact managers, IEP generators, and form makers. Technologists can also purchase scaled-down or simplified versions of extremely complex software (such as PhotoShop Elements rather than PhotoShop), which are simpler to use and less expensive.

Although providing templates, designing databases for educators, buying predesigned productivity tools, and selecting scaled applications are excellent strategies for contextualizing tools and reducing the learning curve, there are trade-offs in these decisions. Predesigned products and scaled software are not as customizable or robust as full-functioning productivity tools. For example, teachers will immediately recognize the function of a grade-book program and be able to use it quickly, but this software can only be used as a grade book. It will not have the broad scope of functions that spreadsheet tools will have. Users also will not have as many opportunities to add features to a predesigned productivity tool. The formulas, the field, and the functionality are constrained by the way it is designed. Designing products for educators and buying highly contextualized productivity tools may also prevent educators from learning higher-level skills. Often users are perfectly willing to let others design technology tools for them, placing technology facilitators and leaders in a chauffeur role with their colleagues (Nardi & O'Day, 1999). In this role, technologists use the technology for users, while users never learn to operate the technology themselves.

These realities do not limit the value of scaled versions and precontextualized tools. Student information systems serve as an excellent example of a commercially developed database that would be nearly impossible for most school systems to develop and implement on their own. However, technologists must understand the possible constraints, as well. Predesigned tools should be reviewed carefully to ensure that the available functions meet the need of the community. Offering scaled versions of software or making templates for educators is acceptable to support or scaffold users as they learn tools, but technologists should be careful not to truncate users' ability to advance to higher levels.

By helping other educators become proficient users of productivity tools, technologists can help transform schools into efficient workplaces reflecting the skills and knowledge students need to be productive members of society in the digital age. Although improving productivity has been an elusive goal for technology facilitators and leaders, TF/TL Standard V provides further guidance on how to approach and accomplish the work.

Technology and Professional Practice

Professional practice refers to the daily professional tasks of educators, including:

- Preparing for instruction
- Implementing instruction
- Assessing instruction

- Reflecting on instruction

- Modifying instruction

- Involving parents in their children's learning

- Communicating with the community

- Completing administrative duties

- Participating in professional growth activities

However, professional practice is a much broader term as well. Professional practice is also a professional context, such as the practice of law, the practice of medicine, and the practice of teaching. These practices are realized in specific professional cultures that either enable or constrain practice in various ways.

Researchers studying these enabling and constraining factors assert that certain types of cultures are more conducive to effective practice than others. Most recently, cultures supporting innovative practice are referred to as learning organizations or professional learning communities (DuFour & Eaker, 1998; DuFour, Eaker, & DuFour, 2005; Eaker, DuFour, & DuFour, 2002; Fullan, 1999; North Central Regional Educational Laboratory, 2000; Senge et al., 1999). Characteristics of cultures that support effective professional practice are summarized in the sidebar on page 106. Conditions for effective practices are summarized in the sidebar on page 107.

As illustrated in TF/TL Standard V, technology facilitators and leaders collaborate with other educators in their system to facilitate these positive aspects of professional culture and practice. Their roles are likely to be very important because technologies have great potential to enable cultures conducive to effective professional practice in education. The following sections explore the characteristics and the conditions for effective practice. Examples of how technology can support desired practices are also presented.

Characteristics of Effective Practice

Ultimately, effective practice must result in meeting established goals. This characteristic of effective practice remains constant. However, strategies to reach those goals in the fast-paced information age most certainly have shifted. Cycles of innovation have been compressed. New ideas and new products are introduced more frequently, and the rapid emergence of new technologies both enables new innovations and necessitates them. In this culture of rapid change, organizations that do not innovate at a sufficient pace face challenges and perhaps even extinction—especially if others are innovating faster.

Schools, like all organizations, are experiencing the pressure to innovate more frequently. Technology has affected the way digital-age students learn, but schools have not fully responded to what these learners need. Many students live in a world where they have ubiquitous access to information and computing power. They have often assumed responsibility for their own learning outside school, forming their own questions, seeking information, collaborating with others, evaluating all the sources of information, and making their final decisions. Yet when students arrive at school, they power down in several significant ways. They pursue content in orderly, linear ways that others have predetermined for them. Their immediate access to information is limited.

Their collaborative tendencies are repressed, and their learning seldom requires them to solve problems, evaluate solutions, and make decisions.

If educators trying to meet the needs of digital-age learners are to be successful, school cultures must change. To innovate at appropriate paces for contemporary change, cultures must support creativity and collaboration. Each system member must generate ideas that influence others ideas. System members must construct knowledge together instead of reinventing the same innovation over and over again. When something is not working, organizations must adapt—quickly. This is why Senge et al. (1999) characterize effective organizations as "fast."

Characteristics of Effective Professional Practice

- Innovative
- Creative
- Generative
- Adaptive
- Collaborative
- "Fast"

When cultural conditions for effective practice are not in place, being "fast" can seem very stressful for system members, such as teachers and administrators. While schools have struggled to make progress, many other organizations have successfully transformed their practices so that "fast" can seem normal. This should provide hope. Schools can also transform their culture. Evidence of progress is already emerging. However, this transformation is utterly impossible without modern technologies helping workers communicate and manage information more quickly and efficiently.

Conditions for Effective Practice

Organizational scientists agree that effective practice must be focused on shared goals uniting workers in a common purpose. The goals for education must focus on improving student learning, and all educators must share collective responsibility for reaching them (Bruce, Calhoun, & Hopkins, 1999; DuFour and Eaker, 1998; Eaker et al., 2002; Fullan, 1999).

To sustain focus on the shared goals, organizations need accountability mechanisms monitoring performance and providing useful, ongoing feedback to system members. This feedback on a system's progress provides important data to inform decision-making. In recent years, student information systems have greatly improved educators' ability to access and analyze attendance, graduation rates, and student test scores.

Although data systems target areas for school improvement, they do not provide solutions for complex issues. Schools must still innovate. In organizations that innovate, system members are constantly learning. To promote learning, organizations ensure that their employees have ample opportunities for ongoing sustained learning, reflection, and inquiry. They also ensure that there is adequate system support for learning, which includes staff dedicated to promote learning, incentives for learning, and expectations for learning.

In professional learning communities, learning opportunities extend beyond training and workshops. Learning is organized around the most important type of work—monitoring progress toward organizational goals and improving performance. Similar strategies are beginning to emerge in schools. Groups of educators frequently form data teams, analyze student performance, and strategize on how best to address existing gaps.

Conditions for Effective Professional Practices in Education

- Shared mission, vision, and goals that are centered on student learning

- Shared responsibility for meeting goals

- Diversity in membership

- Accountability mechanisms that monitor performance and provide useful, ongoing feedback to system members

- Data-informed decision-making processes

- Opportunities for ongoing sustained learning, reflection, and inquiry

- System support, incentives, and expectations for continuous learning

- Collaborative work group structures

- Interdependent tasks among system members

- Well-established, open, and accessible communication infrastructures

- Information-rich ecosystems

- Permeable boundaries

- Mechanisms for articulating, capturing, and sharing knowledge

- Frequent celebrations of success

- Distributed, democratic leadership

These types of collaborative, interdependent task groups encourage learning and fuel innovation. However, system members involved in this collaborative work need technology tools to maximize their learning and productivity.

Desktop applications such as spreadsheets help educators manipulate, analyze, and visually represent data exported from cumbersome student information systems. Presentation technologies aid educators in communicating results of their analysis to others. Synchronous and asynchronous communication tools, such as e-mail, discussion forums, and centralized document files, support collaboration. Information-rich ecosystems with ready access to a wide variety of resources help educators solve problems and implement solutions. These ecosystems include access to the World Wide Web, professional libraries, and databases of instructional materials and best-practice solutions. These professional resources function as knowledge management systems helping educators build on what others have created instead of constantly reinventing new solutions.

Technologists as Professional Learning Specialists

Throughout all the TF/TL standards, technologists serve as specialized types of professional development experts. Technologists have historically helped people learn about technology; in TF/TL V, they also help people learn with technology—regardless of the knowledge domain in which it is applied. In Standard V, technology facilitators are asked to structure both formal and informal professional learning environments.

To do so, they need a strong background in facilitating professional learning and developing professional learning communities. These theoretical constructs must guide the decisions they make about technology and professional practice.

To these ends, technologists need the same type of knowledge and skills as others professional development specialists. Technology leaders must have or acquire an understanding of adult learning and change, understanding that adults prefer learning that is self-directed and directly related to their work. They also understand that adults learn better from actively constructing knowledge through solving problems or producing products with peers than they do from passive, traditional modes of instruction (National Staff Development Council, 2001; National Staff Development Council and Southwest Educational Development Laboratory, 2003).

National Staff Development Council Standards for Staff Development (2001)

CONTEXT STANDARDS

Staff development that improves the learning of all students:

- Organizes adults into learning communities whose goals are aligned with those of the school and district. (Learning Communities)

- Requires skillful school and district leaders who guide continuous instructional improvement. (Leadership)

- Requires resources to support adult learning and collaboration. (Resources)

PROCESS STANDARDS

Staff development that improves the learning of all students:

- Uses disaggregated student data to determine adult learning priorities, monitor progress, and help sustain continuous improvement. (Data-Driven)

- Uses multiple sources of information to guide improvement and demonstrate its impact. (Evaluation)

- Prepares educators to apply research to decision making. (Research-Based)

- Uses learning strategies appropriate to the intended goal. (Design)

- Applies knowledge about human learning and change. (Learning)

- Provides educators with the knowledge and skills to collaborate. (Collaboration)

CONTENT STANDARDS

Staff development that improves the learning of all students:

- Prepares educators to understand and appreciate all students; create safe, orderly, and supportive learning environments; and hold high expectations for their academic achievement. (Equity)

- Deepens educators' content knowledge, provides them with research-based instructional strategies to assist students in meeting rigorous academic standards, and prepares them to use various types of classroom assessments appropriately. (Quality Teaching)

- Provides educators with knowledge and skills to involve families and other stakeholders appropriately. (Family Involvement)

Models of professional development that are generative, meaningful, collaborative, and participant-centered are also best suited to supporting change—a frequent companion to most technology-related initiatives (Fullan, 2001). These principles and others are reflected in the National Staff Development Council's (2001) Standards for Staff Development (see box above). These standards serve as a useful frame for designing all professional learning programs for educators. Technology leaders use them as a framework for design, just as any other professional development expert does. Since their publication in 2001, the NSDC standards have influenced the way most technology-related professional development efforts are accomplished in schools. They serve as an important guide for technologists as they strive to use technology to create professional learning communities in schools. This knowledge about professional learning will serve to establish technology leaders and facilitators as professional development specialists among their peers, and to improve their performance in all other TF/TL standard areas.

Summary of Current Context

TF/TL Standard V relates to productivity and professional practice. In the current context, productivity tools are widely available but underused. To improve this situation, technology facilitators and leaders must contextualize and model the use of productivity software for other educators. Technologists also play a role in transforming schools into professional learning communities. In doing so, facilitators and leaders assume the role of specialized professional learning specialists who deploy technology tools to increase educators' collaboration, communication, and connection to professional learning resources. The NSDC's standards guide technologists' efforts as they help other educators learn about technology and learn with technology.

Implementing the Standard

This section reviews the standard, performance indicators, and performance tasks of TF/TL Standard V, which can be found in the standards table on pages 112–113.

Performance Standards

The previous sections established a conceptual framework for what technology facilitators and leaders must do. Addressing productivity and professional practice in schools is much deeper than helping educators do the same things they have always done, but faster and better. It requires leveraging technology to support the "reculturing" of schools so that they can innovate and be responsive to students' learning needs (Fullan, 1999).

Both technology facilitators and leaders must be prepared to support productivity and professional practice in schools. However, the scope and scale of what they are expected to do differs slightly. Technology facilitators apply technologies to enhance and improve personal productivity and professional practice, whereas technology leaders design, develop, evaluate, and model products for the same purposes.

Performance Indicators

The roles and responsibilities of school technology professionals are further clarified in four performance areas associated with TF/TL Standard V. The first two performance indicators (TF/TL-V.A., B.) emphasize the professional practice component of technology facilitation and leadership. In these areas, technologists fulfill their roles as specialized professional learning experts. These performance indicators also specify how technology leaders and facilitators should approach their professional learning tasks. In keeping with the concept of professional learning communities, technologists are expected to view professional development as an ongoing cycle of reflective inquiry and improvement. While the topic of productivity receives secondary emphasis in these indicators, technology is still viewed as a critical productivity tool enhancing professional learning. In exemplary performances, technology leaders and facilitators use technology to improve professional learning and to foster new practices that were previously impossible without technology.

In TF/TL-V.C., technology facilitators must be skillful users of a wide variety of productivity tools. They are expected to apply these tools to enhance their own productivity and help others become proficient as well. As technologists and other educators improve their technological skills, they move their organization toward a more productive state, enhancing professional practice.

In TF/TL-V.D., technologists are expected to use productivity tools to build three types of communities. First, they are expected to use technology to facilitate collaborative, professional learning environments for educators. Second, they unite educators, parents, and the community for the purpose of supporting student learning, and third, they involve the community in strengthening curriculum and instruction. For example, technologies such as e-mail, wikis, discussion forums, online learning management systems, instant messenger, shared databases of information, and shared files on servers can facilitate collaborative work, informal learning among peers, and online professional learning courses for educators. Technologists are also expected to help parents stay updated on their children's progress by e-mailing teachers, checking online grade books, visiting class blogs where homework is assigned, and viewing student products posted on the Web. With interactive Web-based technologies, practicing professionals in the field can mentor students and provide opportunities for them to participate in real-world scenarios connected to learning standards.

Performance Tasks

TF/TL-V.A. is composed of two performance tasks for technology facilitators and leaders, both of which concern professional learning. In TF-V.A.1., technology facilitators identify resources and participate in professional organizations supporting their own professional knowledge and professional practice. At advanced stages of performance, technology facilitators might find themselves conducting small-scale professional development activities for others or redelivering professional programs that others designed. However, technology leaders assume the full responsibilities associated with professional development experts at the school, district, and national levels. According to the performance indicator TL-V.A.1., technology leaders design, prepare, and conduct professional development supporting ongoing professional growth related to technology.

TF/TL-V.A.2. focuses on policies related to professional learning. In most cases, policy refers to a large-scale, high-level plan of action or set of rules affecting a great number of system members. Policy is not formed in isolation. For example, in a school district setting, policy making usually involves the superintendent, key cabinet members, and the local board of education. When technology leaders enact this performance indicator, they function as key players on a district leadership team setting policy for professional learning. In contrast, the facilitators' role is to disseminate and explain the policies to building-level educators.

The performance tasks in TF/TL-V.B. illustrate how technology facilitators and leaders implement shared decision making. Because facilitators are proximate to classroom practice, they continually evaluate and reflect on the use of technology. Leaders have responsibility to synthesize this evaluation information and make decisions. The difference in these performance tasks illustrates how enacting TF/TL-V.B. is a coordinated effort between facilitators and leaders.

All the performances in TF/TL-V.C. relate to the ability of technology facilitators and leaders to use productivity tools. These sample performances illustrate that leaders are expected to perform at slightly higher levels or to complete more demanding tasks than are facilitators. In TF/TL-V.C.1., facilitators are expected to model advanced features of several different types of productivity software, and leaders are expected to model the integration of data from multiple types of productivity tools. This might include using a spreadsheet in concert with word processing software to do a mail merge or exporting information from a student information database to a spreadsheet for analysis. In TF/TL-V.C.4., both technology facilitators and leaders use distance learning systems. Facilitators are expected to use online learning for professional learning, whereas leaders are expected to design and deliver opportunities for other educators. All other performance tasks in TF/TL-V.C. mirror the same type of enhanced complexity for leaders.

TF/TL-V.D. includes sample performances relating to enhancing collaboration and communication among community members. As with TF/TL-V.C., the leaders' performance tasks are more complex than the facilitators'. Leaders implement, organize, and coordinate the use of telecommunication technologies and online learning environments, including selecting tools that will be available for educators in the district and deciding how these tools will be used. Facilitators model the use of the tools and use the tools to communicate and participate, but they do not have as much responsibility to establish the context of use. For example, in TL-V.D.3., leaders organize and coordinate online curricular projects, while facilitators participate. In TL-V.D.4., leaders have a broader scope of responsibility than do facilitators. Whereas facilitators may manage their school's website and communications with parents and the community, leaders are responsible for structuring local websites and influencing Web-based communication for the district and beyond.

Productivity and Professional Practice (TF/TL-V)

Technology Facilitation Standard	Technology Leadership Standard
(TF-V) Educational technology facilitators apply technology to enhance and improve personal productivity and professional practice.	(TL-V) Educational technology leaders design, develop, evaluate, and model products created using technology resources to improve and enhance their productivity and professional practice, development and lifelong learning.

TF/TL-V.A. Use technology resources to engage in ongoing professional development and lifelong learning

Performance Tasks for Facilitators	Performance Tasks for Leaders
TF-V.A.1. Identify resources and participate in professional development activities and professional technology organizations to support ongoing professional growth related to technology.	TL-V.A.1. Design, prepare, and conduct professional development activities to present at the school/district level and at professional technology conferences to support ongoing professional growth related to technology.
TF-V.A.2. Disseminate information on district-wide policies for the professional growth opportunities for staff, faculty, and administrators.	TL-V.A.2. Plan and implement policies that support district-wide professional growth opportunities for staff, faculty, and administrators.

TF/TL-V.B. Continually evaluate and reflect on professional practice to make informed decisions regarding the use of technology in support of student learning.

TF-V.B.1. Continually evaluate and reflect on practice to make informed decisions regarding the use of technology in support of student learning.	TL-V.B.1. Based on evaluations make recommendations for changes in professional practices regarding the use of technology in support of student learning.

TF/TL-V.C. Apply technology to increase productivity.

TF-V.C.1. Model advanced features of word processing, desktop publishing, graphics programs, and utilities to develop professional products.	TL-V.C.1. Model the integration of data from multiple software applications using advanced features of applications such as word processing, database, spreadsheet, communication, and other tools into a product.
TF-V.C.2. Assist others in locating, selecting, capturing, and integrating video and digital images, in varying formats for use in presentations, publications, and/or other products.	TL-V.C.2. Create multimedia presentations integrated with multiple types of data using advanced features of a presentation tool and model them to district staff using computer projection systems.
TF-V.C.3. Demonstrate the use of specific-purpose electronic devices (such as graphing calculators, language translators, scientific probeware, or electronic thesaurus) in content areas.	TL-V.C.3. Document and assess field-based experiences using specific-purpose electronic devices.

TF-V.C.4. Use a variety of distance learning systems and use at least one to support personal and professional development.	TL-V.C.4. Use distance learning delivery systems to conduct and provide professional development opportunities for students, teachers, administrators, and staff.
TF-V.C.5. Use instructional design principles to develop hypermedia and multimedia products to support personal and professional development.	TL-V.C.5. Apply instructional design principles to develop and analyze substantive interactive multimedia computer-based instructional products.
TF-V.C.6. Select appropriate tools for communicating concepts, conducting research, and solving problems for an intended audience and purpose.	TL-V.C.6. Design and practice strategies for testing functions and evaluating technology use effectiveness of instructional products that were developed using multiple technology tools.
TF-V.C.7. Use examples of emerging programming, authoring, or problem-solving environments that support personal and professional development.	TL-V.C.7. Analyze examples of emerging programming, authoring, or problem solving environments that support personal and professional development, and make recommendations for integration at school/district level.
TF-V.C.8. Set and manipulate preferences, defaults, and other selectable features of productivity tools commonly found in PK–12 schools.	TL-V.C.8. Analyze and modify the features and preferences of productivity tool programs when developing products to solve problems encountered with their operation and/or to enhance their capability.

TF/TL-V.D. Use technology to communicate and collaborate with peers, parents, and the larger community in order to nurture student learning.

TF-V.D.1. Model the use of telecommunications tools and resources for information sharing, remote information access, and multimedia/hypermedia publishing in order to nurture student learning.	TL-V.D.1. Model and implement the use of telecommunications tools and resources to foster and support information sharing, remote information access, and communication between students, school staff, parents, and local community.
TF-V.D.2. Communicate with colleagues and discuss current research to support instruction, using applications including electronic mail, online conferencing, and Web browsers.	TL-V.D.2. Organize, coordinate, and participate in an online learning community related to the use of technology to support learning.
TF-V.D.3. Participate in online collaborative curricular projects and team activities to build bodies of knowledge around specific topics.	TL-V.D.3. Organize and coordinate online collaborative curricular projects with corresponding team activities/responsibilities to build bodies of knowledge around specific topics.
TF-V.D.4. Design, develop, and maintain Web pages and sites that support communication between school and community.	TL-V.D.4. Design, modify, maintain, and facilitate the development of Web pages and sites that support communication and information access between the entire school district and local/state/national/international communities.

ISTE's Essential Conditions and TF/TL Standard V

TF/TL Standard V: Productivity and Professional Practice is related to two ISTE essential conditions, *Skilled Personnel* and *Ongoing Professional Learning*. When implementing this standard, technology facilitators help educators build their skills in using a variety of productivity tools, such as word processing, video editing, and telecommunication tools. These skills can help educators streamline their instructional and administrative practices. These tools also enable new kinds of ongoing, professional learning opportunities, such as online learning, peer-to-peer collaboration, and building online repositories of information. By enacting TF/TL Standard V and strengthening these two essential conditions, technology facilitators and leaders play an important role in transforming schools into modern, efficient learning organizations.

Performance Scenarios

The performance indicators also suggest that technology leaders conduct professional development after they design it. Conducting professional development can involve many things. These professional development programs can be large-scale initiatives and involve train-the-trainer models for redelivery or local coaching to support them. Therefore, technology leaders also frequently monitor professional learning programs and direct the activities of technology facilitators in the local schools.

Technology leaders want teachers to become more adept at using telecommunication tools to support their own professional learning and expand their collegial alliances with teachers from other schools. To promote these learning goals, the technology leader influences a district policy requiring teachers to complete at least one of their next professional learning units via an online course. Local facilitators help their administrators inform teachers of this new policy and explain the rationale behind the action. Facilitators also conduct meetings with each teacher and help the teacher select a course that meets his or her individual learning needs.

To encourage effective technology use in classrooms, a district technology leader establishes a best-practice database in which teachers can link technology-related instructional resources to state learning standards and post them for other teachers to use. The district technology leader also creates criteria to ensure high-quality submissions. The district is requiring each teacher to submit at least three entries in the first year of implementation. The technology leader trains facilitators in how to submit resources, how to meet criteria for submission, and how to search the database for standards-related resources. Facilitators redeliver the training to local teachers, help them select best practice examples, and ensure that submissions meet quality criteria.

The school district needs to train every teacher on the new state curriculum standards for students. Because of his reputation as a professional development expert, the district technology leader is asked to serve on the district leadership team to design the district's professional development plan. Faced with the logistical challenges of training every teacher in the district, the technology leader suggests an online format allowing teachers to progress at their own pace and to complete training as their schedules permit. Although the focus of the learning is on curriculum, the technology leader realizes that if the online training is well designed and well monitored, hundreds of teachers will experience effective online learning for the first time—providing them with a model for designing online learning experiences for their own students. The technology leader co-develops the training with the curriculum directors. A curriculum consultant and a technology facilitator partner moderate each online course.

A principal asks the school's technology facilitator to create a series of video podcasts for parents and community partners. The principal's vision requires the technology facilitator to capture and integrate sound, video, and digital images; create RSS feeds; and publish the final product on the Web. Although familiar with some of these skills, the facilitator lacks some of the knowledge necessary to complete the task. The facilitator contacts a district-level technology leader specializing in multimedia and Web 2.0 technologies to secure assistance in completing the task. The district leader completes the project with the facilitator and helps the facilitator increase her knowledge of and skills in using productivity tools.

case study

TECHNOLOGY AND PLCs

Professional Learning Communities

As Richard DuFour co-developed and co-authored his first books on professional learning communities (PLCs), he also put his ideals into practice at Adlai Stevenson High School in Lincolnshire, IL, where he served as principal from 1983 to 1991 and as district superintendent from 1991 to 2002.

PLCs are characterized by high levels of collaboration and a unified focus on student learning. For example, the entire community at Stevenson constructs a shared vision around student performance and is communally responsible for working toward these common ideals. To achieve the vision, teachers work in collaborative teams where they set student achievement goals, monitor progress, share resources and best practices with one another, and constantly strive to improve their own professional knowledge and skills.

Each year, thousands of people visit this famous high school to better understand how PLCs work. When they do, Charlene Chausis, Stevenson's technology training and integration manager and recipient of the 2007 ISTE Outstanding Leader Award, is quick to point out the role that technology plays in supporting the PLC culture.

At this technology-rich high school, the PLC culture is greatly enhanced and supported by an abundance of telecommunication and productivity tools. Throughout the year, teachers and staff have opportunities to learn how to make use of a variety of collaborative tools such as instant messaging, list servers, discussion forums, wikis, and group calendars during weekly sessions offered in the school's staff development lab.

When new teachers enter Stevenson, they attend three days of orientation focusing on PLCs and how they work. During this orientation, Chausis shows the teachers how to use the student information and data systems that provide teachers with critical information on student achievement. She also shows them how using e-mail and shared folders on the network can help them collaborate with their colleagues.

However, Chausis knows that this cursory introduction isn't enough to support deep learning and the development of expert users. This is why, at Stevenson, teachers are invited to become part of a professional learning community dedicated to exploring how technology can improve productivity, professional practice, and instruction. This group is nicknamed "Power Rangers," and nearly every teacher at Stevenson participates in the community.

"It might be a bit confusing, but we are a PLC exploring how technology can support PLCs!" comments Chausis. "PLCs are a part of everything we do. It is just the way we learn here at Stevenson."

(Continued)

case study *(Continued)*

When teachers join Power Rangers, they are provided with a portable computer—the ultimate productivity tool, according to Chausis. In addition to attending a brief orientation to the "care and feeding" of the hardware, each Ranger develops a yearly individual professional learning plan that includes participating in 16 hours of formal, professional development opportunities related to technology. In fulfilling their professional learning hours, teachers can choose from a full menu of options listed on Chausis' website or a variety of other online or face-to-face courses approved by the school. In addition, Rangers are also expected to attend monthly meetings and participate in online discussions throughout the year.

Chausis has managed the Power Ranger program since 1999. As it has grown from a small cadre of 50 teachers to a group of more than 320, Chausis has established an eight-member, volunteer Ranger Advisory team—commonly referred to as the R.A.T. Pack—that helps her monitor and respond to evolving learning needs of the community. This team, consisting of a representative from each major academic division, helps Chausis place the Rangers in small groups with others who share common interests and similar planning times. The advisory team also helps plan and present on a variety of integration topics at the monthly Power Ranger meetings, late-arrival and release day workshops, and optional "Power Lunches."

Chausis attributes the success of the program to the PLC ideal of letting people guide their own learning and share with one another. In this way, she believes learning becomes "useful" and "meaningful" to people. "I view myself less as a technology expert and more as a person who is able to facilitate learning through technology. This is my job and I love it!"

To view Charlene Chausis' website, visit www6.district125.k12.il.us/staffdev/

Discussion Questions

- What types of productivity tools are available to educators in your local setting? To what extent do they maximize these tools to enhance their professional practice? What are some exemplary uses of productivity tools by educators? How could technology facilitators and leaders improve educators' use of productivity tools?

- How can technology facilitators and leaders help transform school cultures from isolated, individual practice to professional learning communities? What role can technology play in this transformation?

- How can technology be used to involve parents and the larger community in student learning?

- Staff development, professional development, and professional learning are terms referring to enhancing educators' professional knowledge and skills. Which term do you prefer and why? Which term is currently preferred by most educators today and why?

- To what extent do technology facilitators and leaders align technology-related professional learning initiatives to the NSDC Standards? Which standards are strong, and which need improvement? Why do you think these patterns exist?

Resources

As technology facilitators and leaders implement TF/TL Standard V, they may benefit from several types of resources that either assist technologists by deepening their understanding of concepts discussed in the chapter or provide tools technologists may share with other educators. Although all the resources are valuable, we have identified one "Spotlight Resource" in each chapter that has particular utility to technologists.

The resources identified under TF/TL Standard V pertain to productivity and professional practice. A series of blogs have been identified that will help technology facilitators and leaders stay current and connected to leaders in the field. E-newsletters are included to provide technology leaders and facilitators with the latest news on technology in education. Tutorial resources are listed for educators who need to learn basic productivity tools. Finally, websites focusing on various professional development opportunities are included.

Blogs

2 Cents Worth—David Warlick
http://davidwarlick.com/2cents/

Blue Skunk Blog—Doug Johnson
http://doug-johnson.squarespace.com/blue-skunk-blog/

Edu Blog Insights—Ann Davis
http://anne.teachesme.com

Learning Aloud—Mark Grabe
http://studytools.psych.und.nodak.edu/wordpress/

Moving at the Speed of Creativity—Wesley Fryer
www.speedofcreativity.org

Technology and Learning
http://techlearning.com/blog

The Strength of Weak Ties—David Jakes
http://strengthofweakties.org

Weblogg-ed—Will Richardson
http://Weblogg-ed.com

E-Newsletters

ASCD SmartBrief
www.ascd.org
> The ASCD SmartBrief is a free news service that provides summaries and links to major education stories on curriculum, professional development, leadership, emerging technologies, policy, and news from the field. ASCD membership required.

Doyle Report
www.thedoylereport.com
> The Doyle Report is a weekly e-newsletter, published by SchoolNet, at the crossroads of education improvement and the technology revolution.

 Spotlight Resource

eSchool News
www.eschoolnews.com

eSchool News is a monthly newspaper dedicated to covering educational technology news for K–12 educators. It is a subscription-based periodical, but nearly all content is available without paying fees. Nonsubscribers can access current issues via the Web, sign up for e-newsletters, subscribe to content via RSS feeds, access content from previous issues, and search for specific topics in previous issues.

Tutorials

Introduction to Microsoft Word, Part One
http://ctc.aspira.org/PDF files/Intro to Word 1.pdf
> This step-by-step tutorial can be used by technology facilitators to assist educators in their efforts to learn the basics of word processing software. It also serves as a good model for technology facilitators when developing tutorials on various other productivity tools for educators.

Introduction to Microsoft Word, Part Two
http://ctc.aspira.org/PDF files/Intro to Word 2.pdf
> This step-by-step tutorial can be used by technology facilitators to assist teachers in their efforts to learn advanced features of word processing software.

Media Library

http://library.learningtech.net

> This online media library by the Imperial County Office of Education delivers content including productivity tutorials using a variety of tools, such as podcasts, Webcasts, streaming media, and more.

Microsoft Publisher in Pictures

www.inpics.net/publisher.html

> These tutorials help educators learn the basics of creating documents with Microsoft Publisher.

Microsoft Products and Technology Tutorials

www.microsoft.com/education/tutorials.mspx

> These tutorials help educators learn the basics of various Microsoft software with in-depth, step-by-step tutorial guides.

Techtorials

www.educationworld.com/a_tech/techtorial/techtorialintro.shtml

> Techtorials are weekly step-by-step instructions posted on the Web by *Education World* on various software applications, Internet use, and more.

Websites

National Staff Development Council

www.nsdc.org

> The NSDC is a professional association committed to ensuring success for all students through staff development and school improvement.

Online Social Network for Teachers Using Technology

http://teachstrongnetwork.ning.com

> This site is an online professional learning community for educators who use digital technologies.

Podcasts for Teachers

www.teacherspodcast.org

> This site offers a series of podcasts on a variety of educational technology topics that can serve as a powerful new form of professional learning for educators.

Professional Development at Edutopia

www.edutopia.org/professionaldevelopment/

> This section of Edutopia provides a variety of articles focused on providing effective professional development for educators.

Professional Learning Communities

www.sedl.org/pubs/change34/

> This SEDL report provides research on how school educators organize as a learning community, summarizes what professional learning communities look like and how they operate, and identifies outcomes for staff and students when educators organize into a learning community within a school.

References

Bruce, R., Calhoun, E., and Hopkins, D. (1999). *The new structure of school improvement: Inquiring schools and achieving students.* Philadelphia: Open University Press.

DuFour, R., & Eaker, R. (1998). *Professional learning communities at work: Best practices for enhancing student achievement.* Bloomington, IN: National Education Service.

DuFour, R., Eaker, R., & DuFour, R. (Eds.). (2005). *On common ground: The power of professional learning communities.* Bloomington, IN: National Education Service.

Eaker, R., DuFour, R., & DuFour, R. (2002). *Getting started: Reculturing schools to become professional learning communities.* Bloomington, IN: National Education Service.

Fullan, M. (1999). *Change forces: The sequel.* London: Falmer.

Fullan, M. (2001). *Leading in a culture of change.* San Francisco: Jossey-Bass.

Ketelhut, D., McCloskey, E., Dede, C., Breit, L., & Whitehouse, P. (2006). Core tensions in the evolution of online teacher professional development. In C. Dede, (Ed.), *Online professional development for teachers.* Cambridge, MA: Harvard University Press.

Nardi, B., & O'Day, V. (1999). *Information ecologies: Using technology with heart.* Cambridge, MA: MIT.

National Staff Development Council. (2001). *Standards for staff development: Advancing student learning through staff development.* Oxford, OH: National Staff Development Council.

National Staff Development Council and Southwest Educational Development Laboratory. (2003). *Moving NSDC's staff development standards into practice: Innovation configurations.* Oxford, OH: National Staff Development Council.

North Central Regional Educational Laboratory. (2000). *enGauge framework for effective technology use in schools: Culture of learning and innovation.* Retrieved January 1, 2007, from www.ncrel.org/engauge/framewk/sys/culture/sysculin.htm

Senge, P., Roberts, C., Ross, R., Smith, B., Roth, G., & Kleiner, A. (1999). *The dance of change: The challenges of sustaining momentum in learning organizations.* New York: Doubleday.

The issue is not whether we will use
technologies, but which we will choose
and whether we will use them well.

— NARDI AND O'DAY, 1999

Chapter Six

TF/TL STANDARD VI

Social, Ethical, Legal, and Human Issues

In an era of rapid change, technology leaders and facilitators are constantly grappling with how to structure technology programs in positive ways. When new technologies are implemented in school environments, they trigger a host of social, ethical, legal, and human issues. It is difficult to predict how educators and students will use new technologies and what the consequences of those uses will be. Because other educators look to technology facilitators and leaders for guidance, technologists must understand the emerging issues and shape technology use for the common good.

Sometimes existing social norms, school policies, ethical principles, and legal precedents guide the decisions technologists must make. At other times, technology uses will evoke new types of situations, and technologists will operate in areas lacking clear guidelines. In these cases, technology facilitators must forge new ground. TF/TL Standard VI addresses these social, ethical, legal, and human components of technology use in education.

Current Context: Enhancing Benefits and Avoiding Harm

Although this standard will be applied in virtually every decision a technology facilitator or leader makes, some of the most prominent contemporary issues facing school technologists today are digital equity, privacy of electronic student records, students' online safety, and copyright infringement.

Digital Equity

One of the most convincing arguments for technology-supported learning in the classroom is the complex linkage among technology, economic power, and political action. When used properly, information and communication technologies open new opportunities for learning and help students acquire necessary technology-related knowledge and skills for work and citizenship in the digital age. Unfortunately, the opportunities for advancement are inextricably linked to the possibility of disenfranchisement and oppression as well. Deprivation from educational technology—or a lack of informed guidance regarding its use—perpetuates distinctions in the quality of education students receive and opportunities they have. For these reasons, technology facilitators and leaders must be guardians of digital equity, monitoring, advocating, and acting in ways that promote benefits for all and the exclusion of none.

The quest for digital equity is a long standing social issue related to technology in education. Early discussions of digital equity in education were typically framed in terms of closing a "digital divide" between students who have access to computers and high-speed Internet connections at school and those who do not. On this front, the campaign for equity has experienced great success. According to the U.S. Department of Education (Wells & Lewis, 2006), nearly all U.S. schools and classrooms had high-speed access to the Internet in fall 2005 (pp. 4–5)—an achievement due in great part to the Schools and Libraries Program of the Universal Service Fund included in the Telecommunications Act of 1996 and popularly known as E-rate.

According to student-to-computer ratios, student access to computers at school is fairly equitable across historically identified subgroups—confirming the notion that schools continue to be a great equalizer for disadvantaged students. Whereas the national average was calculated at 3.8 computers per student, elementary schools, larger schools, urban schools, schools with higher percentages of minority students, and schools with more low-income students had slightly fewer computers than other schools; however, the difference was not nearly as great as it was in 1998. The greatest difference remained between schools with higher and lower percentages of minority students, but this gap had also significantly decreased over time (see Table 6.1).

TABLE 6.1 ▪ Ratio of public school students to instructional computers with Internet access by school characteristics: 1998–2005

SCHOOL CHARACTERISTICS	1998	2005
All public schools	12.1	3.8
Instructional Level		
Elementary	13.6	4.1
Secondary	9.9	3.3
School Size		
Less than 300	9.1	2.4
300–999	12.3	3.9
1,000 or more	13.0	4.0
Locale		
City	14.1	4.2
Urban fringe	12.4	4.1
Town	12.2	3.4
Rural	8.6	3.0
Percent Minority Enrollment		
Less than 6%	10.1	3.0
6–20%	10.4	3.9
21–49%	12.1	4.0
50% or more	17.2	4.1
Percent of Students Eligible for Free or Reduced-Price Lunch		
Less than 35%	10.6	3.8
35–39%	10.9	3.4
50–74%	15.8	3.6
75% or more	16.8	4.0

Source: Wells, J., & Lewis, L. (2006). Internet access in U.S. Public Schools and Classrooms: 1994–2005 (NCES 2007–0200). U.S. Department of Education. Washington, DC: National Center for Educational Statistics.

Although ensuring equal access to computers and the Internet at school is an important first step, informed educators also know that there are many other dimensions critical to achieving true digital equity. Simply providing students with access to hardware does not correlate with meaningful technology integration in instruction. Present areas of concern in meeting digital equity include:

- Equitable student access to other types of digital tools besides computers and high-speed Internet access at school, such as software, peripherals, online subscription-based resources, and online learning courses

- Equal opportunities for students to use technologies to increase access to channels of civic action and economically valuable knowledge and skills—especially the ability to create original content on the World Wide Web

- Equitable student access to the Internet, broadband services, modern computing devices, and other technical resources beyond the school day

- Access to assistive technologies for students with disabilities as mandated by the Individuals with Disabilities Education Act (IDEA)

- Access to teachers possessing the knowledge and desire to integrate technology and instruction meaningfully, using technology to enable and empower learning

To make informed decisions, K–12 technology professionals must continually monitor these concerns. Available information indicates that there has been progress in many areas; however, reason for concern remains. Too often, race, gender, income, and locale continue to correlate to digital inequities. For example:

- Students and teachers in low-income settings have less access to technology resources and technology support (Ronnkvist, Dexter, & Anderson, 2000).

- Technology-supported instruction in high-poverty settings may focus on drill, skill, and other lower-order cognitive tasks, while students from more affluent areas are using technology to solve problems, create products, and publish on the World Wide Web. This is significant because user-created content (UCC) is an emerging indicator of economic prosperity (Organisation for Economic Co-operation and Development, 2007; Schrum & Bracey, 2003).

- Students from some minority groups may suffer from shortage of software and online content relating to their cultural experiences (Lazarus & Lipper, 2003; Lazarus & Mora, 2000).

- In 2002–2003, White, Asian, and Multiracial students in grades K–12 were approximately twice as likely as Hispanic, Black, and American Indian students to have home Internet access. These trends were slightly more severe when comparing students from high-income (76%) and low-income families (30%)(Corporation for Public Broadcasting, 2003; Wells & Lewis, 2006).

- In 2007, nearly half the American homes had broadband access (47%), with gaps among Whites (48%) and Blacks closing (40%) over the preceding three years, but gaps between low and high-income levels remaining extremely great (Horigan & Smith, 2007).

- In December 2006, the United States had more broadband users than any other country in the world, but the percentage of users ranked 15th among the nations (Organisation for Economic Co-operation and Development, 2006).

- Fifty-five percent (55%) of rural Americans had broadband access compared to 73% in urban/suburban areas (Horigan & Smith, 2007).

- A recent study suggests that a group of female elementary-school students have technology-related attitudes and performance levels comparable to those of their male counterparts; however, others note that women are still not entering the field of computer science as often as do men (Bain & Rice, 2007; Schrum & Geisler, 2003).

- School districts that spent more in technology funds were less likely to experience cuts and were more likely to expect technology-related funding increases in the future. In contrast, districts spending less on technology programs experienced the most severe cuts and had low or no expectations for improvements in future funding cycles (Consortium for School Networking, 2005).

- Inequities must also be examined within a school or district. Even though data on these inequities is not often collected and reported, there can be great disparities in technology implementation across classrooms in the same school and schools in the same district (North Central Educational Laboratory, 2000).

If technology facilitators and leaders aspire to equalize the digital playing field for their students, they must continue to track these national trends, consider the emerging issues, and study the dimensions of equity in their own settings. They may also consider the following five strategies for making progress developed by participants at ISTE's Digital Equity Summit: Engaging and Empowering the 21st Century Learner (Davis, Fuller, Jackson, Pittman, & Sweet, 2007):

1. Legitimize the significant role cultur'e plays in students' educational experience;

2. Continue to challenge perceptions about the role of technology in education;

3. Encourage others to recognize the critical link between professional development and classroom practice;

4. Create opportunities for students to access technology outside the classroom;

5. Continue to seek funding for technology in spite of challenges (Universal Service Administrative Company, 2007).

Privacy and Student Records

As discussed in Chapter 4, schools are collecting, reporting, and storing student information in unprecedented ways, and these practices will continue to expand in the future. Although electronic data collection and warehousing offer great potential for school improvement, educators are obligated to protect the privacy of student records under the Family Educational Rights and Privacy Act (FERPA) of 1974. In the information age, this requires action on many fronts.

For school technologists, the work begins by securing the computers that store information and the networks that transmit it. Security measures may include firewalls, encryption, user authentication, network monitoring, and restricted access to server rooms. But security efforts cannot end there. The National Forum on Education Statistics (NFES, 2006) warns that educators' use of small storage devices, laptops, and handheld computers presents new security risks. Because these devices are portable and easily misplaced, anyone who finds the lost item usually has immediate access to the contents, which often includes student grades and other information. Educators who store FERPA-protected information on their home computers and exchange unencrypted e-mail with student information also place the school district at risk (NFES, 2006, p. 8). However, the most common security threats are uninformed or careless users who create simple or obvious passwords, share accounts with others, write passwords down in accessible places, or leave computers unattended without properly logging out. Dealing with these types of security threats requires training users and creating a "security-conscious" organizational culture (NFES, 1998, p. 37). Although information on data security in schools is scarce, in a recent survey of more than 381 district technologists, 9% reported a security breach in the preceding year (CDW-G, 2007).

Under FERPA, technologists also must be careful how they represent student data in public reports. Although these reports are allowable under FERPA, educators cannot present data that identifies an individual student in any way. For example, if a report on standardized test scores is disaggregated by grade level and racial subgroup and there is only one student of a particular race in that grade, the student is identifiable even though his or her name is not included. The data cannot be published.

These examples serve only as an introduction to the many issues that currently exist in schools, but they illustrate how technology facilitators and leaders need an in-depth knowledge of FERPA and other privacy laws related to education. Technologists can learn more by reading, consulting with other educational leaders, and relying on the school district attorneys for guidance, as needed.

Online Safety

Initial concerns related to Internet safety in schools centered on students' access to inappropriate content on the Web. These concerns led to the enactment of the Children's Internet Protection Act (CIPA) in December 2000. This law requires that, as a condition of participating in federal educational funding programs (such as E-rate), school systems will have protection mechanisms in place to block or filter sites that are obscene, pornographic, or otherwise harmful to children.

Schools have had reasonable success limiting student access to inappropriate Web content; however, educators and the general public have newer concerns about protecting students' privacy and security in online environments—both in and out of school. Today's students socialize in very different ways than did previous generations. Recent survey results suggest that nearly all (96%) online teens have used social networking technologies such as chat, text messaging, blogging, and online communities such as MySpace and Facebook (National School Boards Association, 2007). Nearly three-quarters (71%) of teens participate in online communities at least weekly (NSBA, 2007), and between half (55%) and 71% of children aged 13–18 with Internet access have online profiles (Lenhardt & Madden, 2007). Websites such as Webkins and the chat sections of Nick.com are socializing younger children's communication patterns toward online communities, as well (NSBA, 2007).

Because pedophiles are known to frequent online communities, primary concerns relating to social networking center on the safety of underage minors. By providing personal information online and being lured into face-to-face meetings, children and teens have unwittingly aided pedophiles in committing crimes against them. Encounters with cyberbullies, cyberstalkers, inappropriate material, and vulgar language represent other reasons for caution. In addition, youth report frequently lying about their age and personal information online—sometimes to gain access to inappropriate sites, sometimes to be "playful," and sometimes to protect their identity (Lenhardt & Madden, 2007). Although some youth seem comfortable with misrepresenting personal information online, this practice raises new questions and implications surrounding ethical interpersonal communication. Educators and parents are also concerned that too much time online impedes healthy face-to-face relationships and distracts students from their academic studies—even though nearly 60% of teens report that they use social networking to discuss education-related topics, and 50% talk specifically about homework (NSBA, 2007).

Most online safety concerns center around online profiles on social networking sites, but schools and school districts struggle with online safety in classrooms, as well. Although Web 2.0 technologies facilitate Web-based publication, syndication, and communication in the classroom, they also possess the potential for harm. The Internet is highly promoted as a method of increasing instructional authenticity by giving students a place to publish their work to real audiences and communicate with others beyond the classroom. However, educators and parents are also appropriately concerned with identifying students and exposing them to undesirable online persons in these contexts. Because FERPA interprets "student records" broadly to include student academic work and photos and videotapes of individuals and groups of students, this example represents one of the most perplexing contemporary dilemmas for technology facilitators and leaders in the field.

Balancing equity, safety, and instructional efficacy is often difficult. Although Web 2.0 technologies have propelled online interactivity, the acceptable norms and processes of these methods of communication are still evolving. Primarily, youth—with developing moral structures and limited life experiences—are leading the effort outside of school, with educators and parents knowing very little about the technologies students use and only 8% of schools providing cybersafety training (CDW-G, 2007). In schools, leaders are pondering whether the benefits of Web publishing and communication are worth the risk—with most erring on the side of caution. Although exceptions exist, heightened fear is causing most school districts to limit classroom communications, restrict access to popular social networking sites, and prohibit blogging, Web publishing, or any type of cross-site communication with others (NSBA, 2007). These policies may frustrate teachers and impose restrictions on practices (such as electronic pen pals and publishing work on class websites) that were commonly accepted before the advent of social networking.

In this context, technology facilitators and leaders are challenged to develop and implement policies that harness the potential of social networking technologies for learning, striking a balance between wide-open, unregulated use and unplugged environments that will seem foreign and sterile to today's students. Promising compromises include:

- Publishing Web products anonymously or with pseudonyms.

- Restricting access to student work with passwords for family members and friends.

- Publicizing only products of excellence and purpose and partnering with national or regional programs, such as highschooljournalism.org, that are equipped with policies and procedures about publishing student work. Although this will not eliminate all risks, it reduces the volume of published items, highlights the positive aspects of publishing, and provides models of how online publishing can be managed.

- Allowing parents to make decisions about the risks they want to take. Use parent consent forms either once a year or on a case-by-case basis.

- Publishing work or blog entries anonymously or with pseudonyms. Use avatars instead of pictures of students to protect their identity.

- Using moderated discussions to preapprove published work and to screen participants.

- Leaning on existing public media policies, such as city newspaper or school yearbook photos, as precedents to inform emerging Web-based policies.

- Using online projects that screen participants, such as e-Pals, to reduce the risk of undesirable communication.

- Exploring social networking sites, such as whyville.org, that implement community-based safety measures but do not necessarily promise to prevent a breach in security or cyberbullying from a peer. Instead, they teach children what is acceptable online behavior, what is not, and how they should protect themselves in social online environments should a violation occur. After students complete an initial training and earn their "driver's license," they are allowed to participate in the community and practice the safety measures they have learned.

- Exploring online educational programs, such as imbee.com and think.com, to integrate social networking tools into educational environments.

- Implementing online learning management systems, such as Web CT, Moodle, or BlackBoard, to implement virtual learning or to augment face-to-face instruction can help older students communicate with their local peers about learning in a safe, password-protected, moderated environment.

- Educating parents, students, and educators about online safety and netiquette.

- Publishing policies that specify and prohibit undesirable or unsafe online practices.

Although some of these strategies reduce the benefits and excitement of publishing to broad audiences, they still honor students' need to use the Web for social interaction and learning. They also provide intermediate steps to help students, educators, and parents structure positive online interactions. Social networking fosters creativity and provides students with opportunities to read, write, create multimedia products, and enhance their technical skills. These activities seem to be especially attractive to "nonconformists" who possess an impressive list of knowledge, skills, and abilities but who are not necessarily top academic achievers (NSBA, 2007).

Technology and Copyright

Many of the concerns related to online environments are not new, but new technologies have accelerated or provided a new medium for undesirable behaviors. This is especially true in the cases of plagiarism and the unauthorized duplication of other copyrighted materials, such as movies, music, and graphics. According to reports from practicing educators, the following represent frequent occurrences in and outside of school:

- Cutting text from Internet sites and pasting it into academic papers or homework without adequate citations

- Buying papers online and submitting them as original work

- Downloading music illegally from Internet sites for personal use and for sharing with others

- Making and possibly distributing illegal copies of copyrighted movies

- Using copyrighted music, video clips, and graphics in academic presentations and products without obtaining proper copyright clearance

- Loading illegal copies of software on school and/or personal computers

These actions continue to proliferate for the following reasons: First, most educators do not fully comprehend copyright law and, therefore, are not able to model and teach basic principles to students. For these reasons, some violations are grounded in ignorance and confusion, not necessarily blatant disregard. Second, the violations have become so frequent and commonplace that social resistance and condemnation of some copyright violations are eroding. Third, improving one's knowledge is so complex and time consuming that most educators do not pursue it.

The Copyright Act of 1976 defines intellectual property rights and what constitutes violations of these principles, and Section 107 of this act discusses the fair use defense for teaching, scholarship, and research. This act and all subsequent amendments are available online (see www.copyright.gov/title17/). However, most educators have not read the law, and many of those who have tried find the text tedious and ambiguous. Furthermore, experts agree that a thorough understanding of the Copyright Act also requires studying prior legal cases that establish a context for interpreting the legislation, keeping pace with emerging conflicts, and following changes in current legislation.

These barriers must not prevent educators from being informed, teaching students, and reinforcing legal and ethical behavior in schools. Some common tactics deployed by experienced technology facilitators and leaders include:

- Increasing their own copyright literacy

- Ensuring that key staff members are familiar with copyright laws and tasked with educating others in basic principles and evolving issues

- Using information, curriculum, and guest speakers from key organizations promoting copyright adherence

- Purchasing and training staff and students to use electronic plagiarism detection tools, such as Turn It In

- Using technical solutions to prevent teachers and students from installing software without administrative permission

- Using network-monitoring software to search for unauthorized applications on the network

Policies, Procedures, and Advocacy

Current issues related to digital equity, online safety, copyright, and other social, ethical, legal, and human issues require that technology facilitators and leaders structure technology use and educate parents, educators, and students about key issues. Participating in policy development is one way to accomplish these goals. Policies represent a formal position of the school district—one approved by the school board.

Because policy development requires fully vetting the idea prior to school board action and full dissemination of a policy after approval, policy development maximizes opportunities to inform the school community of key issues. Technologists typically participate in the development and dissemination of at least two types of policies related to the implementation of TF/TL Standard VI—Internet safety policies and acceptable use policies. To encourage reflection on social, ethical, and human issues, state and federal funding programs require these policies as a condition of funding. Internet safety policies explain how the school system will respond to the following:

- Restricting access by minors to inappropriate or harmful content on the Internet

- Protecting the safety and security of minors when using e-mail, chat rooms, and other forms of direct electronic communications

- Preventing unauthorized access, including "hacking," and other unlawful activities by minors online

- Preventing unauthorized disclosure, use, and dissemination of personal information regarding minors. (USAC, 2007)

Internet safety policies convey what actions school districts will take to keep children safe, and acceptable use policies (AUPs) address the responsibilities of users. AUPs set boundaries around technology use and educate teachers and parents about security, online safety, copyright, netiquette, cyberbullying, and other emerging issues. These use policies are usually crafted as agreements between the district and the user, who agrees to certain penalties if acceptable use is violated.

Because these policies are required by law, most school districts have them in place, but the current challenge for technologists is to ensure that the policies are frequently updated to address emerging issues. According to a recent survey of district technology leaders, only slightly more than half of school districts (57%) update their AUPs annually.

Formal policy development is time consuming and inappropriate in many cases. It is the role of school district employees—not the school board—to govern most day-to-day operations. To accomplish this, school leaders are engaged in developing procedures and guidelines that are responsive to local needs and aligned to district policy. For example, most district technologists have development procedures or guidelines related to the distribution of equipment in schools to ensure equity within the system. Most often these distribution methods include a standard set of equipment provided to each school and a rotating schedule for refreshing that equipment. Some school districts even have guidelines to ensure that wealthier schools in the system do not outpace technology programs in other schools with fewer resources by using local funds or grant funding to purchase additional technologies. Other districts have established district-level foundations that raise community support for technology and equitably distribute the benefits to all schools. Developing, implementing, and revising procedures and guidelines related to equity and a host of other social, ethical, and human issues is an integral role for the school technology professional.

School technologists must also constantly monitor and participate in the legislative process. New legislation related to technology in schools is continually evolving, and educators must advocate for their local interests—just as they did when CIPA and the Telecommunications Act of 1994 were being formed. Because the school technology roles are relatively new in education, technologists were not as mobilized to participate in the legislative process as those in other professions. However, professional organizations, such as the International Society for Technology in Education (ISTE), the Consortium for School Networking (CoSN), and the State Education Technology Directors Association (SETDA), have effectively filled that gap. ISTE and CoSN have also partnered to create the EdTech Action Network (ETAN), providing educators with information critical to influencing public policy and legislation (see www.edtechactionnetwork.org).

Summary of Current Context

Standard VI challenges technologists to enter unfamiliar fields, incorporating social, ethical, and legal issues into educational technology practice. Some of these challenges—such as cyberbullying and promoting appropriate netiquette—can be readily addressed through hardware, software, and training intervention; however, others—such as bridging the persistent digital divide—require technologists to consider the social and ethical role of technology in promoting (or denying) educational equity. As daunting as these challenges may be, technologists must embrace them as an opportunity to promote safe, healthy, and equitable education for all students. To accomplish their tasks they often need support from legal experts, other educational leaders, professional organizations, and advocacy groups.

Implementing the Standard

For reference, the full TF/TL Standard VI is listed on pages 136–137.

Performance Standards

Standard TF/TL-VI recognizes that technologists will face social, ethical, legal, and other human issues when implementing technology programs in education. As indicated by the standard, both technology facilitators and leaders must work diligently to understand these issues. Beyond this commonality, the performances for facilitators and leaders differ. Technology leaders create a framework to promote beneficial uses of technology, and facilitators help others understand and implement the framework.

According to the standard, the technology leader is responsible for developing programs that address social, ethical, legal, and human issues related to the use of technology in their district, region, or state. Once programs are in place, technology facilitators assist teachers in understanding and implementing safe, fair, and legal practices in local schools.

Performance Indicators

The five performance indicators for this standard are the same for both technology facilitators and leaders.

1. **Modeling and teaching legal and ethical practice related to technology use (TF/TL-VI.A.).** In this performance indicator, technologists are expected to understand and demonstrate legal and ethical practices related to technology use in schools. This includes, but is not limited to, an awareness of federal and state laws regulating educational technology practice (such as copyright laws) and effective integration of these laws into technology-supported educational practices. This performance indicator is incredibly challenging to technologists because it requires constant vigilance for laws that could affect educational technology practice, consideration of the requirements of those laws, and effective communication of the laws to other educators who must implement them in daily educational practice.

2. **Applying technology resources to enable and empower learners with diverse backgrounds, characteristics, and abilities (TF/TL-VI.B.).** Technology has a unique capacity to enable and empower all students. In this standard area, facilitators and leaders apply technology to meet the needs of individual learners. To accomplish this, technology facilitators and leaders must consider how to use digital-age learning tools to empower students with different learning abilities, learning styles, and achievement needs. Technologists must also consider how to help all students participate in governmental and economic processes, which are increasingly dependent on modern technologies.

3. **Identifying and using technology resources that affirm diversity (TF/TL-VI.C.).** The previous performance indicator addressed the power of technology to address diversity represented in each individual student. In TF/TL-VI.C., facilita-

tors and leaders apply technology to help each individual student gain a greater appreciation for diversity in others. In this standard, technologists identify and use technology to promote pluralism in modern culture and to help students understand a broad spectrum of cultures and linguistic backgrounds.

4. **Promoting safe and healthy use of technology resources (TF/TL-VI.D.).** Technologists must promote safe and healthy use of technology resources. This includes legally mandated provisions, such as FERPA, CIPA, and acceptable use/Internet safety policies, as required for participation in federal funding programs such as E-rate. This standard also addresses a host of nonrequired but recommended strategies to keep students, staff, and data secure from harmful or undesirable technology uses.

5. **Facilitating equitable access to technology resources for all students (TF/TL-VI.E.).** In this performance indicator, technology facilitators and leaders stand as guardians who monitor digital divides and develop strategies to minimize inequities when they occur. It is important for technologists to interpret access beyond simply providing equal amounts of hardware, software, and Internet access to students. As illustrated in this chapter, digital equity also includes students' ability to use technology in ways similar to their counterparts.

Performance Tasks

Adhering to copyright laws (TF/TL-VI.A.2.) and providing adaptive/assistive technology to special-needs students (TF/TL-VI.B.2.) are specifically addressed in the performance tasks for TF/TL Standard VI—noting the importance of these two legal issues in school settings. The rest of the performance indicators are stated in more general terms relating to the need for technologists to help others understand the broad spectrum of legal and ethical issues related to technology in education, including topics related to empowering diverse learners (TF/TL-VI.B.1.), affirming diversity (TF/TL-VI.C.1.), promoting the safe and healthy use of technology (TF/TL-VI.D.1.), and providing equitable access to technology (TF/TL-VI.E.1.).

Although technology facilitators and leaders address the same general topics in these performance tasks, their actual performances are quite different. For technology leaders, many performance tasks focus on using and communicating research related to social, ethical, legal, and human issues (TF/TL-VI.B.1., C.2., D.1., E.1.). The multiple references to research in these performances illustrate how leaders must constantly monitor developments and inform others about what they have learned. Because of the sensitivity, impact, and potential liability associated with these topics, superintendents and board members expect technology leaders to be experts in this content area. To assume this expert role, technology leaders must read broadly and synthesize issues across multiple sources. Other performance tasks illustrate why technology leaders must be well-versed experts in research on social, legal, ethical, and human issues. According to these tasks, technology leaders are clearly responsible for developing, implementing, and communicating rules, plans, policies, and procedures related to Standard VI (TL-VI.A.1., A.2., B.2.). In keeping with the assigned role and responsibilities of technology leaders, they enact these tasks at the district, state, and regional levels.

Facilitators, on the other hand, fulfill critical support and implementation roles at the local school level. Similar to many other standard areas, the facilitator's primary role in Standard VI centers around professional learning—especially for teachers. According to the performance tasks, facilitators assist teachers in understanding district rules, plans, policies, and procedures related to the healthy, safe, ethical, and legal uses of technology in schools. Facilitators also help teachers in selecting and applying specific technologies to maximize the benefit and minimize the harm to users (TF-VI.A.1., A.2., B.1., C.2., D.1.). To accomplish their professional learning functions, facilitators may share materials developed by technology leaders, conduct training sessions, or help teachers in one-to-one settings.

The performance tasks also recognize that facilitators will routinely develop strategies for implementing district goals related to Standard VI (TF-VI.A.1., E.1.). For example, facilitators often must choose which professional learning strategy will be most effective at their school. If the district leadership called for a copyright audit in all schools, facilitators would have to develop strategies to complete the audit in their local setting. Performance Standard TF-VI.E.1. suggests that facilitators frequently implement strategies to ensure equitable access for students and teachers. These scenarios illustrate how facilitators generally have some flexibility in how district rules, procedures, and plans are best accomplished locally—thus bridging the critical gap between policy and practice.

A final role for facilitators includes making recommendations related to the healthy, safe, ethical, and legal use of technology in schools. In the performance tasks, facilitators recommend specific technologies to teachers (TF-VI.B.2.). Facilitators can also recommend policies to technology leaders (TF-VI.E.1.). These performances illustrate how facilitators not only disseminate district, regional, or state level decisions, but influence them. Because of their intimate knowledge of local schools, facilitators can assist technology leaders in developing policies, plans, and procedures that are appropriate and responsive to the needs of educators, staff, students, and parents.

Social, Ethical, Legal, and Human Issues (TF/TL-VI)

Technology Facilitation Standard	Technology Leadership Standard
(TF-VI) Educational technology facilitators understand the social, ethical, legal, and human issues surrounding the use of technology in PK–12 schools and assist teachers in applying that understanding in their practice.	(TL-VI) Educational technology leaders understand the social, ethical, legal, and human issues surrounding the use of technology in PK–12 schools and develop programs facilitating application of that understanding in practice throughout their district/region/state.

TF/TL-VI.A. Model and teach legal and ethical practice related to technology use.

Performance Tasks for Facilitators	Performance Tasks for Leaders
TF-VI.A.1. Develop strategies and provide professional development at the school/classroom level for teaching social, ethical, and legal issues and responsible use of technology.	TL-VI.A.1. Establish and communicate clear rules, policies, and procedures to support legal and ethical use of technologies at the district/regional/state levels.

TF-VI.A.2. Assist others in summarizing copyright laws related to use of images, music, video, and other digital resources in varying formats.	TL-VI.A.2. Implement a plan for documenting adherence to copyright laws.
TF/TL-VI.B. Apply technology resources to enable and empower learners with diverse backgrounds, characteristics, and abilities.	
TF-VI.B.1. Assist teachers in selecting and applying appropriate technology resources to enable and empower learners with diverse backgrounds, characteristics, and abilities.	TL-VI.B.1. Communicate research on best practices related to applying appropriate technology resources to enable and empower learners with diverse backgrounds, characteristics, and abilities.
TF-VI.B.2. Identify, classify, and recommend adaptive/assistive hardware and software for students and teachers with special needs and assist in procurement and implementation.	TL-VI.B.2. Develop policies and provide professional development related to acquisition and use of appropriate adaptive/ assistive hardware and software for students and teachers with special needs.
TF/TL-VI.C. Identify and use technology resources that affirm diversity.	
TF-VI.C.1. Assist teachers in selecting and applying appropriate technology resources to affirm diversity and address cultural and language differences.	TL-VI.C.1. Communicate research on best practices related to applying appropriate technology resources to affirm diversity and address cultural and language differences.
TF/TL-VI.D. Promote safe and healthy use of technology resources.	
TF-VI. D.1. Assist teachers in selecting and applying appropriate technology resources to promote safe and healthy use of technology	TL-VI.D.1. Communicate research and establish policies to promote safe and healthy use of technology.
TF/TL-VI.E. Facilitate equitable access to technology resources for all students.	
TF-VI.E.1. Recommend policies and implement school/classroom strategies for achieving equitable access to technology resources for all students and teachers.	TL-VI.E.1. Use research findings in establishing policy and implementation strategies to promote equitable access to technology resources for students and teachers.

ISTE's Essential Conditions and TF/TL Standard VI

TF/TL Standard VI: Social, Ethical, Legal, and Human Issues affects all of ISTE's essential conditions for effective technology use in schools. The following serve as just a few examples of the connections between ISTE's essential conditions and TF/TL Standard VI:

- A *Shared Vision* and *Implementation Planning* must represent the needs and interests of all stakeholder groups. *Engaged Communities* must be involved in constructing the vision and the implementation plan to ensure that diverse opinions and needs are represented.

- Technology facilitators and leaders must ensure that students not only have equitable access to technology, but also have equitable access to *Student-Centered Learning* opportunities, *Skilled Personnel*, and high-quality *Technical Support*.

- Providing students with equitable learning opportunities is inextricably tied to *Consistent and Adequate Funding*, a well-developed *Curriculum Framework*, and *Ongoing Professional Learning* for teachers, staff, and administrators.

- *Student-Centered Learning* requires addressing the individual needs and interests of students, which may vary based on students' gender; academic performance; and cultural, racial, and linguistic backgrounds.

- Technologists can monitor equity through *Assessment and Evaluation* activities.

- Technology-supported *Assessment and Evaluation* of learning allows educators to diagnose student learning and to differentiate instruction based on students' individual needs.

- To encourage safe and ethical use of technologies, technology facilitators and leaders must create and implement local *Support Policies*. Some of these policies, such as acceptable use and Internet safety policies, are required by law to receive federal funding for technology. Other policies are necessary to avoid violating laws, such as copyright law, or for keeping students safe, such as policies related to blogging, podcasting, and identifying students on the World Wide Web.

Performance Scenarios

A new technology leader preparing an E-rate application learns that the school district is responsible for having an acceptable use policy (AUP) and Internet safety policy (ISP). The AUP must state how teachers and students should use district-owned technology resources at home and at school, and the ISP must explain how the district keeps students safe from undesirable content and social interactions on the Web. The leader reviews the district's existing policies and determines that these policies need updating. To revise the policies, the leader convenes technology facilitators in the district to discuss current issues and practices that need district guidance. The facilitators provide input on problems related to cyberbullying and other issues that have emerged in schools since the last policies were drafted. The technology leader revises the district policies to address these issues and shares a draft of the policies with facilitators for revision. The technology leader then shares the final revisions with the district leadership team and superintendent, who delivers the proposed policy changes to the school board for input and approval.

A technology facilitator is approached by a teacher requesting help determining whether a student-created movie complies with all copyright laws and regulations. The student is entering the movie in the local technology fair and has included a variety of multimedia components downloaded from the Web such as graphics, sound, and video. The technology facilitator watches the movie and explains the copyright guidelines that apply. The student modifies the movie based on the recommendations of the technology facilitator and enters the movie in the technology fair.

Technology facilitators report to the technology leader that teachers hesitate to allow students to use technology to complete homework projects because many of their students do not have access to computers or the Internet beyond the school day. To confirm or reject the teachers' assumptions, the technology leader proposes a plan to collect data on students' beyond-school access. Results of the study find that approximately three-fourths of students have readily available access beyond the school day, while the remaining students do not. The technology leader uses this data to support a proposal for a one-to-one laptop initiative for middle and high school students and to leverage low-cost, high-speed Internet access programs for low-income families. The technology facilitators disseminate the results of the study to local educators in their buildings and share the district's proposed plan for increasing students' beyond-school access.

In response to the needs of special education students within the district, an assistive technology facilitator recommends technology products that meet specifications in student individualized education plans (IEPs). The facilitator studies the individual needs of students, researches various hardware and software, and identifies specific technologies required to provide meaningful access to the general curriculum as required by the Individuals with Disabilities Education Act, 1997.

When designing new computer labs, the district technology leader considers proper lighting to minimize eye strain and ergonomically designed furniture to alleviate back problems and carpal tunnel syndrome.

case study

Technology Facilitator Cathy Greenwald

PODCASTS AND MORE AT THE ELEMENTARY LEVEL

Reflective Decisions about Web 2.0 Technologies at Willowdale

Willowdale Elementary is part of the Millard School District in suburban Omaha, Nebraska. Teachers at this school regularly use Web 2.0 technologies to add new dimensions to teaching and learning. This small elementary school is perhaps most famous for Radio WillowWeb, an ongoing series of podcasts for kids by kids. MP3 files of individual Willowcasts are available on WillowWeb (www.mpsomaha.org/willow/radio/), or iTunes. Regular listeners can also subscribe to Radio WillowWeb via RSS feeds. In addition to audio podcasting, the teachers and students also use blogs and video to create and publish original products on the World Wide Web.

Cathy Greenwald, part-time technology specialist and part-time reading teacher at Willowdale, says that since the advent of the World Wide Web, Willowdale has been attracted to the possibilities of the media for enhancing teaching, learning, and home/school communication. "What the Web does is provide a way to implement our language standards to write for real audiences for specific purposes. Because we are an ELL site for our district, this is very important to us," Greenwald explains. "Web 2.0 technologies simply make publishing the content easier for us and accessing the content easier for readers."

Greenwald also notes that online publishing has positive effects for students, parents and other family members. She explains, "While student writing could be turned in to the teacher or students could do presentations in front of the class, Web publishing takes it a step further by writing for a broader audience. Students have more of an investment in that. Even if just parents see it, that's great. One of our younger students realized, 'My dad can see this at his office!' Grandparents also love it. Since we have English language learners, we often have grandparents in another country, like China or Vietnam, and I've had parents tell me how much it means to them to be able to feel a part of the student's life. Even just for parents who miss a Halloween party or a guest speaker, being able to read a student's account of the event or see a picture is important to them."

However, Greenwald admits that the public aspects of their site also require staff to be reflective about online safety. "Since Willowdale has received a lot of attention for our use of Web 2.0 technologies and Radio WillowWeb is on iTunes, we've come to realize that we are really out there! We aren't just a little school website anymore! Everyone—everyone in the world—can see us! While that's great from a publication standpoint, it's also kind of overwhelming. It's a big responsibility to think about that."

Greenwald explains that she and the staff at Willowdale implement many policies to make sure students are safe. First and foremost, the school lets parents decide whether or not their child's photos or original work will be published online. Second, the school only uses first names on author bylines and does not use children's names in photo captions. Third, the staff only publishes work with a specific purpose and

(Continued)

case study *(Continued)*

a link to the curriculum. Finally, all Web content is proofed by a teacher before publication. Students cannot publish directly online without a teacher, and outsiders cannot post to the school blogs. Greenwald believes that the policies and the reflective use of technology by professionals are what make parents comfortable. According to Greenwald, about 99% of parents sign the consent form, which she describes as a standard media release form modified to incorporate Internet use and publishing. "It is a parent's choice, and we need to be very conscientious and respectful of that. Sometimes it is online safety and sometimes it is other reasons, but whatever it is, we make sure to honor the parent's wishes and not make the child or the parent feel uncomfortable."

Of course, modern students do have the desire for more interactive communication as well, so Greenwald explains that students have e-mail accounts, set up by the district, in which they can only e-mail other students in specified grade levels—for example fourth- and fifth-graders are allowed to e-mail each other. Greenwald, the principal, and teachers are also able to view any e-mails sent or received by their students. More interactive blog environments are also used for book talks and other curriculum discussions, but these are only available to the students and their teachers on the school's local area network. "The key is adult monitoring and decision making," explains Greenwald.

Although Greenwald maintains that her role in keeping students safe is simply following district policy, her stories also illustrate how she monitors the local environment and participates in reflective decision making when new situations arise. For example, last year two students had an inappropriate e-mail conversation, which Greenwald read during routine monitoring activities. She immediately notified the teacher, and together, Greenwald and the teacher talked to the students and their parents about the situation. She also participated in a decision not to go to video podcasting right away, either. "When we watched some of the earlier WillowCam broadcasts we'd done about five years ago, we noted that students were identifying themselves by first name. Somehow to publish video podcasts on the Web and have them use their first names doesn't seem quite right, and so we are holding off and rethinking what we want to do. I know we'll go there, but we're just taking our time," she explains.

Greenwald notes that the decisions she has had to make have made her more reflective. "Many of the staff and I used to have our family websites out there with our kids and our dogs, and now I have scaled back. I am not so sure I want all of that out there without a strong purpose. I love what the Web can do for learning, but I'm just more reflective." She also would like to think that the students would be more thoughtful about online use because of their experiences at Willowdale—even though she notes that the students currently in their care are very young and their future will also shaped by many other influences along the way. "I am a parent of four, so I understand that the message children receive at home is what can really make the difference. Our students still have to navigate middle school and high school, but the parents will be with them all the way through their teen years."

(Continued)

case study (Continued)

When reflecting on why Web 2.0 and other communication technologies work at Willowdale, Greenwald credits past technology leaders who had been reflective decision makers along the way and a current district-level technology staff that is supportive and innovative. "Instead of shutting things down, the district is buying products and developing policies to help us keep using technology effectively. This is groundbreaking, cutting-edge work, but it's important. I don't know what we'd do if we were in one of those districts that just made us stop doing what we do," she says. "I think there'd be a grieving process, that's for sure. Then, I guess we'd just have to go back to finding old ways of doing things, like, maybe, the old-fashioned newsletter for Roving Reporters, or something. It wouldn't be the same, though, that's for sure!"

Visit WillowWeb at: www.mpsomaha.org/willow/

Discussion Questions

- Many districts have policies to ensure that all schools have access to the same number and types of technologies. These policies are in place to ensure equity, but, on occasion, they have stifled innovation and local funding efforts to provide technology. For example, as a technology facilitator or leader, would you allow a school to apply for a grant and receive equipment that other schools would not receive? Would you allow local parent-teacher-community organizations to purchase equipment in addition to the district allocation? Why or why not?

- What is the local process for identifying and securing adaptive and assistive technologies for students in your school district?

- CIPA was challenged by the American Library Association as being censorship, but the law was upheld. Do you agree that CIPA is an appropriate and necessary form of communication regulation for schools? Why or why not?

- This chapter highlights only a few current legal, social, ethical, and human issues associated with technology use in schools. What other contemporary situations in schools relate to this standard?

Resources

As technology facilitators and leaders implement TF/TL Standard VI, they may benefit from several types of resources that either assist technologists by deepening their understanding of concepts discussed in the chapter or provide tools technologists may share with other educators. Although all the resources are valuable, we have identified one "Spotlight Resource" in each chapter that has particular utility to technologists.

The resources identified under TF/TL Standard VI pertain to social, ethical, legal, and human issues. Reports are included providing the latest research on educational technology issues such as cyberbullying and the digital divide. A digital equity toolkit is provided to help technology facilitators and leaders assist teachers in addressing the digital inequities in the classroom. Numerous websites are included for facilitators and leaders to consult when facing legal and ethical issues related to the use of technology.

Reports

Cyberbullying Pew Report
www.pewInternet.org/PPF/r/216/report_display.asp
> This report provides recent statistics on the realities of cyberbullying and online teens.

Education Week's Technology Counts—The New Divides 2001 Report
www.edweek.org/rc/articles/2004/10/15/tc-archive.html
> Education Week publishes an annual report on educational technology providing the latest research and data regarding the status of technology in education. Scroll down and click on the 2001 issue—The New Divides.

Websites

Center for Applied Special Technology (CAST)
www.cast.org
> This mission of CAST is to expand learning opportunities for all individuals, especially those with disabilities, through the research and development of innovative, technology-based educational resources and strategies.

Center for Safe and Responsible Internet Use (CSRIU)
www.cyberbully.org
> This site provides research and outreach services to address issues of the safe and responsible use of the Internet.

Children's Internet Protection Act (CIPA)
www.cybertelecom.org/cda/cipa.htm
> This site provides detailed information on CIPA.

Cyberethics for Kids
www.cybercrime.gov/rules/kidinternet.htm
> This site, developed by the U.S. Department of Justice's Computer Crime and Intellectual Property Section, provides adults, children, and teens with information on how to use the Internet safely and responsibly.

Digital Divide at Edutopia
www.edutopia.org/digitaldivide/
> This section of Edutopia provides educators with information, articles, and resources on the digital divide.

Digital Divide Network (DDN)
www.digitaldividenetwork.org
> The DDN is the largest community for educators, activists, policy makers, and concerned citizens working to bridge the digital divide. Free memberships allow you to build your own online community, publish a blog, share documents and discussions with colleagues, and post news, events, and articles on the digital divide.

Spotlight Resource

Digital Equity Portal
http://digitalequity.edreform.net

This site provides free full-text information on strategies and resources fostering equitable student and educator access to technology resources in schools.

Family Educational Rights and Privacy Act (FERPA)
www.ed.gov/policy/gen/guid/fpco/
> The Ed.gov website contains a section by the Family Policy Compliance Office that has resources dedicated specifically to FERPA.

Plagiarism.org Learning Center
www.plagiarism.org
> This site is designed to provide the latest information on online plagiarism.

Plagiarism Proofing Assignments
www.doug-johnson.com/dougwri/plagiarism-proofing-assignments.html
> Doug Johnson describes the qualities of LPP (Low Probability of Plagiarism) projects.

Universal Service Administrative Company (USAC)
www.universalservice.org/sl/about/overview-program.aspx
> USAC administers the E-Rate program under the direction of the FCC and provides a wealth of information and resources for schools and libraries.

U.S. Copyright Office

www.copyright.gov

The U.S. Copyright Office provides up-to-date news about copyright issues and explains the basics of copyright law.

References

Bain, C., & Rice, M. (2007). The influence of gender on attitudes, perceptions, and uses of technology. *Journal of Research on Technology in Education, 39*(2), 119–132.

CDW-G (2007). *School safety index.* Retrieved August 31, 2007, from http://Webobjects.cdw.com/Webobjects/docs/pdfs/CDWG_School_Safety_Index_2007.pdf

Consortium for School Networking. (2005). *Digital leadership divide.* Available from www.cosn.org/resources/grunwald/digital_leadership_divide.pdf

Corporation for Public Broadcasting. (2003). *Connected to the future: A report on children's Internet use.* Retrieved April 1, 2007, from www.cpb.org/stations/reports/connected/connected_report.pdf

Davis, T., Fuller, M., Jackson, S., Pittman, J., & Sweet, J. (2007). *A national consideration of digital equity.* Available from www.iste.org/digitalequity/

Horigan, J. B., & Smith, A. (2007). *Home broadband adoption 2007.* Retrieved August 27, 2007, from www.pewInternet.org/report_display.asp?r=217

Lazarus, W., & Lipper, L. (2003). *The search for high-quality online content for low-income and underserved Americans: Evaluating and producing what's needed.* Retrieved August 6, 2007, from www.childrenspartnership.org/AM/Template.cfm?Section=Reports1

Lazarus, W., & Mora, F. (2000, March). *Online content for low-income and underserved Americans: The digital divide's new frontier.* Retrieved August 2, 2007, from www.childrenspartnership.org/AM/Template.cfm?Section=Reports1

Lenhardt, A., & Madden, M. (2007). *Social networking sites and teens: An overview.* Retrieved August 2, 2007, from www.pewInternet.org/PPF/r/198/report_display.asp

Nardi, B., & O'Day, V. (1999). *Information ecologies: Using technology with heart.* Cambridge, MA: MIT.

National Forum on Education Statistics (NFES). (1998). *Safeguarding your technology: Practical guidelines for electronic education information security.* (NCES 98–297). U.S. Department of Education. Washington, DC: National Center for Education Statistics. Retrieved August 29, 2007, from http://nces.ed.gov/pubs98/98297.pdf

National Forum on Education Statistics (NFES). (2006). *Forum guide to the privacy of student information: A resource for schools* (NFES 2006–805). U.S. Department of Education. Washington, DC: National Center for Education Statistics. Retrieved August 29, 2007, from http://nces.ed.gov/pubs2006/2006805.pdf

National School Boards Association (NSBA). (2007). *Creating and connecting: Research and guidelines on online social and educational networking.* Retrieved August 2, 2007, from http://files.nsba.org/creatingandconnecting.pdf

North Central Educational Laboratory. (2000). *System-wide equity indicator of enGauge: A framework for effective technology use.* Retrieved August 6, 2007, from www.ncrel.org/engauge/framewk/equ/system/equsysin.htm

Organisation for Economic Co-operation and Development. (2006). *OECD broadband statistics to December 2006.* Retrieved March 3, 2007, from www.oecd.org/sti/ict/broadband

Organisation for Economic Co-operation and Development. (2007). *Participative Web: User created content.* Retrieved June 21, 2007, from www.oecd.org/dataoecd/57/14/38393115.pdf

Ronnkvist, A., Dexter, S., & Anderson, R. (2000). *Technology support: Its depth, breadth, and impact on America's schools, Teaching, learning, and computing* (1998 survey, Rep. No. 5). Retrieved August 6, 2007, from www.crito.uci.edu/tlc/findings/technology-support/

Schrum, L., & Bracey, B. (2003). Refocusing curriculum. In G. Solomon, N. Allen, & P. Resta (Eds.), *Toward digital equity: Bridging the divide in education.* Boston: Pearson.

Schrum, L., & Geisler, S. (2003). Gender issues and considerations. In G. Solomon, N. Allen & P. Resta (Eds.), *Toward digital equity: Bridging the divide in education.* Boston: Pearson.

Universal Service Administrative Company (USAC). (2007). *CIPA Internet safety policy guidance.* Retrieved August 26, 2007, from www.usac.org/sl/applicants/step10/cipa.aspx

Wells, J., & Lewis, L. (2006). *Internet access in U.S. public schools and classrooms: 1994–2005* (NCES 2007–0200). U.S. Department of Education. Washington, DC: National Center for Educational Statistics.

One of the most important steps to developing a successful technology program is hiring a technical director or coordinator. Technology is becoming too complex and too expensive to leave to untrained teachers or administrators. Networking computers and multimedia tools today are presenting a series of difficult challenges to schools. School leaders need to know what type of equipment to purchase, where to obtain the best buys, how to train teachers to use it, and when it should be upgraded. It is therefore important that administrators have access to personnel who have a technology background and understand how to address these problems.

—WHITEHEAD, JENSEN, AND BOSCHEE, 2003, P. 162

Chapter Seven

TF/TL STANDARD VII

Procedures, Policies, Planning, and Budgeting for Technology Environments

Researchers repeatedly suggest that access to technology is the strongest predictor of technology use in the classroom (Norris, Sullivan, Poirot, & Soloway, 2003). Therefore, it is critical that technologists establish a stable technological infrastructure to support the effective use of technology in schools. Implementing technology-supported learning strategies requires computers, peripherals, software, and telecommunications networks that are current, operable, well maintained, and adapted to specific K–12 contexts and goals. Without adequate infrastructure support, teachers are easily frustrated and prone to abandon technology, dismissing it as unreliable (Sandholtz & Reilly, 2004; Zhao, 2004). Once developed, these negative associations are often difficult to dislodge. For these reasons, TF/TL Standard VII: Procedures, Policies, Planning, and Budgeting for

Technology Environments focuses on the managerial and technical tasks associated with providing educators and students with high-quality access to technology.

Technology facilitators and leaders are uniquely responsible for establishing a technical environment that supports integrating technology into instructional and administrative practices. The technical and administrative tasks described in this standard far exceed what is expected of teachers. TF/TL VII has a modified alignment to NETS•A Standard VI: Support, Management, and Operations; however, the TF/TL standards are more focused, specific, and technically demanding than expectations for principals, superintendents, and other school-level and central-office administrators. Although administrators have responsibilities for policy, oversight, implementation, and resource allocation, technology facilitators and leaders must design, implement, and support technology-rich environments. As illustrated through this comparison of standards, TF/TL Standard VII represents a specialized, defining skill area for technology facilitators and leaders. Developing these skills often requires specialized training in technology operations and project management.

Current Context: Providing Access to Technology

In implementing TF/TL VII, school technologists must work closely with educators to create and support modern learning facilities. This includes providing access to modern computers for teaching and learning—a concept usually measured in terms of the ratio of students to instructional computers and the availability of high-speed Internet access in schools and classrooms.

According to national reports, educators have reached the connectivity and student-to-computer ratio goals established by the U.S. Department of Education in the mid-1990s. In 1994, only 34% of schools had Internet access, compared with nearly 100% in fall 2005. Similarly, classrooms are much more connected than they were in the past. In 1994, only 3% of classrooms were connected to the Internet, whereas 94% reported having Internet access in fall 2005 (Wells & Lewis, 2006). Student to high-speed, Internet-connected computer ratios have also dropped dramatically. In 1997, *Ed Week* reported a national average of 21 students per multimedia computer (Market Data Retrieval, 1997). In 2007, student to Internet-connected computer ratios are less than 4:1 nationally and less than 5:1 in every state (Editorial Projects in Education Research Center, 2007).

Despite these achievements, lack of access to technology is still perceived as a common obstacle to implementing technology for instruction. In fact, in a 2006 random national survey of 1,000 teachers, over half (55%) of teachers indicated that insufficient access prevented them from fully integrating technology into the curriculum—making lack of access the most commonly selected barrier, followed by time (48%) and budget (48%). Because more middle school teachers (59%) and high school teachers (57%) cited access as a barrier compared to elementary teachers (49%), access constraints may even be more severe in secondary educational settings (CDW-G, 2006).

It is unclear why teachers perceive a lack of access to technology when student-to-computer ratios are at an all-time low and high-speed Internet access is pervasive in schools and classrooms. However, as TF/TL Standard VII illustrates, providing educators and students with access in schools is a complex, interrelated process that is often difficult for technology facilitators and leaders to implement effectively—especially with limited resources. Reflecting on these steps to providing high-quality access may help technology facilitators and leaders determine where the process may be weak in their own local settings.

The most common duties related to providing educators and students with sufficient access to technology fall into the following four stages: (1) Planning for technology deployments, (2) procurement, (3) implementation, and (4) maintenance/monitoring (see Figure 7.1).

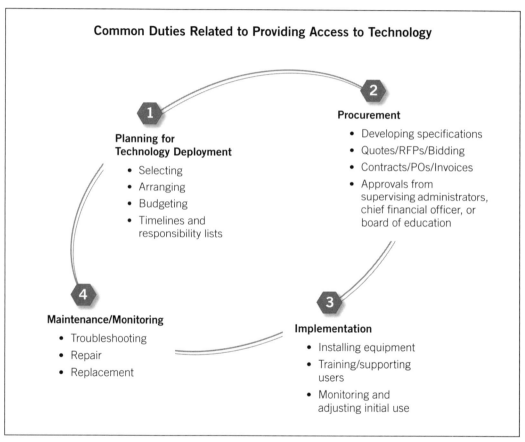

Figure 7.1 Common duties related to providing access to technology

Planning for Technology Deployment

In the initial stages of planning, facilitators and leaders select technologies aligned to learning standards and research-based teaching methodologies, decide how to arrange the new technologies, budget for proposed improvements, and develop a timeline for the project. Each level of this planning process involves the application of a great deal of technical knowledge and managerial skill.

SELECTING TECHNOLOGIES

Selecting appropriate technologies requires the ability to understand the instructional context in which the technologies will be utilized and thorough knowledge of available educational technology best suited to those contexts. It is possible that technologies may be available, but teachers do not see the application of these technologies for learning. While teachers may have access to technologies, they do not have access to the technologies that they want and need to implement the curriculum (Frazier & Bailey, 2004). As discussed in Chapter 3, implementing the NETS•S often requires more than access to an Internet-connected computer. Access to content-related software and other digital resources is critical to implementing technology in the disciplines. Consulting with teachers and involving them in the selection process increases the likelihood of access to the types of technologies teachers and students need for standards-based teaching and learning.

ARRANGING TECHNOLOGIES

Likewise, correctly arranging technology in classrooms and schools is one of the most critical components for providing teachers and students with high-quality access—and a likely point of failure for many schools. Although there are reportedly more Internet-connected computers in schools than ever before, they may not be arranged in accessible ways. For example, in 2007, only 65% of students had access to an Internet-connected computer in the classroom—the center of instructional activity (EPE, 2007). Often classrooms have only one Internet-connected computer for the teacher and no computers for students. In this situation, teachers and students are expected to visit flexibly scheduled labs for instruction. If student computers are provided in the classroom, they are often positioned in ways that make whole-group instruction with the computers very difficult. A growing number of technology professionals believe that the 5:1 student-to-computer ratios commonly recommended in the 1990s are simply inadequate to support full integration of technology into the curriculum. These educators advocate portable computing devices, wireless networks, and 1-to-1 configurations in schools, especially for middle and high school students. To date, no one configuration has emerged as the most effective or has become a standard in schools. Each configuration has strengths and weaknesses (see Table 7.1), and technologists are currently struggling to select and implement the most effective arrangements. In light of these current conditions, inefficient arrangements may be the one of most viable theories to explain why teachers still cite access as a barrier to integrating technology into learning.

TABLE 7.1 ■ Strengths and weaknesses of technology arrangements in schools

Desktops in Computer Labs

Strengths	Weaknesses
a. Desktops are more reliable and durable than laptops.	a. If lab monitor or computer teacher is available, teachers tend to "drop off" students for drill and practice or for technology skill instruction that may or may not be linked to content standards.
b. Desktops, larger monitors, and mice are better suited to some tasks and users than laptops.	b. Teachers have limited access to the labs.
c. Desktops are cheaper than laptops.	c. Scheduling can be time-consuming, disorganized, and conflict-ridden.
d. Desktops are usually networked with wired connections, which are faster and more reliable than wireless.	d. Advance scheduling reduces ability to pursue short-term learning goals as they emerge.
e. It is easier to maintain technology in a central location such as a lab.	e. Labs require physical space, and many schools are already overcrowded.
f. It is easier to secure technology from theft and misuse.	f. Obtaining enough labs to meet daily instructional needs of teachers and students is often impossible.
g. Arrangement provides 1-to-1 access for instruction.	g. Travel to and from class wastes instructional time.
h. Arrangement provides optimum environment for testing, demonstration, and skills training.	h. Furniture for desktops is expensive.
i. Labs can double as teacher training centers beyond school hours.	i. Labs are usually fixed arrangements that cannot easily be modified for different types of instructional tasks. For example, traditional lab arrangements may not be conducive to peer-to-peer conversation and collaborative learning.
	j. Arrangement does not provide students with 24/7 access to a personal computing device.

(Continued)

TABLE 7.1 ■ *(Continued)*

Desktops in Classrooms

Strengths	Weaknesses
a. Desktops are more reliable and durable than laptops.	a. No teacher uses computers during every learning experience, so computers can sit idle in classrooms, even in the best of circumstances.
b. Desktops, larger monitors, and mice are better suited to some tasks and users than laptops.	b. There are usually not enough desktops in classrooms to accommodate either small-group or full-class instruction.
c. Desktops are cheaper than laptops.	c. Computers are usually not arranged effectively for small-group work. Students have to "visit" the computer.
d. Desktops are usually networked with wired connections, which are faster and more reliable than wireless.	d. Classrooms are too small to permit arranging desktops for effective instruction.
e. The presence of desktops in classrooms encourages integration into content standards and daily classroom practice.	e. Too few desktops and poor arrangements cause classroom management issues.
f. Students and teachers do not have to waste instructional time walking to labs.	f. Desktop arrangements in classrooms often impede teachers' ability to rearrange the room for different instructional tasks (e.g., testing).
	g. Furniture for desktops is expensive.
	h. Wiring classrooms is more expensive than using a wireless network.
	i. Wire management (power, network, mouse, keyboard) is awkward in small classroom spaces and may cause safety hazards.
	j. Arrangement does not provide students with 24/7 access to a personal computing device.

(Continued)

TABLE 7.1 ▪ *(Continued)*

Mobile, Wireless Laptop Labs	
Strengths	**Weaknesses**
a. Provide 1-to-1 student-to-computer access. b. Wireless and battery-powered computing devices allow for flexible arrangement of computers in classrooms. c. Laptops ease classroom space requirements and eliminate the need for additional furniture for desktops. d. Wireless networking is cheaper than establishing wired connections. e. Mobile labs are portable and can be moved from classroom to classroom according to instructional needs, thus minimizing downtime or idle computers.	a. Batteries must be charged and will not last the entire instructional day. Extra batteries or charging procedures must be in place. b. Laptops are more fragile than desktops. c. Laptops are more difficult to secure than desktops. d. Laptops are more expensive than desktops. e. Starting up laptops and connecting them to the wireless network often creates more technical problems than wired desktops, placing more technical support demands on the teacher. f. Wireless connections are slower than wired connections. g. Wireless connections cannot support all types of uses, such as video streaming and database management. h. Wireless networks are more difficult to maintain and secure than wired connections. i. School staff members often lack the technical expertise to manage wireless connections. j. Finding storage space for laptop carts in crowded schools is difficult. k. Arrangement does not provide students with 24/7 access to a personal computing device. l. Wireless laptop labs must be scheduled in the same way as physical labs. m. Depending on the number of available labs, access for instruction still may be inadequate. n. Carts containing laptops are heavy and difficult to move from room to room. o. Wireless laptop labs are more difficult to maintain than wired labs with desktops. p. Setup and teardown time reduces instructional time. q. Students must share instructional computing devices and store work on portable media.

(Continued)

TABLE 7.1 ■ *(Continued)*

Laptop Cart (permanently assigned to each classroom)

Strengths	Weaknesses
a. Provide 1-to-1 student-to-computer access.	a. Batteries must be charged and will not last the entire instructional day. Extra batteries or charging procedures must be in place.
b. Wireless and battery-powered computing devices allow for flexible arrangement of computers in classrooms.	b. Laptops are more fragile than desktops.
c. Laptops ease classroom space requirements and eliminate the need for additional furniture for desktops.	c. Laptops are more difficult to secure than desktops.
d. Wireless networking is cheaper than establishing wired connections.	d. Laptops are more expensive than desktops.
e. Assigning a classroom set of laptops to each room minimizes loss of instructional time.	e. Starting up laptops and connecting them to the wireless network often creates more technical problems than wired desktops, which places more technical support demands on the teacher.
f. Permanently assigning laptops eliminates scheduling issues and allows teachers more flexibility in planning for and using technology for instruction.	f. Wireless connections are slower than wired connections.
g. Restricting use of laptop cart to only one classroom may help reduce technical issues.	g. Wireless connections cannot support all types of uses, such as video streaming and database management.
	h. Wireless networks are more difficult to maintain and secure than wired connections.
	i. School staff members often lack the technical expertise to manage wireless connections.
	j. Finding storage space for laptop carts in crowded schools is difficult.
	k. Arrangement does not provide students with 24/7 access to a personal computing device.
	l. Providing a laptop cart in each classroom requires significantly more computers and, therefore, is more expensive than fixed, desktop labs or desktops in classrooms.

(Continued)

TABLE 7.1 ■ *(Continued)*

1-to-1 Laptop Initiatives*

Strengths	Weaknesses
a.–d. from Mobile, Wireless Laptop Labs: Strengths list.	**a.–i.** from Mobile, Wireless Laptop Labs: Weaknesses
e.–f. from Laptop Cart permanently assigned to each classroom: Strengths list.	**j.** Assigning laptops to individual students for use at both home and school increases maintenance needs; software costs; and the risk of viruses, damage, and theft.
g. Arrangement provides students with 24/7 access to a personal computing device. This access may improve students' technology literacy and student achievement in ways other arrangements cannot.	**k.** Lack of models on how to fund additional software, maintenance, repair, and replacement costs associated with 1-to-1.
h. Arrangement reduces digital divide by providing students with equitable access to computing devices.	**l.** Updating operating systems and applications requires new technical support models.
i. Assigning a laptop to each student may further minimize loss of instructional time and eliminates scheduling issues.	**m.** 1-to-1 initiatives may be appropriate only for older students (middle school and up).
j. May reduce setup and teardown time associated with wireless/laptop lab and classroom models.	**n.** Home access increases educators' and parents' concerns over inappropriate use and Internet safety.
k. Exerts the greatest social pressure on teachers to use technology to enrich daily instructional practices.	**o.** Arrangement does not provide for students' home Internet access, and high-speed home access is critical to maximize the potential and justify the cost of 1-to-1 initiatives.
	p. Individual user questions may be overwhelming to the teacher.
	q. Pressure to use technology to enrich daily instructional practices may be overwhelming to teachers.
	r. 1-to-1 initiatives represent the highest cost to school districts of any other arrangement model.
	s. 1-to-1 initiatives potentially involve cost to parents.

*1-to-1 laptop initiatives assign laptop computers to each student. The laptop travels with the student throughout the instructional day. Most 1-to-1 initiatives allow students to take the laptop home with them, but a few programs mandate that the laptops be stored on school premises overnight and on weekends. This discussion of 1-to-1 initiatives assumes that students have access to their computing device 24/7.

Source: Adapted and expanded from Roblyer, M. D. (2006). Integrating technology into teaching (4th ed., p. 20). Upper Saddle River, NJ: Pearson, with assistance from graduate Educational Leadership/Technology Leadership students at Kennesaw State University and practicing technology leaders in Georgia schools during collaborative meetings sponsored by the Georgia Department of Education and Georgia's Educational Technology Training Centers in preparation for the State of Georgia 2007–2009 state technology plan.

BUDGETING FOR TECHNOLOGY

Similarly, budgeting requires a comprehensive knowledge of all the components necessary to ensure sufficient access to technology. When budgeting, technology novices may tend to focus only on the initial costs of the technologies rather than the total cost of ownership (TCO) or the comprehensive costs of technology implementation, support and maintenance. A familiar concept in business, the Consortium for School Networking (CoSN) applied TCO to the educational environment in *Taking TCO to the Classroom: A School Administrator's Guide to Planning for the Total Cost of New Technology* (2001). In this guide, planners are encouraged to adopt a strategic approach to budgeting, considering the costs associated with all of the following elements of technology implementation (adapted from CoSN, 2001, pp. 5, 6):

End-User Equipment. The initial price of computers, peripherals, and other computing devices used by educators, staff, and students. End-user equipment typically refers to technology used in classrooms and other educational environments, such as scientific probeware, printers, assistive technologies, interactive whiteboards, graphing calculators, and global positioning systems (GPS).

Infrastructure/Connectivity. The costs associated with establishing local and wide area networks and providing Internet access. These costs include wiring and/or wireless access points needed to establish local area networks in schools, connecting schools within a district and the central office, and providing Internet access throughout the district. This includes wiring, routers, switches, servers, and software to operate, manage, monitor, and secure the networks. The variety of devices and services needed affects the way technologists view their budgets. For example, some infrastructure items will require budgeting for the purchase of equipment. Other expenses, such as Internet services and equipment leases, will be budgeted as recurring monthly charges.

Installation/Retrofitting. The labor and material costs beyond the price of the technology necessary to make it operable in the school environment. Installation refers to facility alterations accommodating new technologies that do not involve extensive renovation of the physical structure. These include mounting an LCD projector or ordering tables, racks, carts, and safety straps to hold new equipment. Retrofitting is a term usually reserved for more extensive modifications to the physical plant, including upgrading electric, heating, cooling, and ventilation systems and enhanced security. Retrofitting includes the indirect costs associated with altering facilities. For example, upgrading wiring and networking may require asbestos abatement. Costs for retrofitting may be reduced by planning for technology implementation during new construction, combining projects (such as upgrading networking and fire alarms during the same time) to save labor and material costs, or using products (such as wireless solutions) that require fewer physical changes.

Professional Development. The costs of providing end users and technical staff with high-quality learning opportunities related to managing and using the new technologies effectively and efficiently. These costs may include salaries and benefits for local personnel charged with professional development, fees for outside trainers or training, costs for substitutes while teachers attend training, conference registrations, and stipends or other incentives for educators who pursue professional learning opportunities. The

Consortium for School Networking recommends that professional development constitutes 15–30% of the total project budget.

End-User Software and Online Resources. The price of software applications and fees associated with accessing subscription-based online products available for teaching, learning, assessment, and administrative functions. Budgeting for curriculum-based software, productivity tools, subscriptions to online services, and software to adapt technology to needs of special learners are often frequently neglected when planning for technology integration. However, the absence of these software and online products severely restricts the potential functions of computers being purchased and invites legal challenges when students and employees with special needs are not provided reasonable accommodations permitting them to access technology equitably.

Technical Support. The cost of providing human resources to keep new technologies in working order. Whether this function is outsourced or locally managed, networks, equipment, and software require technical support staff to keep technologies in working order.

Operation Costs. Additional costs associated with the regular use of technologies. For example, new computers may increase electricity consumption, and the installation of printers requires the ongoing purchase of paper and ink cartridges in order to operate the technologies as planned.

Replacement/Upgrade Costs. The projected costs for replacing aging equipment and purchasing software titles as new versions appear. Technologists must educate stakeholders on the ongoing need to make equipment purchases. School computers are often replaced on staggered three- to five-year cycles. Predicting when new versions of software will be released or when printers will become inoperable is a bit more difficult, but future budgets must account for these recurring costs as well.

As illustrated throughout CoSN's TCO model, there is a close relationship between the funding available for technology and adequate, equitable access to technology. A budgeting cycle is not complete until funding sources have been assigned to support the adequate acquisition, support, and/or replacement of each action item. Finding and receiving permission to allocate needed funds is another challenge for school technologists.

Local school systems report that a majority of their technology programs are supported with local and state funding; however, since the mid-1990s, the federal government has played an important role in funding technology improvements, as well—especially for school systems with higher percentages of students in poverty. The majority of funds have traditionally been associated with the elementary and secondary education acts (ESEA) and the federal E-Rate program. Competitive grants and business partnerships make up another source of funding available to local schools. These funding sources provide excellent opportunities for local school systems, especially for pilot programs and innovations. Because of the small amount of funding provided and the short-term nature of grants and partnerships, they are usually not perceived as stable funding for core technology operations in schools and districts.

To ensure adequate funding, technologies must integrate all available funding sources appropriately into the technology plan. Insufficient funding can obviously prevent purchase of the technology needed to support instruction or impede a district's ability to choose the most effective technology arrangements.

CONSTRUCTING TIMELINES

Planning includes the ability to accurately project the amount of time required to complete a technology deployment. Novice technologists and other educational leaders unfamiliar with the steps needed to plan, procure, train, install, and test equipment frequently underestimate the time it takes to provide educators with access to the technology tools they need. Allowing adequate time for the procurement phase is perhaps the most difficult skill for new technologists who may be unfamiliar with local policies and procedures. Because of inaccurate timelines, many grant projects and other strategic instructional initiatives have frequently launched without the expected technology in place, thus posing another possible reason why teachers may cite inadequate access as their top barrier to technology integration.

Procuring Technology Products and Services

After the planning stage, technology facilitators and leaders begin the process of acquiring desired technologies and services. At this stage, the school technologist must be very familiar with local purchasing requirements. Small-scale purchases may only require negotiating a best price, drafting a purchase order, and securing permission from a supervising employee or the chief financial officer. Larger-scale purchases are often subject to more stringent policies, including approval by a governing board.

Because public funds are involved in these more expensive purchases, education community policies and procedures are in place to secure the best possible price and product on behalf of the taxpayer. Procurement policies also ensure that all business partners have a fair chance to engage in business with a public entity. Although these policies and procedures vary from site to site, some basic commonalities and terms tend to transcend different settings. For example, in virtually all cases, technologists must specify exactly what type of equipment, materials, and services are required. These specifications (or specs) are generally fairly precise and might include the exact type of processor, the number of USB ports, or the type of monitor desired by the purchaser. These specifications are sent to vendors as either a request for quote (RFQ) or a request for proposal (RFP), depending on the nature of the project and the requirements of local governing bodies.

An RFQ is the simplest of the options and involves requesting prices from a limited number of vendors (maybe even as few as three). This method is used primarily when the cost estimate is very low, the product is well specified, and price is the primary deciding factor in the decision. For larger-scale purchases, entities might use the term "bids" instead of "quotes." Bids are usually submitted in writing by a certain deadline and often sealed to ensure both low and competitive bidding. Sealed bids are opened publicly and awarded to the lowest bidder capable of dependably meeting project specifications.

For larger-scale projects, price frequently is not the determining factor in choosing a vendor. Often the quality and dependability of the vendor's previous work is relevant, as well as the vendor's experience in working with school districts and other educational entities. For these reasons, decision makers need more information from and dialogue with a potential business partner. Vendors may also need more clarification on what educators want and need. In these situations, scoring rubrics are usually developed, and final decisions are most often made by committees after vendors submit initial proposals, present options, and, finally, submit a best and final offer (BAFO).

Although boards of education have a variety of different procurement policies, board members are usually involved in decisions to request quotes, bids, and proposals from vendors; to enter into contracts; and to pay invoices once the work is completed. Consequently, technologists should anticipate board members' inquiries regarding educational technology expenditures and be prepared not only to demonstrate compliance with board procurement policies, but to defend the rationale for technology purchases.

Additionally, corporate, state, and federal funding programs may have procurement requirements independent of local requirements. For example, E-rate programs require a very structured, transparent, and well-documented bidding process, one with which vendors may be unfamiliar. These regulations form a very specialized type of knowledge for technology facilitators and leaders. Administrators in the district lean heavily on local technologists to know the procurement guidelines for technology-related programs.

Regardless of the source of funding or regulation, technology leaders and facilitators must ensure bidder fidelity to procurement process. Public bidding requirements are generally very strict, and a prevailing bidder's failure to adhere to any part of bidding requirements may invite legal challenge from nonprevailing bidders. When any or all bids do not meet bidding requirements, the bid(s) may be declared nonresponsive and stricken from consideration. However, before declaring a bid nonresponsive, technologists should carefully scrutinize the bid advertisement and specifications and be capable of explaining why the bid is not responsive to the advertisement.

These complexities associated with the procurement process often impede securing the technologies that teachers want and need quickly, which may contribute to teachers' opinions about access to technology.

Implementing New Technologies

In the implementation stage, products and services are delivered, and technology is integrated into school sites. Technology facilitators and leaders keep projects on schedule, accomplish installations while minimizing disruptions to teaching and learning, and keep stakeholders informed of progress toward implementation. Because accomplishing these tasks requires high levels of coordination among staff and outside contractors, technologists must possess excellent organizational and communication skills.

Experienced technologists are prepared for adjustments and changes during the implementation stage. Inevitably, some changes will become necessary as plans are executed. No one can completely foresee all of the variables involved in implementing large-scale programs. Technologists are usually the only district employees with sufficient technological expertise to deal with this variability. They must ensure contractor fidelity to proposal requirements and must act as agents of their local school district when working with outside contractors. They employ strategies to keep projects within scope and on time. They minimize change orders that increase cost. Before finishing an installation, technologists also make sure that newly installed equipment and services are tested and ready to be used by teachers, students, and others.

The final stages of implementation usually involve training educators and other staff to use equipment. Scheduling training after hardware and software implementation stage ensures that users have access to their new equipment or services upon the conclusion of training, and they can begin to apply their new skills immediately—a factor frequently linked to improved learning and performance (Broad & Newstrom, 1992).

Concluding the implementation phase, technology facilitators and leaders monitor new users after training to ensure they are using the new technologies effectively. Technologists monitor early stages of actual use, collecting data on the frequency and quality of use, permitting analysis and reporting. This initial data collection allows technologists to locate and eliminate barriers to desired use patterns and improve performance. The data also serves as a baseline against which future data can be compared. Technologists continue monitoring initial use until the technologies have been well integrated into daily work activities, and teachers and other users reach a sufficient level of comfort and independence with new tools.

All of these steps in the implementation process are critical in providing teachers with access. If any elements are neglected, teachers may not be able to access the new technologies, even if they are physically present and operable. For example, teachers who do not know passwords or basic operating functions for newly installed machines cannot use them. Therefore, weaknesses in training or other implementation components may also contribute to teacher access levels.

Providing High-Quality Maintenance and Support

The hallmark of a good technology program is providing ongoing and continued technical support to teachers and other technology users. Many immature and ineffective programs fail in this area. After implementing new equipment and services, the technologies soon fall into disrepair or disuse. Districts also may fail to realize the scope of technical support needed. North Central Regional Educational Laboratory (2000) lists the following types of technical support needed in local schools:

LOCAL AREA NETWORK (LAN) SUPPORT

- Moving, adding, or changing machines that are registered on the network
- Managing network software and user access to the network (includes setting up and maintaining user accounts)
- Setting up and maintaining Internet and file servers
- Backing up servers and user machines on a regular basis
- Configuring and managing the devices that connect all segments of the network: switches, hubs, routers, etc.

HARDWARE SUPPORT

- Installing, configuring, troubleshooting, maintaining, repairing, upgrading, and replacing user workstations and workstation hardware

USER SUPPORT

- Installing, configuring, and maintaining workstation software

- Training users (through one-on-one training, the development of user guides, and help desk maintenance and operation)

- Troubleshooting as needed

MANAGEMENT AND ADMINISTRATIVE SUPPORT

- Planning, collaborating, supervising

OTHER TECHNICAL SUPPORT

- Website managing (coordinating content development, integrating Web applications with organizational operations)

- Telephone services (coordinating with provider, supporting internal systems)

- Videoconferencing (supporting digital video, satellite, broadcast services)

Additionally, school districts need support for wide area networks (WAN) linking schools and Internet services, including filtering, firewalls, e-mail, and Web management. Also increasing the need for highly technical staff are online learning management systems, Web 2.0 technologies, centralized media services, and data systems.

To meet these needs, the Consortium for School Networking recommends one support person for every 50–70 computers or—in a closely managed network environment—one person for every 500 computers. Additionally, exemplary technology support programs will have the following characteristics:

- Routine maintenance tasks to prevent disruption of services

- A standard procedure—often a Web-based trouble ticket—by which users can request support

- Policies to prioritize requests based on instructional needs

- Prompt responses to requests

- Low incidences of computer and network downtime

- High client satisfaction ratings related to technical support

- The presence of acceptable use policies and security/monitoring software to minimize user error and disruptive activities resulting in down time

- No security breaches, theft, or vandalism to interrupt services

- Centralized management systems that allow for remote management, thus optimizing technician work time

Most districts have equipment, software, and network infrastructure rivaling corporate environments. Schools also have a unique user population of underage minors, a more challenging user base with a wider range of experience levels, and a wide variety of applications and practices varying across age levels and disciplines. Yet, school settings have fewer and less experienced technical staff than most business settings. Although schools are reporting high volumes of computers, it is unclear to what extent those computers are reliable, operable, and well maintained. A lack of technical support may also attribute to teachers' reported access problems.

Summary of Current Context

Because access to technology is the primary predictor of technology use, TF/TL Standard VII highlights the need for highly technical staff who can plan for, procure, implement, and maintain technological equipment. Although access levels are reportedly at an all-time high, teachers are still citing access as a barrier to classroom use. This chapter explored reasons why this apparent disconnect is occurring, including ineffective configurations of technology in classrooms and/or poor technology support programs. However, the reason for this disconnect is still unclear. To ensure adequate access, technology facilitators and leaders must reflect on their practice and ensure that all components for successful technology deployments are implemented. The performance indicators and tasks in TF/TL Standard VII provide a framework for this reflection and evaluation.

Implementing the Standard

This section reviews the standard, performance indicators, and performance tasks of TF/TL Standard VII, which can be found in the standards table on pages 165–166.

Performance Standards

In implementing Standard VII, technology leaders play a critical role in ensuring the overall success of technology programs in PK–12 schools. The importance of coordinating the development and implementation of technology infrastructure, procedures, policies, plans, and budgets cannot be overemphasized. Sophisticated computer technology requires leaders to analyze and coordinate infrastructure issues, implement policies ensuring that systems are maintained and upgraded, and plan and budget the necessary resources to support and strategically grow a robust technology program supporting instruction and administrative practice. Technology facilitators assist leaders by promoting the development and implementation of technology infrastructure, procedures, policies, plans, and budgets at the school site. Working with educators, facilitators ensure that the use of technology is aligned with the plans and policies developed at the district level.

Performance Indicators

The performance indicators for Standard VII outline three broad categories of technology-related tasks that technology facilitators and leaders are expected to perform.

1. **Using the school technology facilities and resources to implement classroom instruction (TF/TL-VII.A.).** Under this performance indicator, technologists must ensure that technology facilities and resources support classroom instruction. This requires technologists to make effective use of instructional facilities—classrooms, laboratories, and media centers—and configure hardware and software to support a variety of proven instructional methodologies. Technology leaders and facilitators must ensure that the school facility sufficiently supports technology integration by providing an infrastructure with adequate bandwidth for Internet access, well-maintained equipment, updated software, and immediate technical support when problems occur.

2. **Follow procedures and guidelines used in planning and purchasing technology resources (TF/TL-VII.B.).** Technology leaders should ensure that technology hardware and software acquisitions and instructional integration occur on a planned, strategic basis, following a well-developed and clear policy for technology procurement, integration, and support. Recognizing the dynamic nature of technology, this policy should contain a proactive technology replacement cycle. Both technology leaders and facilitators must strategize with educators and administrators, providing technological expertise to schools and districts when planning hardware and software acquisition and implementation. As educational objectives change, technologists ensure that technology continues to align with and promote school and district improvement goals.

3. **Participate in professional development opportunities related to management of school facilities, technology resources, and purchases (TF/TL-VII.C.).** Performance indicator VII.C. concerns technologists' responsibility to provide professional expertise to educators, increasing their ability to manage and maintain technology-rich learning environments. Under this indicator, technologists are expected to design and participate in professional development opportunities for educators at the district and building level, communicating district policies and best practices supporting technology procurement and facility planning and use.

Performance Tasks

In TF/TL-VII, the performance tasks address three separate, yet interrelated components of effective planning, budgeting, and use. In TF/TL-VII.A., the performance tasks relate to planning and supporting technology-ready facilities. TF/TL-VII.B. performance tasks concern planning and purchasing technology resources. TF/TL-VII.C. relates to communicating technology facility and resource policies and practices to educators, permitting strategic planning and acquisition at the district and school levels.

Under performance tasks for TF/TL-VII.A.1.–8., technologists develop and configure methods to provide technology-ready facilities to support classroom instruction. These tasks essentially subdivide into two components: facility planning and technology support. In facility planning, technology leaders develop plans to configure and integrate software/computer/technology systems to best support the instructional purposes for which they are intended. This includes analyzing the need for technology facilitators and other support personnel necessary for technology implementation and support at school sites. Technology facilitators then use facility plans to work with educators in integrating these systems to support school-site instruction. Other tasks in facility planning include installing and using mass-storage devices to store and retrieve data and instructional resources securely and ensuring that adequate wide area network support exists and is maintained to support instruction. The technology support component requires technology leaders to develop and disseminate strategies for inventorying and integrating software to support instruction and for effective and timely "troubleshooting" of hardware and software problems. Facilitators are then expected to apply these strategies at the school site, applying them to maintain hardware configurations. Facilitators are additionally expected to install, maintain, inventory, and manage software libraries at the school site, modeling integration of software in classroom and administrative settings and reporting the effectiveness of these materials in the classroom environment. This permits leaders to evaluate the district's and the school's practices of software installation, integration, and support.

For TF/TL-VII.B.1.–7., technologists must consider many of the fundamental problems and misunderstandings stemming from technology implementation—strategic planning, support, and maintenance. Technology leaders must strategically align hardware and software purchasing with a district's or school's larger instructional mission, carefully differentiating among specifications identified and recommended for purchasing by technology facilitators. To this end, leaders must develop, maintain, and disseminate current research and district practices involving technology-related facility planning, software acquisition, and budgeting and managing educational computing and technology facilities and resources. Technology facilitators must then implement these practices at the school site, using their experience to suggest policies and procedures concerning staging, scheduling, and security for managing technology. Technology leaders in turn will use these reports to design and develop policies relating to technology management. Additionally, leaders must research and recommend systems supporting distance learning that will be utilized by technology facilitators and educators at the school level.

TF/TL-VII.C.1. describes how technologists are expected to communicate district and school policies and practices related to facility planning and technology acquisition to other educators. This communication should particularly include indirect costs and facility needs associated with education, including ensuring adequate power and network support in classrooms designed to integrate technology. Technologists should assist educators in considering the total cost of ownership (TOC) when planning software and hardware acquisition, and must be particularly vigilant for technology purchased during "end of the year" spending drives, some of which may not be strategically integrated into a larger technology plan.

Procedures, Policies, Planning, and Budgeting for Technology Environments (TF/TL-VII)

Technology Facilitation Standard	Technology Leadership Standard
(TF-VII) Educational technology facilitators promote the development and implementation of technology infrastructure, procedures, policies, plans, and budgets for PK–12 schools.	(TL-VII) Educational technology leaders coordinate development and direct implementation of technology infrastructure procedures, policies, plans, and budgets for PK–12 schools.

TF/TL-VII.A. Use the school technology facilities and resources to implement classroom instruction.

Performance Tasks for Facilitators	Performance Tasks for Leaders
TF-VII.A.1. Use plans to configure software/computer/technology systems and related peripherals in laboratory, classroom cluster, and other appropriate instructional arrangements.	TL-VII.A.1. Develop plans to configure software/computer/technology systems and related peripherals in laboratory, classroom cluster, and other appropriate instructional arrangements.
TF-VII.A.2. Use local mass storage devices and media to store and retrieve information and resources.	TL-VII.A.2. Install local mass storage devices and media to store and retrieve information and resources.
TF-VII.A.3. Discuss issues related to selecting, installing, and maintaining wide area networks (WAN) for school districts.	TL-VII.A.3. Prioritize issues related to selecting, installing, and maintaining wide area networks (WAN) for school districts and facilitate integration of technology infrastructure with the WAN.
TF-VII.A.4. Model integration of software used in classroom and administrative settings including productivity tools, information access/ telecommunication tools, multimedia/ hypermedia tools, school management tools, evaluation/portfolio tools, and computer-based instruction.	TL-VII.A.4. Manage software used in classroom and administrative settings including productivity tools, information access/telecommunication tools, multimedia/ hypermedia tools, school management tools, evaluation/portfolio tools, and computer-based instruction.
TF-VII.A.5. Utilize methods of installation, maintenance, inventory, and management of software libraries.	TL-VII.A.5. Evaluate methods of installation, maintenance, inventory, and management of software libraries.
TF-VII.A.6. Use and apply strategies for troubleshooting and maintaining various hardware/software configurations found in school settings.	TL-VII.A.6. Develop and disseminate strategies for troubleshooting and maintaining various hardware/software configurations found in school settings.
TF-VII.A.7. Use network software packages to operate a computer network system.	TL-VII.A.7. Select network software packages for operating a computer network system and/ or local area network (LAN).
TF-VII.A.8. Work with technology support personnel to maximize the use of technology resources by administrators, teachers, and students to improve student learning.	TL-VII.A.8. Analyze needs for technology support personnel to manage school/district technology resources and maximize use by administrators, teachers, and students to improve student learning.

TF/TL-VII.B. Follow procedures and guidelines used in planning and purchasing technology resources.

TF-VII.B.1. Identify instructional software to support and enhance the school curriculum and develop recommendations for purchase.	TL-VII.B.1. Investigate purchasing strategies and procedures for acquiring administrative and instructional software for educational settings.
TF-VII.B.2. Discuss and apply guidelines for budget planning and management procedures related to educational computing and technology facilities and resources.	TL-VII.B.2. Develop and utilize guidelines for budget planning and management procedures related to educational computing and technology facilities and resources.
TF-VII.B.3. Discuss and apply procedures related to troubleshooting and preventive maintenance of technology infrastructure.	TL-VII.B.3. Develop and disseminate a system for analyzing and implementing procedures related to troubleshooting and preventive maintenance on technology infrastructure.
TF-VII.B.4. Apply current information involving facilities planning issues and computer-related technologies.	TL-VII.B.4. Maintain and disseminate current information involving facilities planning issues and computer-related technologies.
TF-VII.B.5. Suggest policies and procedures concerning staging, scheduling, and security for managing computers/technology in a variety of school/ laboratory/classroom settings.	TL-VII.B.5. Design and develop policies and procedures concerning staging, scheduling, and security for managing hardware, software, and related technologies in a variety of instructional and administrative school settings.
TF-VII.B.6. Use distance and online learning facilities.	TL-VII.B.6. Research and recommend systems and processes for implementation of distance learning facilities and infrastructure.
TF-VII.B.7. Describe and identify recommended specifications for purchasing technology systems in school settings.	TL-VII.B.7. Differentiate among specifications for purchasing technology systems in school settings.

TF/TL-VII.C. Participate in professional development opportunities related to management of school facilities, technology resources, and purchases.

TF-VII.C.1. Support technology professional development at the building/school level utilizing adult learning theory.	TL-VII.C.1. Implement technology professional development at the school/district level utilizing adult learning theory.

ISTE's Essential Conditions and TF/TL Standard VII

TF/TL Standard VII: Procedures, Policies, Planning, and Budgeting for Technology Environments is the primary standard addressing ISTE's Essential Conditions for *Equitable Access* and *Technical Support*. *Equitable Access* is defined as the "robust and reliable access to current and emerging technologies, digital resources, and connectivity for all students."

Technical Support is defined as "consistent and reliable assistance for maintaining, renewing, and using technology."

TF/TL Standard VII also relates to the more managerial and practical aspects of ISTE's essential conditions for *Implementation Planning, Consistent and Adequate Funding*, and *Support Policies*. For example, technology facilitators and leaders may complete an E-rate application, construct a budget for proposed technology acquisitions, develop policies for purchasing technology, and plan for the installation of new computers when addressing TF/TL Standard VII.

As will be illustrated in Chapter 8, technology facilitators and leaders grapple with the higher-level, leadership-oriented elements of *Implementation Planning, Consistent and Adequate Funding*, and *Support Policies* when they enact TF/TL Standard VIII.

Performance Scenarios

To assess the quality of technical support in a school district, the technology leader reviews online trouble tickets to determine the average length of time required to solve most technical issues. The technology leader also administers a survey to measure educators' satisfaction level with current technical support services. The technology leader then reviews these data with technologists responsible for technology support in the schools and develops strategies to reduce downtime and increase client satisfaction.

Employing a full staff of technology support specialists across a large school district is difficult for most school districts to manage and afford. Therefore, a technology leader investigates the possibility of outsourcing technology maintenance and support services to accommodate the level of support needed in schools. The technology leader reads about the pros and cons of outsourcing and visits school districts to determine how successful outsourcing strategies have affected service levels and responsiveness. The technology leader uses this information to make recommendations appropriate to meet local district needs.

Technology facilitators manage desktop security software to ensure that educators and teachers do not install unauthorized software on school-district machines. They also update locally installed software titles in the districts' online inventory management system to assist technology leaders in determining when software upgrades are needed.

A technology facilitator serves on the local technology committee at his school. The committee has drafted the school's technology plan and needs to identify software and hardware to support the school's math and science goals. The technology facilitator will be attending an upcoming state technology conference and is asked to research technologies available to support science and math and make recommendations aligned to the school improvement plan.

case study

ESTABLISHING A RELIABLE INFRASTRUCTURE FOR SOUTHWEST INDEPENDENT SCHOOL DISTRICT

When Rick Martinez interviewed to become the assistant superintendent for technology for Southwest Independent School District (SWISD) in San Antonio, Texas, he shared his vision of infusing technology into all teaching, learning, and administrative practices. Martinez's vision resonated with district leaders, and he joined the central office team in 2005.

Eager to implement his vision, Martinez began his job by carefully assessing the current condition of technology implementation in SWISD schools. Through this needs assessment, he realized that the gap between his ideal future and the current reality in his new district was wider than expected.

"Basically, we found that there was little use of technology in the schools. When we explored the reasons why, we uncovered the most fundamental types of problems. Limited hardware, software, Internet resources, training, and accessibility to a reliable infrastructure were all causes for the nonuse. In addition, it was the philosophy of the previous technology administration that the more they locked down the systems, the fewer problems would arise. Teachers were unable to utilize instructional CDs or external storage devices, which limited access to instructional resources. The technology infrastructure was so unreliable that teachers didn't even consider using it anymore," Martinez commented.

After this needs analysis, Martinez knew that the first step in his plan must focus on infrastructure. Although Martinez's background is in education, he has supplemented his traditional bachelor's and master's degrees with industry-standard training in network administration and engineering. This technical background helped him assess the technical difficulties in SWISD, communicate with the district's technical staff, and draft a plan to correct the problems.

"Although most servers were centralized, many of the servers were running multiple tasks such as DHCP, DNS, and e-mail on a single server. Bandwidth to the Internet was minimal, causing most resources to be unavailable during peak times. Wireless access was isolated to a few areas at two campuses. Storage and data backup were nonexistent or insufficient," recalled Martinez.

Based on this analysis, an initial infrastructure plan was developed to reconfigure the existing flat network and fix issues related to network devices. One school at a time, switches were reconfigured to accommodate for multiple VLANs for the district's data, proposed wireless, and video network. Routing was deployed to isolate traffic within each of the campuses. SWISD also utilized E-Rate funding to provide a 10 Mb Ethernet connection to the Internet and add to the existing Gigaman circuits, tying campuses together through a core router.

(Continued)

case study (Continued)

An additional plan was drafted and presented to the superintendent's cabinet to provide additional storage and backup capacity for all district servers, an expenditure costing around $300,000. With this plan fully implemented, SWISD's storage capacity is 7.5 terabytes and is expandable to 200 terabytes.

Over time, wireless technologies were installed in all of the district's 13 campuses, servers were replaced because of obsolescence, and an additional 30 servers were installed to support the instructional resources provided to teachers and students. Local funds, the technology allotment from Title II, Part D, and other NCLB title funds supported these advancements.

"With these actions, the most serious problems were corrected within a six-month period. It was important to be able to place users back on the system as soon as possible and restore their confidence in using technology for instruction and the business of the district. I think we did that fairly quickly and successfully," Martinez said.

Finally, Martinez felt that the network configuration issues had stabilized. His next step was to supply educators with the technical support needed to maintain equipment and network operations.

Under Martinez's supervision, the district already had a director of technical services and six district technicians in place, but the technical team addressed the quality of their service. Teachers and staff were provided with an electronic help-desk system to report problems. This system generates an e-mail verification when teachers submit an issue and another e-mail when the issue is resolved. District technicians use the data from this system to improve their response time and to monitor how long it takes to complete the service cycle.

"We continue to work on developing a culture of great customer service—considering teachers, students, and administrators as our clients. It's not about the technology at all, it's about learning. To be successful, district-based technicians must understand the critical nature of technology for instruction," noted Martinez.

With a revitalized network and more effective technology support, Martinez turned his attention to providing educators with up-to-date software and online resources. Accomplishing this feat required some creativity.

"The technology budget was insufficient to do all the things we needed to do," explained Martinez. "Besides, I believe technology should be infused throughout the whole system, and everyone should see the advantages of it. We looked at the software we needed and who would benefit from it. We presented our proposals to the other departments in the district and showed them what they could do with collaborative meeting software, for example. Everyone saw the potential, and we pooled money from various budgets to purchase the necessary tools."

(Continued)

case study (Continued)

Martinez sees his early days in the district as a series of fast-paced, innovative strategies to address basic technical needs. Now, he feels like the district is in a more functional state. With the urgency of an inoperable network behind him, he is able to create a more systematic cycle for planning and implementation.

"Currently, we are working with our technology advisory committee, superintendent's cabinet, and the SWISD Board of Education on a long-range plan to maintain our current systems. We can't sit still and rest. We have to plan for obsolescence. Right now we are researching every sort of funding model available—purchasing through local funds, leasing, grants and bonds. We are also planning for expansion in certain areas, as well. For example, we are constantly monitoring bandwidth, and it is likely we will have to address this issue in the next two years," explained Martinez.

Martinez is pleased with the technological progress SWISD has made under his leadership, but he is more excited about what this new infrastructure is making possible. Since Martinez began working at SWISD, he has implemented a technology proficiency program and built a new Instructional Technology Department, with a director, 14 campus instructional technologists, and 100 teacher-technology leaders throughout the district.

"Really, I try to spend the least amount of time on the technical aspects of my job as possible—even though it is very important, of course. As we have seen here at SWISD, if people don't have stable access to technology, it is impossible to move forward to the things that make a difference—like our technology proficiency program, which helps all teachers gain the skills they need to use technology in the classroom. With the basics in place, we are now seeing an amazing difference in the use of technology. This is exciting! This is why the boxes and wires are important," Martinez said.

SWISD Technology Division Homepage: www.swisd.net/Technology/

Discussion Questions

- After reading all the possible explanations in this chapter, how do you explain the disconnect between the high levels of access reported by schools and the fact that teachers still find access as the top barrier preventing them from implementing technology for instruction?

- Study the pros and cons of different types of configurations in schools and discuss which you would use and why.

- To ease the need for technology support, some schools have enlisted students to help. What are the pros and cons of having students participate in technical support?

- Some researchers have observed that technical concerns can overwhelm the schedule of many technologists, and technical support occurs at the expense of other important performances related to curriculum and instruction (Hearrington & Strudler, 2007). How do technologists in your local setting balance the needs for technical and instructional support?

- Standard VII highlights the need for highly trained technical staff and experienced project managers. What do you think about hiring technical staff from business environments to work in schools? Must K–12 technology specialists have an educational background? How can educators without formal technical training prepare themselves for highly technical positions in schools?

Resources

As technology facilitators and leaders implement TF/TL Standard VII, they may benefit from several types of resources that either assist technologists by deepening their understanding of concepts discussed in the chapter, or provide tools that technologists may share with other educators. Although all the resources are valuable, we have identified one "Spotlight Resource" in each chapter that has particular utility to technologists.

The resources identified under TF/TL Standard VII relate to procedures, policies, planning, and budgeting. Electronic journals and newsletters are included to provide in-depth, up-to-date resources to keep technology leaders abreast of the latest issues and trends, and include links permitting technologists to subscribe. Guidebooks and reports are included on topics ranging from assessing technology use in schools to the challenge of sustainability. Several tools are provided to assist technology leaders and facilitators in analyzing TCO, or the total cost of ownership. A series of websites provide a variety of resources including grant funding for educational technology.

Electronic Journal

T.H.E. Journal
www.thejournal.com
> The Technology Horizons in Education (T.H.E.) online journal contains numerous useful websites for technology leaders, providing information on trends and developments in educational technology.

Electronic Newsletters

T.H.E. Journal eNewsletters
www.thejournal.com/the/newsletters/k12techtrends/
> T.H.E. Journal's eNewsletters provide technologists with a free subscription resource containing in-depth education technology resources. They include T.H.E. News Update, T.H.E. SMARTClassroom, School Security, T.H.E. Focus, and EduHound Weekly. Subscribe to all of these eNewsletters at the URL listed above.

TCO/VOI e-Newsletter

http://classroomtco.cosn.org

> This newsletter is sponsored by CoSN and provides resources for determining the total cost of ownership of technology in schools.

Guidebooks

Technology in Schools: Suggestions, Tools and Guidelines for Assessing Technology in Secondary Education

http://nces.ed.gov/pubs2003/2003313.pdf

> This guidebook, published by the National Center for Education Statistics (NCES) and its National Forum on Education Statistics, provides guidelines and tools for gathering information on the presence and use of technology in schools.

The Secret Life of Grantwriters

www.grantwrangler.com/pdfs/GrantWriting3_07.pdf

> This guide contains useful information for technologists seeking outside financial support for building technological capacity, including a list of grant providers.

Reports

Lessons Learned About Providing Laptops for All Students

www.neirtec.org/laptop/

> This report by NEIR*TEC reports on many laptop initiatives around the country.

The Sustainability Challenge: Taking EdTech to the Next Level

http://cct.edc.org/admin/publications/report/EdTechSustainability.pdf

> This report summarizes critical issues related to sustaining good educational technology practice over time.

Tools

K12TCO Calculator

http://129.71.174.252/tcov2/

> This calculator helps schools estimate the multiyear cost of implementing and maintaining technology systems in K–12 schools.

Technology Support Index (TSI)

http://tsi.iste.org

> ISTE's TSI framework and self-assessment tool allows school districts to appraise the quality and efficiency of their current technology support program and learn about possible improvements they can employ.

Spotlight **Resource**

Total Cost of Ownership (TCO) Tool
http://classroomtco.cosn.org/gartner_intro.html

This tool specifically investigates the workstation, network, and server costs of ownership in the K–12 environment, providing an instrument and a process schools and districts can use in determining their total cost of ownership for technology.

Value of Investment (VOI)
www.edtechvoi.org
> This tool allows technology leaders to determine the estimated costs and benefits of proposed technology projects.

Websites

CoSN
www.cosn.org
> The Consortium for School Networking (CoSN) engages in programs and activities such as reports, analysis tools, and professional development resources improving the capabilities of school leaders at the national, state and local levels.

GenYES
http://www.genyes.com
> GenYES is a student-centered research-based solution for school-wide technology integration. Students work with teachers to design technology-infused lessons and provide tech support.

Grants and Funding
www.4teachers.org/archive/index.php?cat=4
> This site is maintained by 4Teachers.org and contains a list of grant providers.

Grants.gov
www.grants.gov
> This site allows organizations to find and apply online for competitive grant opportunities from all federal grant-making agencies.

Open Source Software Solutions for K–12
www.netc.org/openoptions/
> This site helps educators make decisions regarding the use of open-source software solutions.

Sheryl Abshire's Grant List
www.cpsb.org/Scripts/abshire/grants.asp
> This list—developed by Sheryl Abshire, an administrative coordinator of technology in Louisiana—is comprehensive and an outstanding single source for information on grants funding technology.

TechLearning.com

www.techlearning.com

> This site provides technology leaders with comprehensive, relevant, and authoritative information on technology trends, new products, news, and funding sources for their technology programs.

U.S. Department of Education

www.ed.gov

> This site provides information, regulations, and applications for grants and other programs available through the U.S. Department of Education.

References

Broad, M., & Newstrom, J. (1992). *Transfer of training: Action-packed strategies to ensure high payoff from training investments.* New York: Perseus.

CDW-G. (2006). *Teacher Talks survey.* Retrieved August 23, 2007, from http://newsroom.cdwg.com/features/feature-06-26-06.html

Consortium for School Networking (CoSN). (2001). *Taking TCO to the classroom: A school administrator's guide to planning for the total cost of new technology.* Retrieved August 11, 2007, from http://classroomtco.cosn.org/gartner_intro.html

Consortium for School Networking (CoSN). (2005). *Digital leadership divide.* Available from www.cosn.org/resources/grunwald/digital_leadership_divide.pdf

Editorial Projects in Education (EPE) Research Center. (2007). Annual state technology survey, as reported in C. Bausell & E. Klemick. Tracking U.S. trends. *Education Week Special Issue: Technology Counts 2007, 26*(30), 42–44.

Frazier, M., & Bailey, G. (2004). *The technology coordinator's handbook.* Eugene, OR: ISTE.

Hearrington, D., & Strudler, N. (2007, June). *The effects of barriers and enabling factors, homophily, and technical support on instructional support time.* Poster session presented at the annual meeting of the American Educational Research Association. Chicago, IL.

Norris, C., Sullivan, T., Poirot, J., & Soloway, E. (2003). No access, no use, no impact: Snapshot surveys of educational technology in K–12 schools. *Journal of Research on Technology in Education, 36*(1), 15–26.

North Central Regional Educational Laboratory. (2000). *EnGauge: A framework for effective technology use in schools. Condition: Practice, Indicator: Technology support.* Retrieved on August 23, 2007, from www.ncrel.org/engauge/framewk/acc/support/accsupin.htm

Roblyer, M. D. (2006). *Integrating technology into teaching* (4th ed.). Upper Saddle River, NJ: Pearson.

Sandholtz, J., & Reilly, B. (2004). Teachers, not technicians: rethinking technical expectations for teachers. *Teachers College Record, 106,* 487–512.

Wells, J., & Lewis, L. (2006). *Internet access in U.S. public schools and classrooms: 1994–2005* (NCES 2007–0200). U.S. Department of Education. Washington, DC: National Center for Educational Statistics.

Whitehead, B., Jensen, D., & Boshchee, F. (2003). *Planning for technology: A guide for school administrators, technology coordinators, and curriculum leaders.* Thousand Oaks, CA: Corwin.

Zhao, Y. Pugh, K., Sheldon, S., & Byers, J. (2002). Conditions for classroom technology innovations. *Teachers College Record, 104*(3) 482–515.

Capable leadership and careful planning are critical factors that are consistently interwoven within the fabric of successful school technology initiatives.

— WHITEHEAD, JENSEN, & BOSCHEE, 2003, P. 21

Chapter Eight

TF/TL STANDARD VIII

Leadership and Vision

Both TF/TL Standard VII and Standard VIII have a strong administrative focus, but they address different types of functions and tasks. As described in the previous chapter, in Standard VII, technology facilitators and leaders manage daily technical responsibilities and projects. They execute these managerial tasks in support of a community vision and a strategic direction for technology use established within the organization. By comparison, Standard VIII describes how technologists lead others in creating a research-based vision and developing a long-range strategic plan moving the vision into reality. The contrast between management (Standard VII) and leadership (Standard VIII) tasks may be helpful in distinguishing between these two areas (see Table 8.1). These descriptions illustrate that—although TF/TL Standard VII describes performances that are absolutely essential to high-quality technology programs—the work is incomplete without TF/TL Standard VIII, focusing on the ability of technologists to:

- Inspire a shared vision among members of an organization and their key stakeholders

- Generate goals and strategies to move the organization toward the vision

- Sustain and garner support for change along the way

TABLE 8.1 ■ Characteristics of management (Standard VII) and leadership (Standard VIII)

MANAGEMENT	LEADERSHIP
Produces order and consistency	**Produces change and movement**
Planning and Budgeting • Establish agendas • Set timetables • Allocate resources	**Establishing a Direction** • Create a vision • Clarify big picture • Set strategies
Organizing and Staffing • Provide structure • Make job placements • Establishes rules and procedures	**Aligning People** • Communicate goals • Seek commitment • Build teams and coalitions
Controlling and Problem Solving • Develop incentives • Generate creative solutions • Take corrective action	**Motivating and Inspiring** • Inspire and energize • Empower subordinates • Satisfy unmet needs

Source: P. Northouse. (2007) Leadership theory and practice *(p. 10). Thousand Oaks, CA: Sage; adapting content from J. P. Kotter. (1990).* A force for change: How leadership differs from management *(pp. 3–8). New York: Free Press.*

Current Context: The Importance of Leadership and Vision

Inspiring a diverse group of people to establish and accomplish common goals is a critical enabling factor in the success of any school improvement effort. Technology programs are no exception (Anderson & Dexter, 2000; Baylor & Ritchie, 2002).

In the absence of a strong vision for effective use, technologies will be underutilized. Technology, like all tools, can be adapted for many purposes. For example, technology can be used to promote student-centered, performance-based instruction, higher-order thinking, and problem solving. Technology can also be used to reinforce teacher-centered presentations or rote memorization of discrete facts. Although all instructional modes have their place in supporting student learning, research suggests that current instructional models are more teacher-centered than student-centered. Leadership and a strong vision are necessary to push technology use into less familiar, but promising, constructivist contexts. Without this leadership and vision for instructional change, technology may be used to reinforce traditional forms of instruction, but not to enable new ways of teaching and learning in classrooms.

The foundation for successful technology implementation requires educators and policy makers to possess a viable vision for technology use, enact the vision, and link the vision to other important organizational endeavors. In the absence of strong leadership and a shared vision for how technology can positively affect education, implementation efforts can flounder, and stakeholders may lack incentives to allocate the necessary funds to acquire, support, and maintain modern learning environments (CoSN, 2005).

Challenges to Constructing a Vision

When technology facilitators and leaders attempt to construct a shared vision for technology use, they may face some unique types of challenges. For example, technologies having the greatest potential to enhance education today were not available when many educators, parents, and policy makers were elementary and secondary students themselves. Consequently, stakeholders often have difficulty imagining how new technologies can support educational endeavors. This limited awareness may create apathy, or even resistance, to technology programs.

In addition to helping the school community develop an appropriate, research-based vision for technology use, leaders must sustain the community's focus on this vision until it becomes entrenched in the local culture. Often, vision statements are created at the national, state, and district levels. Even if the committees who developed the vision statements are representative, it is not truly a shared vision until all members of the community—teachers, students, administrators, staff members, business partners, and parents—also understand, adopt, and enact it.

Recently, technology leaders reported to us that educators, administrators, board members, and other key stakeholders in the community are reluctant to focus on technology-supported learning. Although they may not oppose technology, stakeholders seem overwhelmed by other pressing needs in the district, such as meeting adequate yearly progress (AYP) for NCLB.

Successful Strategies for Creating and Sustaining a Vision

Because it is difficult for people to conceptualize technology-supported instruction without experiencing it, technologists frequently strive to immerse stakeholders in technology-rich environments and provide them with multiple models of successful practice in the classroom. In Chapter 2, we discussed how modeling effective practice is critical for supporting teacher transformation. However, administrators, parents, and board members can also benefit from participating in professional learning and reviewing movies, research reports, and news articles related to effective technology use.

To sustain the vision, these types of activities must be ongoing. To capture the attention of busy leaders, the use of technology must be relevant. Stakeholders must be able to see how technology use will help them achieve school improvement goals. Technology needs to be seen as a critical "have-to-do" rather than an additional "nice-to-do."

Associate superintendent Rick Martinez from Southwest Independent School District in San Antonio, Texas, deploys a very effective strategy that illustrates these principles. A few years ago, he hired a technology specialist who works only with the central office and local board of education members. This specialist holds regularly scheduled training sessions to show the board members what technologies are available in schools and how they are being used to support learning. The training sessions also address how board members can use available technologies to support their administrative role in the district. The specialist's work mirrors the type of professional learning that teachers receive in local schools. Through these learning experiences, board members gain the knowledge and the experience they need to construct and embrace a vision for technology's role in learning. The results have been increased technology literacy among board members and heightened support for the district's technology initiatives.

The Culture of Long-Range Technology Planning

Leadership and vision in the field of instructional technology are often associated with long-range strategic planning, which is a prominent feature in job descriptions of technology professionals. The planning process permits schools to construct a cohesive vision for technology, set measurable goals, chart an action plan, and monitor progress. Local board members and other political decision makers rely on such plans to understand proposed technology expenditures and ensure accountability, and local technologists use the plans to guide their daily work.

Although technology plans were part of school cultures for many years, the primary motivator for wide-scale strategic planning for technology has been state and federal policy. As a condition of receiving funds for technology, these policies mandate technology plans containing a strategic vision for technology acquisition and implementation. For example, when the Elementary and Secondary Education Act was reauthorized and amended by the Improving America's Schools Act (IASA) of 1994, Congress allocated significant public funding for technology. In the same legislation, Congress also called for the first national educational technology plan, providing structure and direction for this massive funding initiative. In response to this mandate, the U.S. Department of Education published *Getting America's Students Ready for the 21st Century: Meeting the Technology Literacy Challenge* in 1996. Two other national technology plans have subsequently been published—*e-Learning: Putting a World-Class Education at the Fingertips of All Children* (2000) and *Toward A New Golden Age in American Education: How the Internet, the Law and Today's Students Are Revolutionizing Expectations* (2004).

Federal policy initiatives have traditionally required state education agencies and local school districts to develop and submit technology plans as a condition of federal funding from such programs as the Technology Innovation Challenge Grants (authorized under Title III of IASA, 1994); Enhancing Education through Technology (authorized under Title II, Part D of NCLB, 2001); and E-Rate (authorized by the Telecommunications Act of 1996). These requirements have resulted in the U.S. Department of Education and states publishing guidelines and providing technical support for technology planning and implementation.

Although some have viewed these planning and approval requirements as burdensome, the mandates encourage the educational community to reflect on how technology will be utilized, why it will be used in these ways, and what will be needed to accomplish their goals. As a result of these technology planning policies, strategic visioning and planning for technology is now a regular part of state and school district culture, requiring technology facilitators and leaders at the local, state, and national levels.

Components of Technology Plans

Federal and state policies and guidelines, along with local professional learning efforts, have created a general consensus as to what components are necessary in a well-constructed technology plan. Although most plans add other elements, nearly all plans are designed to include:

- A vision describing the community's ideal and preferred future related to technology use and student learning. The vision usually consists of a short statement that can be readily communicated and understood and a more lengthy description of what community members should see and experience when the vision is realized. A vision answers the question, "Where do we want to go?"

- A description of the current reality of the local culture, a comparison of this current reality to the vision, and an analysis of what needs must be met for the organization to move forward. An effective needs analysis is generally based on data collected from multiple sources. If conducted well, this needs analysis can serve as baseline data for an evaluation plan. A current reality section answers the question, "Where are we now?"

- An action plan describing goals and strategies. Goals are shorter-term, specific, and measurable outcomes that will bring the community closer to realizing the vision. Goals are related to the current reality in that they address the current needs or deficiencies obstructing progress toward the vision. Strategies are specific actions or activities designed to help the community reach its goals. Strategies are usually accompanied by budgets, timelines, and responsibility lists. The action plan answers the question, "How do we achieve our vision?"

- An evaluation plan, which is a description of how the community will measure and report progress toward its goals. The evaluation plan answers the question, "How do we know we are making progress?"

Qualities of Exemplary Technology Plans

Simply including certain components in a technology plan does not ensure an exemplary plan. In addition to containing the essential requirements just outlined, exemplary technology plans are expected to be:

- **Focused on student learning.** Historically, technology plans were criticized for their overemphasis on acquiring technologies, with little or no indication of how these technologies were to be used or how they would improve student learning. However, more recent state and national guidelines have directed planners to ensure that student learning—especially in areas of low performance—is a central, organizing feature of the plan. As a result, exemplary plans explicitly describe how technologies will be implemented and how student learning will increase.

- **Grounded in research and best practices.** As with all school improvement initiatives, policy makers and stakeholders must ensure that proposed actions reflect research and best practice. Constructing a technology plan is important, but if that plan does not represent current knowledge and best thinking in the field, it does not serve the best interests of students in the school, district, region, or state.

- **Aligned to other strategic initiatives.** Technology plans should be aligned to other strategic initiatives in the district, state, and nation. School improvement and change experts claim that schools have suffered from implementing too many and sometimes even competing initiatives at the same time. Therefore, technology programs cannot make the mistake of launching individual or isolated programs. Leadership is needed to ensure that technology is linked to the other high-profile school improvement efforts—which often means cooperating with top leaders in the organization and advocating for the inclusion of technology into comprehensive strategic plans (Creighton, 2003).

- **Comprehensive.** Although we have aligned TF/TL Standard VIII to ISTE's Essential Conditions for *Shared Vision* and *Implementation Planning*, technology facilitators and leaders must have a strong understanding of all of the essential conditions for effective technology use. Because practitioners and scholars have expressed a clear understanding that effective technology implementations are possible only when certain enabling factors are in place, technology plans must be comprehensive. Plans cannot only address a few essential conditions, such as access, funding, and technical support, without also addressing remaining essential conditions, such as student-centered learning, skilled personnel, and ongoing professional learning. To plan successfully for technology, facilitators and leaders must be able to assess the current strength of the essential conditions in their schools, districts, states, or regions. They must also design strategies to address weak areas. Good technology plans address all of the essential conditions.

- **Simple and clear.** Many experts have noted that overly elaborate planning, in general, can drain resources and even have a negative effect on student achievement (Creighton, 2003; Schmoeker, 2006). For these reasons, technology plans—especially those to be distributed to stakeholders and the public—should contain powerful ideas but should also be brief and easy to comprehend.

- **Useful and achievable.** The best technology plans are actionable and achievable. Technology plans should provide a clear plan for technology professionals and other educators, and the need for the results offered by technology implementation should be readily understandable and clearly communicated. Importantly, the plan should contain tasks that are achievable. Many plans remain unimplemented because they are too ambitious, overestimating what current staff and financial resources have the capacity to accomplish.

- **Measurable.** Stakeholders should be able to determine to what extent the desired outcomes in the plan—usually in the form of goals—are being accomplished. Because reporting progress and celebrating successes are important components of community-based planning, a plan must be measurable, and there must be assigned staff and resources to implement the ongoing evaluation (Kotter, 1996).

- **Logical.** Given the current needs of the community, established goals should seem logical and reasonable to educators and other stakeholders. Additionally, the goals should be aligned to achieving the vision and enacting strategies that will improve the community's likelihood of meeting the goals. Many poorly constructed plans do not contain these logical links between components. To correct this, SERVE (2004) recommends using logic maps to connect individual strategies to the goals they are intended to target. This practice also helps in the evaluation process. Because evaluation usually targets whether or not the community is meeting goals, the logic map provides a way to trace the evaluation to specific strategies that might be ineffective or poorly implemented.

Managing a Planning Process

Identifying the components and qualities of technology planning is useful, but it does not describe how facilitators and leaders create high-quality plans. Being able to manage this planning process is tightly related to the performance standards and tasks in TF/TL Standard VII and the very definition of what it means to be a leader. Northouse (2007), for example, notes that whereas leadership has been described by traits or characteristics in the past, most modern definitions focus on leadership as "a process whereby an individual influences a group of individuals to achieve a common goal" (p. 3).

Though the processes for creating high-quality technology plans vary, there is a high expectation that technology planning will be community based. Evidence of community input is often required for state and federal approval processes. Community-based planning offers several advantages to technologists. Most importantly, perhaps, an open, actively inclusive approach provides an opportunity to build understanding and consensus among key decision makers in the community—especially in areas where some may not understand or have misconceptions about technology and learning (Porter, 1999). With broad-based support, technologists have a better chance of acquiring resources necessary for implementation and avoiding a negative community response. A community-based approach provides technologists with the opportunity to assemble advocates who can help explain why technology is important for learning. These advocates can serve as a support team for technologists, add new dimensions to the conversation, and prevent the planning process from being overwhelmed by those with negative views. Although community-based planning is time consuming and will include opinions both for and against technology in schools, vetting the issues and arriving at consensus can provide both short- and long-term benefits for program implementation. Figure 8.1 illustrates some common phases in a typical community-based technology planning model.

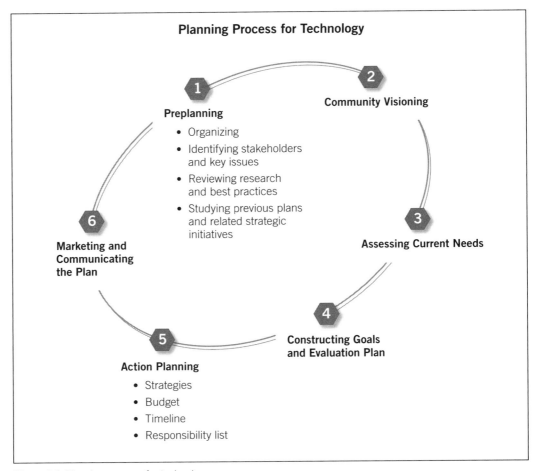

Figure 8.1 Planning process for technology

The first stage is preplanning—a time-consuming phase often underestimated by planners. In this stage, technology leaders and facilitators work together to design the planning process, identify key stakeholders who should participate, and list key issues influencing local planning. To plan effectively, technologists must be thoroughly familiar with previous technology plans and other current strategic planning initiatives to which technology planning must be aligned. Many planners use preplanning time to collect current research, best practices, and innovations that will keep the planning process fresh and focused.

The preplanning stage should include a discussion of why the proposed plan is necessary. Whereas the need to integrate technology into instruction may seem self-evident to technologists and those familiar with educational research, it will not be to many stakeholders whose political and resource support may be critical to success. Technologists must create a sense of urgency, explaining both why the status quo is unacceptable and why the proposed changes are necessary for success.

In stage 2, technologists lead stakeholders in a collaborative, democratic visioning process. Experienced planners agree that visioning should involve as many stakeholders as possible. However, they also warn that in broad-based community planning initiatives, participants need information on technology-related research, innovations, and best practices before constructing a vision. If stakeholders are not informed, the vision may be flawed or limited. Infusing research into planning helps stakeholders make informed decisions and serves as an effective strategy for changing current perceptions about technology—thus highlighting the educative as well as the administrative purposes of planning.

After constructing a vision, technologists frequently engage stakeholders in a reflective assessment of the distance between the current reality in their school and the vision. In doing so, the community identifies barriers obstructing realization of the vision. This process, often referred to as a needs assessment or gap analysis, leads into the next stage of the process—establishing goals and an evaluation plan.

Because needs usually outpace available or realistically acquirable resources, stakeholders must prioritize current needs and establish related short-term goals. As goals are identified, stakeholders should decide what constitutes progress toward each goal. Combining goal setting and evaluation keeps evaluation activities streamlined, simple, and focused on goals instead of strategies, which are formed in the next stage of the process.

After the goals and evaluation plan have been drafted, stakeholders construct an action plan. In this phase, leaders must identify strategies likely to help them reach their goals. As with vision, a strategy should be selected after consideration of available or acquirable resources and their ability to realize multiple goals. Strategies should include budgets, timelines, and responsibilities, identifying discrete duties of individuals and teams. Often novice planners begin and end with this step, which is actually more managerial than leadership oriented. In the context of the TF/TL standards, most of the action planning tasks are addressed in TF/TL Standard VII, whereas other stages of the planning process are leadership functions associated with TF/TL Standard VIII.

Once the plan is drafted, technologists and stakeholders must create a guiding coalition, strategically marketing the plan and building support and momentum to overcome the inevitable barriers to its implementation and sustainability. During this process, technologists should provide data demonstrating progress toward goals, and celebrate incremental short-term wins as goals are achieved toward realization of the vision. If goals are not realized, technologists should consider what barriers are obstructing progress and identify methods for removing or overcoming those obstacles.

Summary of Current Context

In current school cultures, technology facilitators and leaders will be expected to lead the community in constructing a community-based vision and a long-range strategic plan for the comprehensive use of technology. Creating a strategic direction requires a unique skill set, including managing groups of people with divergent viewpoints and achieving consensus. Because most strategic initiatives involve change, this complicates the process even further. Although TF/TL Standard VIII represents one of the most difficult performance areas, the performance indicators outline the specific knowledge and skills that will help technology facilitators and leaders successfully engage in this important process of leading technology programs and constructing a shared vision.

Implementing the Standard

This section reviews the standard, performance indicators, and performance tasks of TF/TL Standard VIII, which can be found in the standards table on pages 190–191.

Performance Standards

In implementing standard VIII, both technology leaders and facilitators assume a leadership role in uniting community stakeholders as they construct a shared vision for technology use and work toward realizing that vision. However, technology leaders are central in designing and implementing the collaborative visioning process, whereas technology facilitators are expected only to contribute to the shared vision. For this reason, leaders are expected to be more skilled in managing group processes, leading change, and fostering collaborative cultures. In enacting this standard, facilitators are likely to learn from observing technology leaders as they work with large groups of people, manage conflict, keep the process focused on key ideas, synthesize ideas, prioritize issues, and build consensus.

Performance Indicators

The performance indicators for Standard VIII outline five broad categories of technology-related tasks that technology facilitators and leaders are expected to perform.

1. **Identify and apply educational and technology related research, the psychology of learning, and instructional design principles in guiding the use of computers and technology in education (TF/TL-VIII.A.).** According to this performance indicator, technology facilitators and leaders must possess strong foundational knowledge of human learning and understand how it serves as a basis for instructional design incorporating the use of technology. Technologists must stay abreast of best practices and other related research and disseminate these findings to educators using technology to enhance the teaching and learning process. By identifying and applying learning theory and instructional design principles, technologists ensure that the vision represents what current research and best practice suggests is best for student learning.

2. **Apply strategies for and knowledge of issues related to managing the change process in schools (TF/TL-VIII.B.).** Implementing a technology-related vision is inextricably tied to advancing new ways of teaching and learning. When constructing a vision, all stakeholders must rethink their current beliefs about teaching and learning. Teachers must learn new skills, implement new practices, and reflect on their roles in the classroom. Because change has a ripple effect through a system, school leaders may find themselves revising school schedules, redefining policies, changing definitions of an instructional resource, and redesigning funding models to accommodate these new instructional practices. For these reasons, technology leaders and facilitators must be well schooled in managing change.

3. **Apply effective group process skills (TF/TL-VIII.C.).** Creating a vision and managing change include designing and facilitating a collaborative process where new ideas are vetted, prioritized, evaluated, and implemented. Technology facilitators and leaders are responsible for effectively communicating a research-based vision to foster collaborations, alliances, and partnerships, but technologists must also ensure that the voices of all stakeholders are heard equally. To manage this democratic process, technologists must deploy proven strategies to encourage diversity and to unify disparate stakeholders toward the common objectives.

4. **Lead in the development and evaluation of district technology planning and implementation (TF/TL-VIII.D.).** Creating and utilizing a district technology plan is perhaps the most important objective of technology leaders and facilitators as they promote comprehensive integration of technology. Technology leaders and facilitators advocate for a plan that strategically integrates technology based on analysis of district technology resources and needs. Once the plan is implemented, technology leaders and facilitators must continually evaluate and adjust it to ensure that it supports instructional and administrative goals.

5. **Engage in supervised field-based experiences with accomplished technology facilitators and/or directors (TF/TL-VIII.E.).** This final performance objective recognizes that aspiring technology leaders and facilitators cannot learn their craft solely from reading about the standards. Knowledge building must also include appropriately supervised field-based experiences. Readers should be aware that this standard applies to all of the TF/TL Standards and not only to TF/TL Standard VIII. By participating in practical application in all TF/TL standard areas, developing technology leaders and facilitators will gain experience in the instructional, technical, and administrative performances associated with being a technology professional in K–12 schools.

Performance Tasks

In TF/TL-VIII, the performance tasks address five components of leadership and vision. These components include research, change, collaboration, planning, and field experiences.

In TF/TL-VIII.A.1., the performance tasks relate to understanding and applying research in educational technology. This skill is critical in helping stakeholders construct a vision that is aligned with researched-based best practices. The tasks suggest that both technology facilitators and leaders will remain knowledgeable about best practices in educational technology, but the performances for leaders require higher levels of synthesis, evaluation, and application. According to the performance tasks, facilitators are expected to discuss and evaluate current research, whereas leaders are expected to communicate and apply principles and practices of research. In practice, facilitators often support leaders by finding individual research relevant to local issues in a district, region, or state; however, leaders are expected to be able to synthesize the content from multiple sources and to communicate broad generalizations. Leaders are also expected to apply these generalizations to improve practice. Facilitators are not expected to engage in these higher levels of performance.

In TF/TL-VIII.B.1. the performance tasks require technology facilitators and leaders to understand and apply the social and historical foundations of education as they relate to change in schools. In this performance task, technology facilitators demonstrate some basic knowledge of these principles by discussing them. However, leaders describe how they relate to the use of technologies in schools. Based on these performance indicators, technology leaders are expected to apply the principles in a deeper, more profound way than are facilitators. In their performances, foundational principles are used to guide the way technology leaders' actions implement change. Although facilitators are only expected to understand these principles, they often advance by watching leaders enact them.

In TF/TL-VIII.C.1., performance tasks focus on building alliances to support the use of technology in schools. Facilitators are expected to discuss the need or the rationale for these partnerships and examine examples from local practice. However, leaders must be able to discuss the issues related to building collaborations, alliances, and partnerships involving educational technology initiatives. The leaders' performances imply that they have already had some experience leading such initiatives and can intimately discuss the related issues and tensions that can emerge from this complex process. The facilitators' performance tasks do not require this level of experience. To prepare them for future performance, the facilitators' tasks center on understanding why such processes are important and looking at models implemented by technology leaders.

All of the performance tasks in TF/TL-VIII.D.1.–7. relate to technology planning. In two of these tasks, technology facilitators play a supportive or peripheral role at the local school level, whereas leaders fully execute tasks associated with high-quality planning at the district, state, and/or regional levels. In TF/TL-VIII.D.1., technology facilitators participate in the group processes associated with technology planning, but the technology leader is expected to design and lead these processes. Similarly, in TF/TL-VIII.D.2., the technology facilitator is expected to be able to conduct an evaluation of a local school environment, perhaps listing the strengths and weaknesses associated with each essential condition for successful technology programs. However, the leader is expected to use evaluation findings to recommend modifications in technology implementations on a broader scale. Both of these performance tasks illustrate how technology facilitators can use their emerging skills and their intimate local knowledge of schools to contribute to the technology planning process, but not to assume full responsibility for planning at the district, state, or regional level.

In performance tasks TF/TL-VIII.D.3.–7., facilitators' performances are better described as preparatory. Unlike TF-VIII.D.1. and 2., facilitators are not required to participate in district, state, or regional technology planning processes but to reflect on them. In TF-VIII.D.3.–7., facilitators identify, discuss, describe, and examine technology planning principles. Through these activities, facilitators are expected to become aware of the issues of technology planning and to study the processes and products produced by technology leaders. In this phase, observations and reflections are key for the development of technology facilitators. Through this learning, facilitators can better support technology leaders during technology planning and/or prepare to assume more active leadership functions in the future. Technology leaders, on the other hand, are already assuming these leadership roles as described TL-VIII.D.3.–7. In these standards, technology leaders exhibit high-level, strategic skills as they plan, develop, compare, and implement strategies that result in high-quality technology plans.

Because of the nature of TF/TL Standard VIII: Leadership and Vision, the role of the technology leader is central throughout all of the performance tasks, and technology facilitators play more supportive roles. The most active roles that technology facilitators play in this standard are to contribute to the technology processes designed and implemented by leaders (TF/TL-VIII.D.1.) and to conduct evaluations of their local schools to inform technology planning (TF/TL-VIII.D.2.). These two performance areas illustrate how technology facilitators leverage their intimate knowledge of schools to improve district-, state-, or regional-level planning.

However, the rest of the performance tasks cast technology facilitators in a less central role. Facilitators who wish to advance to a technology leadership position should seek every opportunity to engage in field experiences with technology leaders, serving as their active apprentices whenever possible.

This kind of apprenticeship is what is reflected in TF/TL-VIII.E.1., though field-based experiences should not be limited to technology planning, but should include all the standard areas. As reflected in performance task TF-VIII.E.1., aspiring technology facilitators are expected to examine components needed for effective field-based experiences, whereas future technology leaders are expected to participate actively.

The differences between facilitators' and leaders' performance tasks may reflect some current realities and constraints in schools and graduate education programs. For example, aspiring technology facilitators enacting TF-VIII.E.1. are likely to be classroom teachers who are preparing to assume school-based technology jobs. Based on their current responsibilities in the classroom, their field-based experiences may be slightly more limited and hypothetical than those addressing TL-VIII.E.1. Teachers training to be technology facilitators may lack experience and familiarity with content and concepts related to the field of educational technology. Because of these needs and constraints, their course work may be less field-based and more centered on building the content knowledge necessary for successful performance.

In contrast, aspiring technology leaders have already mastered the TF standards and are often functioning as technology facilitators, making possible a higher level of performance in field-based activities. Technology leaders need a greater level of foundational knowledge to participate in leadership activities. Their current jobs also afford more access to field-based experiences. Practicing facilitators aspiring to be technology leaders have more mobility than a classroom teacher, and their current job performances are already related to technology program goals.

Leadership and Vision (TF/TL-VIII)

Technology Facilitation Standard	Technology Leadership Standard
(TF-VIII) Educational technology facilitators will contribute to the shared vision for campus integration of technology and foster an environment and culture conducive to the realization of the vision.	(TL-VIII) Educational technology leaders will facilitate development of a shared vision for comprehensive integration of technology and foster an environment and culture conducive to the realization of the vision.

TF/TL-VII.A. Identify and apply educational and technology related research, the psychology of learning, and instructional design principles in guiding the use of computers and technology in education.

Performance Tasks for Facilitators	Performance Tasks for Leaders
TF-VIII.A.1. Discuss and evaluate current research in educational technology.	TL-VIII.A.1. Communicate and apply principles and practices of educational research in educational technology.

TF/TL-VIII.B. Apply strategies for and knowledge of issues related to managing the change process in schools.

TF-VIII.B.1. Discuss the history of technology use in schools.	TL-VIII.B.1. Describe social/historical foundations of education and how they relate to use of technology in schools.

TF/TL-VIII.C. Apply effective group process skills.

TF-VIII.C.1. Discuss the rationale for forming school partnerships to support technology integration and examine an existing partnership within a school setting.	TL-VIII.C.1. Discuss issues relating to building collaborations, alliances, and partnerships involving educational technology initiatives.

TF/TL-VIII.D. Lead in the development and evaluation of district technology planning and implementation.

TF-VIII.D.1. Participate in cooperative group processes and identify the processes that were effective.	TL-VIII.D.1. Design and lead in the implementation of effective group process related to technology leadership or planning.
TF-VIII.D.2. Conduct an evaluation of a school technology environment.	TL-VIII.D.2. Use evaluation findings to recommend modifications in technology implementations.
TF-VIII.D.3. Identify and discuss national, state, and local standards for integrating technology in the school environment.	TL-VIII.D.3. Use national, state, and local standards to develop curriculum plans for integrating technology in the school environment.
TF-VIII.D.4. Describe curriculum activities or performances that meet national, state, and local technology standards.	TL-VIII.D.4. Develop curriculum activities or performances that meet national, state, and local technology standards.
TF-VIII.D.5. Discuss issues related to developing a school technology plan.	TL-VIII.D.5. Compare and evaluate district-level technology plans.

TF-VIII.D.6. Discuss the elements of and strategies for developing a technology strategic plan.	TL-VIII.D.6. Use strategic planning principles to lead and assist in the acquisition, implementation, and maintenance of technology resources.
TF-VIII.D.7. Examine issues related to hardware and software acquisition and management.	TL-VIII.D.7. Plan, develop, and implement strategies and procedures for resource acquisition and management of technology-based systems including hardware and software.
TF/TL-VIII.E. Engage in supervised field-based experiences with accomplished technology facilitators and/or directors.	
TF-VIII.E.1. Examine components needed for effective field-based experiences in instructional program development, professional development, facility and resource management, WAN/LAN/wireless systems, or managing change related to technology use in school-based settings.	TL-VIII.E.1. Participate in a significant field-based activity involving experiences in instructional program development, professional development, facility and resource management, WAN/LAN/wireless systems, or managing change related to technology use in school-based settings.

ISTE's Essential Conditions and TF/TL Standard VIII

TF/TL Standard VIII: Leadership and Vision is a comprehensive standard addressing at least six of ISTE's Essential Conditions. TF/TL Standard VIII is the primary standard addressing the *Shared Vision* and *Engaged Communities* essential conditions. Shared Vision is defined as "proactive leadership in developing a shared vision for educational technology among school personnel, parents, students, and the community." Engaged Communities is defined as "partnerships and collaborations within the community to support and fund use of technology and digital resources." As illustrated through the definitions, these two essential conditions are inextricably linked to one another. An engaged community is essential for constructing, disseminating, and sustaining a shared vision.

TF/TL Standard VIII is also critical to promoting *Student-Centered Learning*. Because student-centered learning represents a radical departure from prevalent, traditional models of instruction, leadership is needed to encourage and support a new vision for learning.

Finally, TF/TL Standard VIII shares the following three essential conditions with TF/TL Standard VII: *Implementation Planning, Consistent and Adequate Funding,* and *Support Policies*. Whereas TF/TL Standard VII addresses the practical and managerial aspects of these essential conditions, TF/TL Standard VIII addresses higher-level, leadership-type goals necessary for successfully implementing technology programs.

For example, TF/TL Standard VIII addresses the need for higher-level, comprehensive strategic planning for technology, whereas TF/TL Standard VII focuses on implementing the plan. In TF/TL Standard VIII, technology facilitators engage in advocacy to ensure funding for technology and in developing new funding streams via grants and partnerships. In TF/TL Standard VII, technology facilitators concentrate on spending and/or creatively allocating funding sources that have already been identified. In TF/TL Standard VII, technology facilitators and leaders grapple with procedures to implement policy and make suggestions related to policy in a few, isolated areas related to technology deployments, but TF/TL Standard VIII addresses policy in a broader context. The primary responsibilities associated with collaboratively constructing policy and navigating the approval process are best represented by TF/TL Standard VIII.

Performance Scenarios

In preparation for developing a district technology plan, a technology leader reviews current research on effective technology use in schools and collects models of research-based technology implementations. The technology leader incorporates this information into a brief presentation about how technology is enhancing student learning in schools. This information is presented to community members, technology facilitators, and other educators to inspire their thinking and shape their vision for technology use in their own local classrooms.

In preparation for leading a collaborative process to create a district technology plan, technology leaders review criteria for exemplary technology plans and review other district-level technology planning documents. From these documents, the leaders gather ideas on how to organize and format the local district plan. The district leader shares a proposed format with technology facilitators and considers their responses and suggestions.

To help technology facilitators reach teachers and administrators who resist implementing technology, district technology leaders plan a "change retreat." At this retreat, the group explores various theories of how to encourage teachers to shift their practices. They also share strategies that have been successful for them in the past.

A technology facilitator examines current research in educational technology and discovers ISTE's essential conditions needed to implement the national technology standards. Using these essential conditions as a guiding framework, she conducts an evaluation of her school environment. After determining the school's strengths and weaknesses, she consults with a district technology leader to devise the next steps in moving the school toward meeting these important essential conditions. The district technology leader is so impressed with the facilitator's evaluation process that she requires all other technology facilitators to assess the essential conditions at their schools. The technology leader then aggregates the results and uses the information for district technology planning.

STRATEGIC PLANNING FOR ALABAMA DISTANCE LEARNING

In 2004, Governor Bob Riley and State Superintendent of Education Joseph B. Morton envisioned how distance learning could provide Alabama high school students with the opportunity to engage in Advanced Placement (AP), elective, and other courses often unavailable in many local schools. However, to move the vision forward to other key stakeholders and the legislature for funding, they knew they needed a plan. They entrusted Melinda Maddox, director of technology initiatives for the Alabama State Department of Education, with the task.

As an experienced leader of other planning initiatives, including several Alabama State Technology Plans, Maddox began where she always does—marshalling human resources. "In any planning project, I start with the same question: Who do we need on board to get things done?" In this case, Maddox solicited the involvement of those experienced in either online learning or video-based distance education, including representatives from four Alabama public school districts, two state universities, and the Southern Regional Board of Education (SREB). Representatives of other groups most likely to be affected by the plan, such as the state network, the governor's office, the curriculum and instruction division of the state department, and professional organizations for educators, were also asked to participate.

In addition to ensuring broad representation, Maddox also considered various roles that members would be able to assume once the work began. "For example, I always want to have four or five good writers on the team," she explained. "I also enlisted the help of an experienced, trained meeting facilitator who would be able to acknowledge all the divergent viewpoints but still help us reach consensus around an end product. Having a facilitator for face-to-face sessions allowed me to participate more in shaping the vision, as well."

When planning the task force, Maddox did not believe in "stacking the deck" with only those who were in favor of distance education. "It is good to involve naysayers— especially if you think you can turn them around! You just have to listen to them and respond to their objections, but mostly just really listen—often outside of the big meetings. Sometimes they just want you to understand their heartfelt concerns, and many times, they will actually save you from pitfalls."

Once the task force was in place, Maddox designed a series of meetings and a timeline to produce the planning document. Governor Riley and Superintendent Morton were present to deliver the charge to the group during the first meeting. "Having the governor and the superintendent there—in person—to launch the event was perfect. Planners have to involve the most influential people they can in the process," Maddox explained. "Influential people can convince the team that the work is worthwhile and there are top people who will roll up their sleeves and work with them to make it happen. The governor and the superintendent did that. Their support sustained team members when the work was tough. The work back at their real jobs didn't go away, but they kept planning with us because they knew it was important."

(Continued)

case study *(Continued)*

During the process, Maddox was a taskmaster. "Everyone loves to sit around and tell you their opinions at meetings all day long, but that doesn't get the job done. Every leader has to remind people of deadlines and set up the work so that the work of each member is essential to the completed plan. The aspect of shared responsibility for work kept people motivated. No one wanted to let the team down."

Maddox and the other task force members also collected research on online learning and information from other state initiatives for the group. "We posted these resources online, and they helped to open people's minds. Most of the time, people come to meetings with their way of doing things, but research and examples show them that there are other ways—maybe better ways—to think about things. The research also helped us to make sure that our decisions were informed and that we were making the best possible choices for the students of Alabama."

The team met face-to-face several times over a span of two months and also used online collaborative tools to share drafts and ideas. Finally, they published a document for a proposed program called ACCESS Distance Learning (Alabama Connecting Classrooms, Educators, and Students Statewide) that went forward to the legislature. "The time frame was very short and it was difficult, but you have to take a call from leaders like the governor and the superintendent as an honor, and you just say 'Yes! Thank you!' I've learned that we can never predict how wonderful a project can be. Just look how ACCESS has evolved!" Maddox pointed out.

Many of the original planners are still involved in the ongoing planning, implementation, and evaluation of ACCESS. ACCESS received $10.3 million in both FY06 and FY07 budgets, and $20.3 million in FY08. Maddox now manages a new staff and three regional support centers for the program. "Finding these key people has been essential to our success," Maddox noted. However, Maddox is most pleased with some of the unintended benefits that are emerging. "In working with students part-time via distance learning, high school teachers are now understanding how technology can enhance their traditional, face-to-face classes, as well," concluded Maddox. "Since I am a former high school teacher, I'm absolutely thrilled that ACCESS is also influencing high school reform. In the beginning, I had no idea what would become of this idea for distance learning, but Alabama is a case study of how the willingness to have a vision and develop a plan can help others."

To view more information and the strategic plans for ACCESS, visit http://accessdl. state.al.us/. To view IMPACT (Indicators for Measuring Progress in Advancing Classroom Technology), the State of Alabama's K–12 Technology Plan, visit www.alsde.edu/html/sections/documents.asp?section=61&sort=10&footer=sections/.

Discussion Questions

- What is the vision for technology use in your school, district, state, and/or region? How many system members are able to articulate the vision clearly? How many buy into the vision? What could be done to help key people adopt the vision?

- Read the following excerpt from Michael Schmoeker's (2006) book *Results Now* (p. 34) and respond to it. Although he is speaking in general about school improvement planning, his comments provoke thought about long-range strategic planning for technology, as well. Do you think technology planning should be a common practice? Why or why not?

   > Certainly, by now, schools should know that "strategic planning doesn't work"—and never did (Kouzes & Posner, 1995, p. 244). Like so many initiatives, it was embraced on a massive scale in the absence of any evidence of effectiveness. As Bruce Joyce writes, elaborate improvement planning "has failed miserably and in plain sight" (2004, p. 76).

   > But . . . schools, districts, and state departments of education continue to commit to these multipage planning templates that guarantee "fragmentation and overload" (Fullan, 1996, p. 420)— and thus failure. A recent study in Kentucky confirmed what was already abundantly clear: that the most common, elaborate forms of improvement planning have a negative relationship to achievement (Kannapel & Clements, 2005); they reduce the chances for improvement.

- State and federal policies mandate technology plans for school districts, not schools. As a result, there may have been a decrease in the number of school-level technology plans. Does your school have a technology plan? Do schools in your district, state, or region have technology plans? Why or why not? Do you think each individual school needs a technology plan? Why or why not?

- In Theodore Creighton's (2003) book *The Principal as Technology Leader*, the author quotes Cheryl Lemke, president and CEO of the Metiri Group, as saying there should be no technology plans—only school improvement plans with technology-related components (p. 28). What do you think of this idea? What are the pros and cons of integrated plans?

- Constructing a shared vision and managing a community-based planning process requires excellent facilitation skills and a deep understanding of how to manage organizational change. How do you rank your current abilities in this area? How could you improve and/or maintain your skills?

Resources

As technology facilitators and leaders implement TF/TL Standard VIII, they may benefit from several types of resources that either assist technologists by deepening their understanding of concepts discussed in the chapter or provide tools technologists may share with other educators. Although all the resources are valuable, we have identified one "Spotlight Resource" in each chapter that has particular utility to technologists.

The resources identified under TF/TL Standard VIII pertain to leadership and vision. Links to guidebooks for technology planning are provided to assist technology facilitators and leaders in developing a high-quality plan ensuring the effective use of technology in schools. Several reports are included that establish the essential conditions necessary to improve student learning through technology and provide a vision for technology use far into the future. Additionally, a series of websites are included to facilitate the technology planning process.

Guidebooks

Guidebook for Developing an Effective Instructional Technology Plan
www.nctp.com/downloads/guidebook.pdf
> This guide describes the elements of a technology plan and how the elements are created, evaluated, and distributed.

Guiding Questions for Technology Planning
www.ncrtec.org/capacity/guidepdf/guide.pdf
> This detailed planning guide was developed by the North Central Regional Technology in Education Consortium.

Reports

Milken's Seven Dimensions
www.mff.org/publications/publications.taf?page=158
> This report provides a framework of indicators to consider when assessing whether a school has established the essential conditions necessary to begin improving student learning through technology.

National Trends Reports
www.setda.org/web/guest/nationaltrendsreport
> The State Educational Technology Directors Association (SETDA) is the principal association representing the state directors for educational technology. SETDA's national report highlights state trends in implementing Title II, Part D of No Child Left Behind.

Visions 2020
www.technology.gov/reports/TechPolicy/2020Visions.pdf
> This report guides leaders in creating a technology vision by providing a series of visions for schools in the year 2020.

Visions 2020.2

www.ed.gov/about/offices/list/os/technology/plan/2004/site/documents/visions_20202.pdf

This report provides student views on transforming education and training through advanced technologies.

Books

Whitehead, B., Jensen, D., & Boshchee, F. (2003). *Planning for technology: A guide for school administrators, technology coordinators, and curriculum leaders.* Thousand Oaks, CA: Corwin.

Picciano, A. (2002). *Educational leadership and planning for technology.* (3rd ed.). Upper Saddle River, NJ: Merrill Prentice Hall.

Websites

Educational Leadership Toolkit

www.nsba.org/sbot/toolkit/

This website contains tools developed by the National School Board Association walking you through the entire technology planning process.

ISTE's Essential Conditions

www.iste.org/nets/

This website contains a list of the essential conditions that must be in place in order to implement the ISTE standards for students, teachers, and administrators effectively.

National Center for Technology Planning

www.nctp.com

The National Center for Technology Planning (NCTP) is a clearinghouse for the exchange of many types of information related to technology planning and has many technology plans available for downloading.

 Spotlight Resource

National Educational Technology Plan
www.ed.gov/about/offices/list/os/technology/plan/2004/site/edlite-default.html

This plan examines the progress that the United States has made after a decade of increased federal, state, local, and private investments connecting classrooms to the Internet, providing students with computers, and equipping teachers with the skills they need to use technology as an instructional tool. The plan also provides a set of action steps and recommendations for schools as they begin or continue to transform.

Partnership for 21st Century Skills' Mile Guide

www.21stcenturyskills.org/images/stories/otherdocs/p21up_MILE_Guide_Chart.pdf

The Milestones for Improving Learning and Education (MILE) Guide for 21st Century Skills is designed to assist educators and administrators in measuring the progress of their schools in defining, teaching, and assessing 21st-century skills.

Planning into Practice

www.seirtec.org/P2P.html

SEIR*TEC presents valuable tools (resources, tools, and worksheets) that are particularly useful in helping districts and schools create effective technology plans. These tools are presented in chapter format on this site.

Technology Planning

www.doug-johnson.com/dougwri/maslow-and-motherboards-technology-planning.html

Doug Johnson describes a hierarchical view of technology planning and provides a link to an assessment tool to determine the areas that should be priorities for technology planning and budgeting.

Technology Information Center for Administrative Leadership (TICAL)

http://portical.org

This site is a portal specifically designed for school administrators and a great source of information for technology leaders.

School Technology Needs Assessment (STNA)

www.serve.org/Evaluation/Capacity/EvalFramework/resources/STNA.php

The site by SEIR*TEC assists school leaders—administrators, technology facilitators, media coordinators, or technology committee members—in collecting data to make decisions relating to educational technology in schools (e.g., purchasing, resource deployment, and professional development activities).

References

Anderson, R., & Dexter, S. (2000). *School technology leadership: Incidence and impact.* Retrieved on August 29, 2007, from www.crito.uci.edu/tlc/findings/report_6/startpage.html

Baylor, A., & Ritchie, D. (2002). What factors facilitate teacher skills, teacher morale, and perceived student learning in technology-using classrooms? *Computers in Education, 39,* 395–414.

Consortium for School Networking (CoSN). (2005). *Digital leadership divide.* Available from www.cosn.org/resources/grunwald/digital_leadership_divide.pdf

Creighton, T. (2003). *The principal as technology leader.* Thousand Oaks, CA: Corwin.

Fullan, M. (1996, February). Turning systemic thinking on its head. *Phi Delta Kappan, 77*(6), 420.

Joyce, B. (2004, September). How are professional learning communites created? *Phi Delta Kappan, 86*(1), 76–83.

Kannapel, P.J., & Clements, S.K. (with Taylor, D., & Hibpshman, T.). (2005, February). *Inside the black box of high-performing poverty schools: A report from the Prichard Committee for Academic Excellence.* Available from www.prichardcommittee.com

Kotter, J. (1990). *LA force for change: How leadership differs from management.* New York: Free Press.

Kotter, J. (1996). *Leading change.* Boston: Harvard University Press.

Kouzes, J.M., & Posner, B.Z. (1995). *The leadership challenge.* San Francisco: Jossey-Bass.

International Society for Education. (2007). Essential Conditions. Available from www.iste.org/Content/NavigationMenu/NETS/ForStudents/2007Standards/NETS-S_2007_Essential_Conditions.pdf

Northouse, P. (2007). *Leadership theory and practice* (4th ed.). Thousand Oaks, CA: Sage.

Porter, B. (1999). *Grappling with accountability: Resource tools for organizing and assessing technology results.* Sedalia, CO: Educational Technology Planners, Inc.

Schmoeker, M. (2006). *Results now: How we can achieve unprecedented improvements in teaching and learning.* Alexandria, VA: ASCD.

SERVE (2004). *CAPE evaluation framework.* Retrieved August 29, 2007, from www.serve.org/Evaluation/Capacity/EvalFramework/cape01.php

Whitehead, B., Jensen, D., & Boshchee, F. (2003). *Planning for technology: A guide for school administrators, technology coordinators, and curriculum leaders.* Thousand Oaks, CA: Corwin.

Conclusion

Frazier & Bailey (2004) aptly note that K–12 technology jobs are often "positions without a protocol." However, the TF/TL standards correct this weakness by specifically describing what school technology professionals must know and be able to do. The standards also make useful distinctions between the roles of technology facilitators and technology leaders and illustrate how both roles are necessary to ensure successful educational technology programs.

The TF/TL standards capture the complex and comprehensive nature of supporting and leading K–12 technology initiatives. The content presented in this book supports a balanced, integrated approach to technology facilitation and leadership. Because each standard plays an important role in a systemic approach to change, no single standard area can ensure successful technology programs. Some technology facilitators and leaders may specialize in particular performance areas, but school systems must address all the TF/TL standards to achieve desired results.

TF/TL standards should help all educators—including school technologists themselves—see technology professionals as educational leaders. As the standards illustrate, technology facilitators and leaders must engender shared visions for learning, lead instructional change, engage in policy making, seek funding, manage budgets, understand educational law and ethics, and interface with the community in the same ways as more established educational leadership roles. Because of this, technologists need preparation and professional learning programs that extend beyond building their technological expertise to include leadership development.

The work of technology professionals is critical to successful technology implementations that lead to improved student achievement. Without the presence of well-prepared, capable educational technology professionals to shape the future of K–12 technology integration, we cannot meet the learning goals established in our national, state, district, and school-level improvement plans. As we have illustrated, the TF/TL standards offer a foundation and rationale for the professionalization of technology facilitators and leaders, but the work has only begun.

The following represent some practical "next steps" toward fully leveraging the potential of the TF/TL standards:

- Study the standards documents and supporting rubrics.

- Provide the standards to key stakeholders and brief them on their importance.

- Use the standards to recruit and mentor aspiring technology facilitators and leaders.

- Ensure that local universities are implementing standards-based programs that produce strong technology facilitators and leaders.

- Use the standards to reflect on current levels of technology leadership and facilitation positions in your school, district, or region.

- Use the standards to reflect on your current practice and seek professional learning opportunities in areas that would strengthen your performance.

- Identify areas where standards are weak in your organization, and design strategies, including professional learning programs, to address the gaps.

- Review and revise local job descriptions based on the standards.

- Develop evaluation tools and other job performance documents for technology facilitators and leaders.

- Communicate the results of your standards-based needs assessment to foster needed change.

- Participate in the ongoing professional dialogue about what the TF/TL standards are and what they should be. As with any other educational role, technology professionals need a strong set of professional standards to guide and validate their work.

Reference

Frazier, M., & Bailey, G. (2004). *The technology coordinator's handbook*. Eugene, OR: ISTE.

Appendix A

The TF Standards

Technology Facilitation Standard I. (TF-I)

Technology Operations and Concepts. Educational technology facilitators demonstrate an in-depth understanding of technology operations and concepts.

Educational technology facilitators:

TF-I.A. Demonstrate knowledge, skills, and understanding of concepts related to technology (as described in the ISTE National Educational Technology Standards for Teachers).

Candidates:

1. Assist teachers in the ongoing development of knowledge, skills, and understanding of technology systems, resources, and services that are aligned with district and state technology plans.

2. Provide assistance to teachers in identifying technology systems, resources, and services to meet specific learning needs.

TF-I.B. Demonstrate continual growth in technology knowledge and skills to stay abreast of current and emerging technologies.

Candidates:

1. Model appropriate strategies essential to continued growth and development of the understanding of technology operations and concepts.

Technology Facilitation Standard II. (TF-II)

Planning and Designing Learning Environments and Experiences. Educational technology facilitators plan, design, and model effective learning environments and multiple experiences supported by technology.

Educational technology facilitators:

TF-II.A. Design developmentally appropriate learning opportunities that apply technology-enhanced instructional strategies to support the diverse needs of learners.

Candidates:

1. Provide resources and feedback to teachers as they create developmentally appropriate curriculum units that use technology.

2. Consult with teachers as they design methods and strategies for teaching computer/technology concepts and skills within the context of classroom learning.

3. Assist teachers as they use technology resources and strategies to support the diverse needs of learners including adaptive and assistive technologies.

TF-II.B. Apply current research on teaching and learning with technology when planning learning environments and experiences.

Candidates:

1. Assist teachers as they apply current research on teaching and learning with technology when planning learning environments and experiences.

TF-II.C. Identify and locate technology resources and evaluate them for accuracy and suitability.

Candidates:

1. Assist teachers as they identify and locate technology resources and evaluate them for accuracy and suitability based on district and state standards.

2. Model technology integration using resources that reflect content standards.

TF-II.D. Plan for the management of technology resources within the context of learning activities.

Candidates:

1. Provide teachers with options for the management of technology resources within the context of learning activities.

TF-II.E. Plan strategies to manage student learning in a technology-enhanced environment.

Candidates:

1. Provide teachers with a variety of strategies to use to manage student learning in a technology-enhanced environment and support them as they implement the strategies.

TF-II.F. Identify and apply instructional design principles associated with the development of technology resources.

Candidates:

1. Assist teachers as they identify and apply instructional design principles associated with the development of technology resources.

Technology Facilitation Standard III. (TF-III)

Teaching, Learning, and the Curriculum. Educational technology facilitators apply and implement curriculum plans that include methods and strategies for utilizing technology to maximize student learning.

Educational technology facilitators:

TF-III.A. Facilitate technology-enhanced experiences that address content standards and student technology standards.

Candidates:

1. Use methods and strategies for teaching concepts and skills that support integration of technology productivity tools (refer to NETS for Students).

2. Use and apply major research findings and trends related to the use of technology in education to support integration throughout the curriculum.

3. Use methods and strategies for teaching concepts and skills that support integration of research tools (refer to NETS for Students).

4. Use methods and strategies for teaching concepts and skills that support integration of problem solving/decision-making tools (refer to NETS for Students).

5. Use methods and strategies for teaching concepts and skills that support use of media-based tools such as television, audio, print media, and graphics.

6. Use and describe methods and strategies for teaching concepts and skills that support use of distance learning systems appropriate in a school environment.

7. Use methods for teaching concepts and skills that support use of Web-based and non Web-based authoring tools in a school environment.

TF-III.B. Use technology to support learner-centered strategies that address the diverse needs of students.

Candidates:

1. Use methods and strategies for integrating technology resources that support the needs of diverse learners including adaptive and assistive technology.

TF-III.C. Apply technology to demonstrate students' higher-order skills and creativity.

Candidates:

1. Use methods and facilitate strategies for teaching problem-solving principles and skills using technology resources.

TF-III.D. Manage student learning activities in a technology-enhanced environment.

Candidates:

1. Use methods and classroom management strategies for teaching technology concepts and skills in individual, small group, classroom, and/or lab settings.

TF-III.E. Use current research and district/regional/state/national content and technology standards to build lessons and units of instruction.

Candidates:

1. Describe and identify curricular methods and strategies that are aligned with district/regional/state/national content and technology standards.

2. Use major research findings and trends related to the use of technology in education to support integration throughout the curriculum.

Technology Facilitation Standard IV. (TF-IV)

Assessment and Evaluation. Educational technology facilitators apply technology to facilitate a variety of effective assessment and evaluation strategies.

Educational technology facilitators:

TF-IV.A. Apply technology in assessing student learning of subject matter using a variety of assessment techniques.

Candidates:

1. Model the use of technology tools to assess student learning of subject matter using a variety of assessment techniques.

2. Assist teachers in using technology to improve learning and instruction through the evaluation and assessment of artifacts and data. [Note: Today, samples of candidates' work are called assessments. In the past, they were called artifacts.]

TF-IV.B. Use technology resources to collect and analyze data, interpret results, and communicate findings to improve instructional practice and maximize student learning.

Candidates:

1. Guide teachers as they use technology resources to collect and analyze data, interpret results, and communicate findings to improve instructional practice and maximize student learning.

TF-IV.C. Apply multiple methods of evaluation to determine students' appropriate use of technology resources for learning, communication, and productivity.

Candidates:

1. Assist teachers in using recommended evaluation strategies for improving students' use of technology resources for learning, communication, and productivity.

2. Examine and apply the results of a research project that includes evaluating the use of a specific technology in a P–12 environment.

Technology Facilitation Standard V. (TF-V)

Productivity and Professional Practice. Educational technology facilitators apply technology to enhance and improve personal productivity and professional practice.

Educational technology facilitators:

TF-V.A. Use technology resources to engage in ongoing professional development and lifelong learning.

Candidates:

1. Identify resources and participate in professional development activities and professional technology organizations to support ongoing professional growth related to technology.

2. Disseminate information on district-wide policies for the professional growth opportunities for staff, faculty, and administrators.

TF-V.B. Continually evaluate and reflect on professional practice to make informed decisions regarding the use of technology in support of student learning.

Candidates:

1. Continually evaluate and reflect on professional practice to make informed decisions regarding the use of technology in support of student learning.

TF-V.C. Apply technology to increase productivity.

Candidates:

1. Model advanced features of word processing, desktop publishing, graphics programs, and utilities to develop professional products.

2. Assist others in locating, selecting, capturing, and integrating video and digital images in varying formats for use in presentations, publications and/or other products.

3. Demonstrate the use of specific-purpose electronic devices (such as graphing calculators, language translators, scientific probeware, or electronic thesaurus) in content areas.

4. Use a variety of distance learning systems and use at least one to support personal/professional development.

5. Use instructional design principles to develop hypermedia and multimedia products to support personal and professional development.

6. Select appropriate tools for communicating concepts, conducting research, and solving problems for an intended audience and purpose.

7. Use examples of emerging programming, authoring or problem-solving environments that support personal/professional development.

8. Set and manipulate preferences, defaults, and other selectable features of operating systems and productivity tool programs commonly found in P–12 schools.

TF-V.D. Use technology to communicate and collaborate with peers, parents, and the larger community in order to nurture student learning.

Candidates:

1. Model the use of telecommunications tools and resources for information sharing, remote information access, and multimedia/hypermedia publishing in order to nurture student learning.

2. Communicate with colleagues and discuss current research to support instruction, using applications including electronic mail, online conferencing, and Web browsers.

3. Participate in online collaborative curricular projects and team activities to build bodies of knowledge around specific topics.

4. Design, develop, and maintain Web pages and sites that support communication between the school and community.

Technology Facilitation Standard VI. (TF-VI)

Social, Ethical, Legal, and Human Issues. Educational technology facilitators understand the social, ethical, legal, and human issues surrounding the use of technology in P–12 schools and assist teachers in applying that understanding in their practice.

Educational technology facilitators:

TF-VI.A. Model and teach legal and ethical practice related to technology use.

Candidates:

1. Develop strategies and provide professional development at the school/classroom level for teaching social, ethical, and legal issues and responsible use of technology.

2. Assist others in summarizing copyright laws related to use of images, music, video, and other digital resources in varying formats.

TF-VI.B. Apply technology resources to enable and empower learners with diverse backgrounds, characteristics, and abilities.

Candidates:

1. Assist teachers in selecting and applying appropriate technology resources to enable and empower learners with diverse backgrounds, characteristics, and abilities.

2. Identify, classify, and recommend adaptive/assistive hardware and software for students and teachers with special needs and assist in procurement and implementation.

TF-VI.C. Identify and use technology resources that affirm diversity.

Candidates:

1. Assist teachers in selecting and applying appropriate technology resources to affirm diversity and address cultural and language differences.

TF-VI.D. Promote safe and healthy use of technology resources.

Candidates:

1. Assist teachers in selecting and applying appropriate technology resources to promote safe and healthy use of technology.

TF-VI.E. Facilitate equitable access to technology resources for all students.

Candidates:

1. Recommend policies and implement school/classroom strategies for achieving equitable access to technology resources for all students and teachers.

Technology Facilitation Standard VII. (TF-VII)

Procedures, Policies, Planning, and Budgeting for Technology Environments. Educational technology facilitators promote the development and implementation of technology infrastructure, procedures, policies, plans, and budgets for P–12 schools.

Educational technology facilitators:

TF-VII.A. Use the school technology facilities and resources to implement classroom instruction.

Candidates:

1. Use plans to configure software/computer/technology systems and related peripherals in laboratory, classroom cluster, and other appropriate instructional arrangements.

2. Use local mass storage devices and media to store and retrieve information and resources.

3. Discuss issues related to selecting, installing, and maintaining wide area networks (WAN) for school districts.

4. Model integration of software used in classroom and administrative settings including productivity tools, information access/telecommunication tools, multimedia/hypermedia tools, school management tools, evaluation/portfolio tools, and computer-based instruction.

5. Utilize methods of installation, maintenance, inventory, and management of software libraries.

6. Use and apply strategies for troubleshooting and maintaining various hardware/ software configurations found in school settings.

7. Use network software packages to operate a computer network system.

8. Work with technology support personnel to maximize the use of technology resources by administrators, teachers, and students to improve student learning.

TF-VII.B. Follow procedures and guidelines used in planning and purchasing technology resources.

Candidates:

1. Identify instructional software to support and enhance the school curriculum and develop recommendations for purchase.

2. Discuss and apply guidelines for budget planning and management procedures related to educational computing and technology facilities and resources.

3. Discuss and apply procedures related to troubleshooting and preventive maintenance of technology infrastructure.

4. Apply current information involving facilities planning issues and computer-related technologies.

5. Suggest policies and procedures concerning staging, scheduling, and security for managing computers/technology in a variety of school/laboratory/classroom settings.

6. Use distance and online learning facilities.

7. Describe and identify recommended specifications for purchasing technology systems in school settings.

TF-VII.C. Participate in professional development opportunities related to management of school facilities, technology resources, and purchases.

Candidates:

1. Support technology professional development at the building/school level utilizing adult learning theory.

Technology Facilitation Standard VIII. (TF-VIII)

Leadership and Vision. Educational technology facilitators will contribute to the shared vision for campus integration of technology and foster an environment and culture conducive to the realization of the vision.

Educational technology facilitators:

TF-VIII.A. Use the school technology facilities and resources to implement classroom instruction.

Candidates:

1. Discuss and evaluate current research in educational technology.

TF-VIII.B. Apply strategies for and knowledge of issues related to managing the change process in schools.

Candidates:

1. Discuss the history of technology use in schools.

TF-VIII.C. Apply effective group process skills.

Candidates:

1. Discuss the rationale for forming school partnerships to support technology integration and examine an existing partnership within a school setting.

TF-VIII.D. Lead in the development and evaluation of district technology planning and implementation.

Candidates:

1. Participate in cooperative group processes and identify the processes that were effective.

2. Conduct an evaluation of a school technology environment.

3. Identify and discuss national, state, and local standards for integrating technology in the school environment.

4. Describe curriculum activities or performances that meet national, state, and local technology standards.

5. Discuss issues related to developing a school technology plan.

6. Discuss the elements of and strategies for developing a technology strategic plan.

7. Examine issues related to hardware and software acquisition and management.

TF-VIII.E. Engage in supervised field-based experiences with accomplished technology facilitators and/or directors.

Candidates:

1. Examine components needed for effective field-based experiences in instructional program development, professional development, facility and resource management, WAN/LAN/wireless systems, or managing change related to technology use in school-based settings.

Appendix B

The TL Standards

Technology Leadership Standard I. (TL-I)

Technology Operations and Concepts. Educational technology leaders demonstrate an advanced understanding of technology operations and concepts.

Educational technology leaders:

TL-I.A. Demonstrate knowledge, skills, and understanding of concepts related to technology (as described in the ISTE National Educational Technology Standards for Teachers).

Candidates:

1. Identify and evaluate components needed for the continual growth of knowledge, skills, and understanding of concepts related to technology.

2. Offer a variety of professional development opportunities that facilitate the ongoing development of knowledge, skills, and understanding of concepts related to technology.

TL-I.B. Demonstrate continual growth in technology knowledge and skills to stay abreast of current and emerging technologies.

Candidates:

1. Offer a variety of professional development opportunities that facilitate the continued growth and development of the understanding of technology operations and concepts.

Technology Leadership Standard II. (TL-II)

Planning and Designing Learning Environments and Experiences. Educational technology leaders plan, design, and model effective learning environments and multiple experiences supported by technology.

Educational technology leaders:

TL-II.A. Design developmentally appropriate learning opportunities that apply technology-enhanced instructional strategies to support the diverse needs of learners.

Candidates:

1. Research and disseminate project-based instructional units modeling appropriate uses of technology to support learning.

2. Identify and evaluate methods and strategies for teaching computer/technology concepts and skills within the context of classroom learning and coordinate dissemination of best practices at the district/state/regional level.

3. Stay abreast of current technology resources and strategies to support the diverse needs of learners including adaptive and assistive technologies and disseminate information to teachers.

TL-II.B. Apply current research on teaching and learning with technology when planning learning environments and experiences.

Candidates:

1. Locate and evaluate current research on teaching and learning with technology when planning learning environments and experiences.

TL-II.C. Identify and locate technology resources and evaluate them for accuracy and suitability.

Candidates:

1. Identify technology resources and evaluate them for accuracy and suitability based on the content standards.

2. Provide ongoing appropriate professional development to disseminate the use of technology resources that reflect content standards.

TL-II.D. Plan for the management of technology resources within the context of learning activities.

Candidates:

1. Identify and evaluate options for the management of technology resources within the context of learning activities.

TL-II.E. Plan strategies to manage student learning in a technology-enhanced environment.

Candidates:

1. Continually evaluate a variety of strategies to manage student learning in a technology-enhanced environment and disseminate through professional development activities.

TL-II.F. Identify and apply instructional design principles associated with the development of technology resources.

Candidates:

1. Identify and evaluate instructional design principles associated with the development of technology resources.

Technology Leadership Standard III. (TL-III)

Teaching, Learning, and the Curriculum. Educational technology leaders model, design, and disseminate curriculum plans that include methods and strategies for applying technology to maximize student learning.

Educational technology leaders:

TL-III.A. Facilitate technology-enhanced experiences that address content standards and student technology standards.

Candidates:

1. Design methods and strategies for teaching concepts and skills that support integration of technology productivity tools (refer to NETS for Students).

2. Design methods for teaching concepts and skills that support integration of communication tools (refer to NETS for Students).

3. Design methods and strategies for teaching concepts and skills that support integration of research tools (refer to NETS for Students).

4. Design methods and model strategies for teaching concepts and skills that support integration of problem-solving/decision-making tools (refer to NETS for Students).

5. Design methods and model strategies for teaching concepts and skills that support use of media-based tools such as television, audio, print media, and graphics.

6. Evaluate methods and strategies for teaching concepts and skills that support use of distance learning systems appropriate in a school environment.

7. Design methods and model strategies for teaching concepts and skills that support use of Web-based and non Web-based authoring tools in a school environment.

TL-III.B. Use technology to support learner-centered strategies that address the diverse needs of students.

Candidates:

1. Design methods and strategies for integrating technology resources that support the needs of diverse learners, including adaptive and assistive technology.

TL-III.C. Apply technology to demonstrate students' higher-order skills and creativity.

Candidates:

1. Design methods and model strategies for teaching hypermedia development, scripting, and/or computer programming, in a problem-solving context in the school environment.

TL-III.D. Manage student learning activities in a technology-enhanced environment.

Candidates:

1. Design methods and model classroom management strategies for teaching technology concepts and skills used in P–12 environments.

TL-III.E. Use current research and district/state/national content and technology standards to build lessons and units of instruction.

Candidates:

1. Disseminate curricular methods and strategies that are aligned with district/regional/state/national content and technology standards.

2. Investigate major research findings and trends relative to the use of technology in education to support integration throughout the curriculum.

Technology Leadership Standard IV. (TL-IV)

Assessment and Evaluation. Educational technology leaders communicate research on the use of technology to implement effective assessment and evaluation strategies.

Educational technology leaders:

TL-IV.A. Apply technology in assessing student learning of subject matter using a variety of assessment techniques.

Candidates:

1. Facilitate the development of a variety of techniques to use technology to assess student learning of subject matter.

2. Provide technology resources for assessment and evaluation of artifacts and data.

TL-IV.B. Use technology resources to collect and analyze data, interpret results, and communicate findings to improve instructional practice and maximize student learning.

Candidates:

1. Identify and procure technology resources to aid in analysis and interpretation of data.

TL-IV.C. Apply multiple methods of evaluation to determine students' appropriate use of technology resources for learning, communication, and productivity.

Candidates:

1. Design strategies and methods for evaluating the effectiveness of technology resources for learning, communication, and productivity.

2. Conduct a research project that includes evaluating the use of a specific technology in P–12 environments.

Technology Leadership Standard V. (TL-V)

Productivity and Professional Practice. Educational technology leaders design, develop, evaluate and model products created using technology resources to improve and enhance their productivity and professional practice.

Educational technology leaders:

TL-V.A. Use technology resources to engage in ongoing professional development and lifelong learning.

Candidates:

1. Design, prepare, and conduct professional development activities to present at the school/district level and at professional technology conferences to support ongoing professional growth related to technology.

2. Plan and implement policies that support district-wide professional growth opportunities for staff, faculty, and administrators.

TL-V.B. Continually evaluate and reflect on professional practice to make informed decisions regarding the use of technology in support of student learning.

Candidates:

1. Based on evaluations make recommendations for changes in professional practices regarding the use of technology in support of student learning.

TL-V.C. Apply technology to increase productivity.

Candidates:

1. Model the integration of data from multiple software applications using advanced features of applications such as word processing, database, spreadsheet, communication, and other tools into a product.

2. Create multimedia presentations integrated with multiple types of data using advanced features of a presentation tool and model them to district staff using computer projection systems.

3. Document and assess field-based experiences and observations using specific-purpose electronic devices.

4. Use distance learning delivery systems to conduct and provide professional development opportunities for students, teachers, administrators, and staff.

5. Apply instructional design principles to develop and analyze substantive interactive multimedia computer-based instructional products.

6. Design and practice strategies for testing functions and evaluating technology use effectiveness of instructional products that were developed using multiple technology tools.

7. Analyze examples of emerging programming, authoring or problem-solving environments that support personal and professional development, and make recommendations for integration at school/district level.

8. Analyze and modify the features and preferences of major operating systems and/or productivity tool programs when developing products to solve problems.

TL-V.D. Use technology to communicate and collaborate with peers, parents, and the larger community in order to nurture student learning.

Candidates:

1. Model and implement the use of telecommunications tools and resources to foster and support information sharing, remote information access, and communication between students, school staff, parents, and local community.

2. Organize, coordinate, and participate in an online learning community related to the use of technology to support learning.

3. Organize and coordinate online collaborative curricular projects with corresponding team activities/responsibilities to build bodies of knowledge around specific topics.

4. Design, modify, maintain, and facilitate the development of Web pages and sites that support communication and information access between the entire school district and local/state/national/international communities.

Technology Leadership Standard VI. (TL-VI)

Social, Ethical, Legal, and Human Issues. Educational technology leaders understand the social, ethical, legal, and human issues surrounding the use of technology in P–12 schools and develop programs facilitating application of that understanding in practice throughout their district/region/state.

Educational technology leaders:

TL-VI.A. Model and teach legal and ethical practice related to technology use.

Candidates:

1. Establish and communicate clear rules, policies, and procedures to support legal and ethical use of technologies at the district/regional/state levels.

2. Implement a plan for documenting adherence to copyright laws.

TL-VI.B. Apply technology resources to enable and empower learners with diverse backgrounds, characteristics, and abilities.

Candidates:

1. Communicate research on best practices related to applying appropriate technology resources to enable and empower learners with diverse backgrounds, characteristics, and abilities.

2. Develop policies and provide professional development related to acquisition and use of appropriate adaptive/assistive hardware and software for students and teachers with special needs.

TL-VI.C. Identify and use technology resources that affirm diversity.

Candidates:

1. Communicate research on best practices related to applying appropriate technology resources to affirm diversity and address cultural and language differences.

TL-VI.D. Promote safe and healthy use of technology resources.

Candidates:

1. Communicate research and establish policies to promote safe and healthy use of technology.

TL-VI.E. Facilitate equitable access to technology resources for all students.

Candidates:

1. Use research findings in establishing policy and implementation strategies to promote equitable access to technology resources for students and teachers.

Technology Leadership Standard VII. (TL-VII)

Procedures, Policies, Planning, and Budgeting for Technology Environments. Educational technology leaders coordinate development and direct implementation of technology infrastructure procedures, policies, plans, and budgets for P–12 schools.

Educational technology leaders:

TL-VII.A. Use the school technology facilities and resources to implement classroom instruction.

Candidates:

1. Develop plans to configure software/computer/technology systems and related peripherals in laboratory, classroom cluster, and other appropriate instructional arrangements.

2. Install local mass storage devices and media to store and retrieve information and resources.

3. Prioritize issues related to selecting, installing, and maintaining wide area networks (WAN) for school districts, and facilitate integration of technology infrastructure with the WAN.

4. Manage software used in classroom and administrative settings, including productivity tools, information access/telecommunication tools, multimedia/hypermedia tools, school management tools, evaluation/portfolio tools, and computer-based instruction.

5. Evaluate methods of installation, maintenance, inventory, and management of software libraries.

6. Develop and disseminate strategies for troubleshooting and maintaining various hardware/software configurations found in school settings.

7. Select network software packages for operating a computer network system and/or local area network (LAN).

8. Analyze needs for technology support personnel to manage school/district technology resources and maximize use by administrators, teachers, and students to improve student learning.

TL-VII.B. Follow procedures and guidelines used in planning and purchasing technology resources.

Candidates:

1. Investigate purchasing strategies and procedures for acquiring administrative and instructional software for educational settings.

2. Develop and utilize guidelines for budget planning and management procedures related to educational computing and technology facilities and resources.

3. Develop and disseminate a system for analyzing and implementing procedures related to troubleshooting and preventive maintenance on technology infrastructure.

4. Maintain and disseminate current information involving facilities planning issues and computer-related technologies.

5. Design and develop policies and procedures concerning staging, scheduling, and security for managing hardware, software, and related technologies in a variety of instructional and administrative school settings.

6. Research and recommend systems and processes for implementation of distance learning facilities and infrastructure.

7. Differentiate among specifications for purchasing technology systems in school settings.

TL-VII.C. Participate in professional development opportunities related to management of school facilities, technology resources, and purchases.

Candidates:

1. Implement technology professional development at the school/district level utilizing adult learning theory.

Technology Leadership Standard VIII. (TL-VIII)

Leadership and Vision. Educational technology leaders will facilitate development of a shared vision for comprehensive integration of technology and foster an environment and culture conducive to the realization of the vision.

Educational technology leaders:

TL-VIII.A. Identify and apply educational and technology-related research, the psychology of learning, and instructional design principles in guiding the use of computers and technology in education.

Candidates:

1. Communicate and apply principles and practices of educational research in educational technology.

TL-VIII.B. Apply strategies for and knowledge of issues related to managing the change process in schools.

Candidates:

1. Describe social/historical foundations of education and how they relate to use of technology in schools.

TL-VIII.C. Apply effective group process skills.

Candidates:

1. Discuss issues relating to building collaborations, alliances, and partnerships involving educational technology initiatives.

TL-VIII.D. Lead in the development and evaluation of district technology planning and implementation.

Candidates:

1. Design and lead in the implementation of effective group process related to technology leadership or planning.

2. Use evaluation findings to recommend modifications in technology implementations.

3. Use national, state, and local standards to develop curriculum plans for integrating technology in the school environment.

4. Develop curriculum activities or performances that meet national, state, and local technology standards.

5. Compare and evaluate district-level technology plans.

6. Use strategic planning principles to lead and assist in the acquisition, implementation, and maintenance of technology resources.

7. Plan, develop, and implement strategies and procedures for resource acquisition and management of technology-based systems, including hardware and software.

TL-VIII.E. Engage in supervised field-based experiences with accomplished technology facilitators and/or directors.

Candidates:

1. Participate in a significant field-based activity involving experiences in instructional program development, professional development, facility and resource management, WAN/LAN/wireless systems, or managing change related to technology use in school-based settings.

Appendix C

Technology Facilitation and Leadership Scoring Rubrics

Technology Facilitation (TF) Standards and Rubrics

Supporting Explanation

Units preparing candidates for this program may collect artifacts demonstrating candidates' performances in addressing the program standards, assess performance by evaluating artifacts (i.e., samples of work; also called assessments) using the above ISTE/ NCATE Technology Facilitation Rubrics and aggregate the performance data collected to provide program-level data. The standards and rubrics should help faculty to identify the kinds of experiences they provide in their courses and whether or not those experiences generate candidate performance that approaches, meets, or exceeds the standards. Each major assignment or experience should be planned to address the performance indicators at levels appropriate to prepare candidates for the essential benchmark assessments. Candidates should be aware of the level of expectations for their performance on each assignment and that their performances will be measured against the "meets standard" performance level of the rubric.

Rubrics, observation tools, self assessments, and test scores with quantifiable performance assessment ratings are often used to collect performance data that can be used to measure individual performance and be aggregated as evidence of program-level performance. When artifacts are collected in a portfolio, it is preferred to have that portfolio available for online review to substantiate the quality of work of your candidates. The performance artifacts used as evidence in the matrix should be selective, representing benchmark assessment points.

Technology Facilitation Scoring Rubrics

Technology Facilitation Standard I. (TF-I)

Technology Operations and Concepts. Educational technology facilitators demonstrate an in-depth understanding of technology operations and concepts. Educational technology facilitators:

Performance Indicator	Approaches Standard	Meets Standard	Exceeds Standard
A. Demonstrate knowledge, skills, and understanding of concepts related to technology (as described in the ISTE National Educational Technology Standards for Teachers). Candidates:			
TF-I.A.1	Make appropriate choices about technology systems, resources, and services that are aligned with district and state standards.	Assist teachers in the ongoing development of knowledge, skills, and understanding of technology systems, resources, and services that are aligned with district and state technology plans.	Conduct needs assessment to determine baseline data on teachers' knowledge, skills, and understanding of concepts related to technology.
TF-I.A.2	Demonstrate an awareness of knowledge and skills related to technology concepts.	Provide assistance to teachers in identifying technology systems, resources, and services to meet specific learning needs.	Evaluate the effectiveness of modeling used to demonstrate teachers' knowledge, skills, and understanding of concepts related to technology.
B. Demonstrate continual growth in technology knowledge and skills to stay abreast of current and emerging technologies. Candidates:			
TF-I.B.1	Identify capabilities and limitations of current and emerging technology resources and assess the potential of these systems and services to address personal, lifelong learning, and workplace needs.	Model appropriate strategies essential to continued growth and development of the understanding of technology operations and concepts.	Evaluate the effectiveness of modeling appropriate strategies essential to continued growth and development of the understanding of technology operations and concepts.

Technology Facilitation Standard II. (TF-II)

Planning and Designing Learning Environments and Experiences. Educational technology facilitators plan, design, and model effective learning environments and multiple experiences supported by technology. Educational technology facilitators:

Performance Indicator	Approaches Standard	Meets Standard	Exceeds Standard
A. Design developmentally appropriate learning opportunities that apply technology-enhanced instructional strategies to support the diverse needs of learners. Candidates:			
TF-II.A.1	Arrange equitable access to appropriate technology resources that enable students to engage successfully in learning activities across subject/content areas and grade levels.	Provide resources and feedback to teachers as they create developmentally appropriate curriculum units that use technology.	Model the creation of developmentally appropriate curriculum units that use technology.
TF-II.A.2	Plan for, implement, and evaluate the management of student use of technology resources to support the diverse needs of learners including adaptive and assistive technologies.	Consult with teachers as they design methods and strategies for teaching computer/ technology concepts and skills within the context of classroom learning.	Model methods and strategies for teaching computer/ technology concepts and skills within the context of classroom learning.
TF-II.A.3	Demonstrate an awareness of technology resources and strategies to support the diverse needs of learners including adaptive and assistive technologies.	Assist teachers as they use technology resources and strategies to support the diverse needs of learners including adaptive and assistive technologies.	Model strategies to support the diverse needs of learners including adaptive and assistive technologies and disseminate information to teachers.
B. Apply current research on teaching and learning with technology when planning learning environments and experiences. Candidates:			
TF-II.B.1	Engage in ongoing planning of lesson sequences that effectively integrate technology resources and are consistent with current best practices for integrating the learning of subject matter and student technology standards.	Assist teachers as they apply current research on teaching and learning with technology when planning learning environments and experiences.	Model strategies reflecting current research on teaching and learning with technology when planning learning environments and experiences.

C. Identify and locate technology resources and evaluate them for accuracy and suitability. Candidates:

TF-II.C.1	Demonstrate an awareness of technology systems, resources, and services that are aligned with district and state standards.	Assist teachers as they identify and locate technology resources and evaluate them for accuracy and suitability based on district and state standards.	Model the use of technology resources reflecting district and state standards.
TF-II.C.2	Make appropriate choices about technology systems, resources, and services that are aligned with district and state standards.	Model technology integration using resources that reflect content standards.	Create professional development lessons integrating technology resources that reflect content standards.

D. Plan for the management of technology resources within the context of learning activities. Candidates:

TF-II.D.1	Engage in ongoing planning of lesson sequences that ensure the management of technology resources within the context of learning activities.	Provide teachers with options for the management of technology resources within the context of learning activities.	Model the use of technology resources within the context of learning activities.

E. Plan strategies to manage student learning in a technology-enhanced environment. Candidates:

TF-II.E.1	Engage in ongoing planning of lesson sequences that manage student learning in a technology-enhanced environment.	Provide teachers with a variety of strategies to use to manage student learning in a technology-enhanced environment and support them as they implement the strategies.	Model a variety of strategies to manage student learning in a technology-enhanced environment and support the teachers as they implement the strategies.

F. Identify and apply instructional design principles associated with the development of technology resources. Candidates:

TF-II.F.1	Plan and implement technology-based learning activities that include an understanding of instructional design principles.	Assist teachers as they identify and apply instructional design principles associated with the development of technology resources.	Model the use of appropriate instructional design principles associated with the development of technology resources.

Technology Facilitation Standard III. (TF-III)

Teaching, Learning, and the Curriculum. Educational technology facilitators apply and implement curriculum plans that include methods and strategies for utilizing technology to maximize student learning. Educational technology facilitators:

Performance Indicator	Approaches Standard	Meets Standard	Exceeds Standard
A. Facilitate technology-enhanced experiences that address content standards and student technology standards. Candidates:			
TF-III.A.1	Demonstrate an awareness of methods and strategies for teaching concepts and skills that support integration of technology productivity tools (refer to NETS for Students).	Use methods and strategies for teaching concepts and skills that support integration of technology productivity tools (refer to NETS for Students).	Analyze methods and facilitate strategies for teaching concepts and skills that support integration of technology productivity tools (refer to NETS for Students).
TF-III.A.2	Demonstrate an awareness of methods and strategies for teaching concepts and skills that support integration of communication tools (refer to NETS for Students).	Use and apply major research findings and trends related to the use of technology in education to support integration throughout the curriculum.	Summarize major research findings and trends related to the use of technology in education to support integration throughout the curriculum.
TF-III.A.3	Demonstrate an awareness of methods and strategies for teaching concepts and skills that support integration of research tools (refer to NETS for Students).	Use methods and strategies for teaching concepts and skills that support integration of research tools (refer to NETS for Students).	Analyze methods and facilitate teachers as they use strategies for teaching concepts and skills that support integration of research tools (refer to NETS for Students).
TF-III.A.4	Demonstrate an awareness of methods and strategies for teaching concepts and skills that support integration of problem-solving/decision-making tools (refer to NETS for Students).	Use methods and strategies for teaching concepts and skills that support integration of problem-solving/decision-making tools (refer to NETS for Students).	Analyze methods and facilitate strategies for teaching concepts and skills that support integration of problem-solving/decision-making tools (refer to NETS for Students).
TF-III.A.5	Demonstrate an awareness of methods and strategies for teaching concepts and skills that support use of media-based tools such as television, audio, print media, and graphics.	Use methods and strategies for teaching concepts and skills that support use of media-based tools such as television, audio, print media, and graphics.	Analyze methods and facilitate strategies for teaching concepts and skills that support use of media-based tools such as television, audio, print media, and graphics.

TF-III.A.6	Demonstrate an awareness of methods and strategies for teaching concepts and skills that support use of distance learning systems appropriate in a school environment.	Use and describe methods and strategies for teaching concepts and skills that support use of distance learning systems appropriate in a school environment.	Analyze methods and strategies for teaching concepts and skills that support use of distance learning systems appropriate in a school environment.
TF-III.A.7	Demonstrate an awareness of methods for teaching concepts and skills that support use of Web-based and non Web-based authoring tools in a school environment.	Use methods for teaching concepts and skills that support use of Web-based and non Web-based authoring tools in a school environment.	Analyze methods for teaching concepts and skills that support use of Web-based and non Web-based authoring tools in a school environment.

B. Use technology to support learner-centered strategies that address the diverse needs of students. Candidates:

TF-III.B.1	Demonstrate an awareness of methods and strategies for integrating technology resources that support the needs of diverse learners including adaptive and assistive technology.	Use methods and strategies for integrating technology resources that support the needs of diverse learners including adaptive and assistive technology.	Analyze methods and strategies for integrating technology resources that support the needs of diverse learners including adaptive and assistive technology.

C. Apply technology to demonstrate students' higher-order skills and creativity. Candidates:

TF-III.C.1	Demonstrate an awareness of methods and strategies for teaching problem-solving principles and skills using technology resources.	Use methods and facilitate strategies for teaching problem-solving principles and skills using technology resources.	Analyze methods and facilitate strategies for teaching problem-solving principles and skills using technology resources.

D. Manage student learning activities in a technology-enhanced environment. Candidates:

TF-III.D.1	Develop an awareness of methods and classroom management strategies for teaching technology concepts and skills in individual, small group, classroom, and/or lab settings.	Use methods and classroom management strategies for teaching technology concepts and skills in individual, small group, classroom, and/or lab settings.	Analyze methods and classroom management strategies for teaching technology concepts and skills in individual, small group, classroom, and/or lab settings.

E. Use current research and district/region/state/national content and technology standards to build lessons and units of instruction. Candidates:

TF-III.E.1	Develop an awareness of curricular methods and strategies that are aligned with district/region/state/national content and technology standards.	Describe and identify curricular methods and strategies that are aligned with district/region/state/national content and technology standards.	Disseminate information regarding curricular methods and strategies that are aligned with district/region/state/national content and technology standards.
TF-III.E.2	Develop an awareness of major research findings and trends related to the use of technology in education to support integration throughout the curriculum.	Use major research findings and trends related to the use of technology in education to support integration throughout the curriculum.	Summarize and disseminate major research findings and trends related to the use of technology in education to support integration throughout the curriculum.

Technology Facilitation Standard IV. (TF-IV)

Assessment and Evaluation. Educational technology facilitators apply technology to facilitate a variety of effective assessment and evaluation strategies. Educational technology facilitators:

Performance Indicator	Approaches Standard	Meets Standard	Exceeds Standard
A. Apply technology in assessing student learning of subject matter using a variety of assessment techniques. Candidates:			
TF-IV.A.1	Develop an awareness of technology tools to collect, analyze, interpret, represent, and communicate data for the purposes of instructional planning and school improvement.	Model the use of technology tools to assess student learning of subject matter using a variety of assessment techniques.	Analyze methods and facilitate the use of strategies to assess student learning of subject matter using a variety of assessment techniques.
TF-IV.A.2	Use results from assessment measures to improve instructional planning, management, and implementation of learning strategies.	Assist teachers in using technology to improve learning and instruction through the evaluation and assessment of artifacts and data.	Analyze methods and facilitate the use of strategies to improve learning and instruction through the evaluation and assessment of artifacts and data.
B. Use technology resources to collect and analyze data, interpret results, and communicate findings to improve instructional practice and maximize student learning. Candidates:			
TF-IV.B.1	Implement a variety of instructional technology strategies and grouping strategies that include appropriate embedded assessment for meeting the diverse needs of learners.	Guide teachers as they use technology resources to collect and analyze data, interpret results, and communicate findings to improve instructional practice and maximize student learning.	Examine the validity and reliability of technology resources to collect and analyze data, interpret results, and communicate findings to improve instructional practice and maximize student learning.
C. Apply multiple methods of evaluation to determine students' appropriate use of technology resources for learning, communication, and productivity. Candidates:			
TF-IV.C.1	Guide students in applying self- and peer-assessment tools to critique student-created technology products and the process used to create the products.	Assist teachers in using recommended evaluation strategies for improving students' use of technology resources for learning, communication, and productivity.	Recommend evaluation strategies for improving students' use of technology resources for learning, communication, and productivity.

Technology Facilitation Standard V. (TF-V)

Productivity and Professional Practice. Educational technology facilitators apply technology to enhance and improve personal productivity and professional practice. Educational technology facilitators:

Performance Indicator	Approaches Standard	Meets Standard	Exceeds Standard
A. Use technology resources to engage in ongoing professional development and lifelong learning. Candidates:			
TF-V.A.1	Participate in professional development activities and professional technology organizations to support ongoing professional growth related to technology.	Identify resources and participate in professional development activities and professional technology organizations to support ongoing professional growth related to technology.	Use resources and professional development activities available from professional technology organizations to support ongoing professional growth related to technology.
TF-V.A.2	Develop an awareness of district-wide policies for the professional growth opportunities for staff, faculty, and administrators.	Disseminate information on district-wide policies for professional growth opportunities for staff, faculty, and administrators.	Implement policies that support district-wide professional growth opportunities for staff, faculty, and administrators.
B. Continually evaluate and reflect on professional practice to make informed decisions regarding the use of technology in support of student learning. Candidates:			
TF-V.B.1	Reflect on professional practice to make informed decisions regarding the use of technology in support of student learning.	Continually evaluate and reflect on professional practice to make informed decisions regarding the use of technology in support of student learning.	Continually evaluate professional practice to make informed decisions regarding the use of technology in support of student learning and disseminate findings to district administrators.
C. Apply technology to increase productivity. Candidates:			
TF-V.C.1	Model features of word processing, desktop publishing, graphics programs, and utilities to demonstrate professional products.	Model advanced features of word processing, desktop publishing, graphics programs, and utilities to develop professional products.	Model the integration of advanced features of word processing, desktop publishing, graphics programs, and utilities to demonstrate professional products.

TF-V.C.2	Locate, select, capture, and integrate video and digital images, in varying formats for use in presentations, publications and/or other products.	Assist others in locating, selecting, capturing, and integrating video and digital images, in varying formats for use in presentations, publications, and/or other products.	Facilitate activities to help others in locating, selecting, capturing, and integrating video and digital images, in varying formats for use in presentations, publications and/or other products.
TF-V.C.3	Use specific-purpose electronic devices (such as graphing calculators, languages translators, scientific probeware, or electronic thesaurus) in content areas.	Demonstrate the use of specific-purpose electronic devices (such as graphing calculators, language translators, scientific probeware, or electronic thesaurus) in content areas.	Facilitate the use of specific-purpose electronic devices (such as graphing calculators, languages translators, scientific probeware, or electronic thesaurus) in content areas.
TF-V.C.4	Develop an awareness of several distance-learning systems to support personal/ professional development.	Use a variety of distance learning systems and use at least one to support personal and professional development.	Use a variety of distance learning systems to support personal/professional development.
TF-V.C.5	Develop an awareness of instructional design principles and its importance in the development of hypermedia and multimedia products.	Use instructional design principles to develop hypermedia and multimedia products to support personal and professional development.	Apply instructional design principles to demonstrate hypermedia/multimedia products to support professional development.
TF-V.C.6	Describe appropriate tools for communicating concepts, conducting research, and solving problems for an intended audience and purpose.	Select appropriate tools for communicating concepts, conducting research, and solving problems for an intended audience and purpose.	Model the use of appropriate tools for communicating concepts, conducting research, and solving problems for an intended audience and purpose.
TF-V.C.7	Develop an awareness of examples of emerging programming, authoring or problem-solving environments that support personal/professional development.	Use examples of emerging programming, authoring, or problem-solving environments that support personal and professional development.	Use examples of emerging programming, authoring or problem-solving environments that support personal/professional development.

TF-V.C.8	Identify preferences and defaults of operating systems and productivity tool programs that can be set to support personal and professional development.	Set and manipulate preferences, defaults and other selectable features of operating systems and productivity tool programs commonly found in P–12 schools.	Set and manipulate preferences and defaults of operating systems and productivity tool programs, and troubleshoot problems associated with their operation.

D. Use technology to communicate and collaborate with peers, parents, and the larger community in order to nurture student learning. Candidates:

TF-V.D.1	Use telecommunications tools and resources for information sharing, remote information access, and multimedia/hypermedia publishing in order to nurture student learning.	Model the use of telecommunications tools and resources for information sharing, remote information access, and multimedia/hypermedia publishing in order to nurture student learning.	Stay abreast of current telecommunications tools and resources for information sharing, remote information access, and multimedia/hypermedia publishing in order to nurture student learning.
TF-V.D.2	Communicate with colleagues about current research to support instruction, using electronic mail and Web browsers.	Communicate with colleagues and discuss current research to support instruction, using applications including electronic mail, online conferencing and Web browsers.	Communicate with colleagues and apply current research to support instruction, using applications including electronic mail, online conferencing and Web browsers.
TF-V.D.3	Participate in online collaborative curricular projects and team activities.	Participate in online collaborative curricular projects and team activities to build bodies of knowledge around specific topics.	Investigate and disseminate online collaborative curricular projects and team activities to build bodies of knowledge around specific topics.
TF-V.D.4	Design, demonstrate and maintain Web pages and sites that support personal productivity.	Design and maintain Web pages and sites that support communication between the school and community.	Design, maintain, and facilitate the development of Web pages and sites that support communication between teachers, school, and community.

Technology Facilitation Standard VI. (TF-VI)

Social, Ethical, Legal, and Human Issues. Educational technology facilitators understand the social, ethical, legal, and human issues surrounding the use of technology in P–12 schools and assist teachers in applying that understanding in their practice. Educational technology facilitators:

Performance Indicator	Approaches Standard	Meets Standard	Exceeds Standard
A. Model and teach legal and ethical practice related to technology use. Candidates:			
TF-VI.A.1	Demonstrate and advocate legal and ethical behaviors among students, colleagues, and community members regarding the use of technology and information.	Develop strategies and provide professional development at the school/classroom level for teaching social, ethical, and legal issues and responsible use of technology.	Analyze rules, policies, and procedures to support the legal and ethical use of technology.
TF-VI.A.2	Summarize copyright laws related to use of images, music, video, and other digital resources in varying formats.	Assist others in summarizing copyright laws related to use of images, music, video, and other digital resources in varying formats.	Plan activities that focus on copyright laws related to use of images, music, video, and other digital resources in varying formats.
B. Apply technology resources to enable and empower learners with diverse backgrounds, characteristics, and abilities. Candidates:			
TF-VI.B.1	Facilitate students' use of technology that addresses their social needs and cultural identity and promotes their interaction with the global community.	Assist teachers in selecting and applying appropriate technology resources to enable and empower learners with diverse backgrounds, characteristics, and abilities.	Analyze and recommend appropriate technology resources to enable and empower learners with diverse backgrounds, characteristics, and abilities.
TF-VI.B.2	Facilitate students' use of technology that addresses their special needs.	Identify, classify and recommend adaptive/assistive hardware and software for students and teachers with special needs and assist in procurement and implementation.	Analyze and recommend appropriate adaptive/assistive hardware and software for students and teachers with special needs and assist in procurement and implementation.

C. Identify and use technology resources that affirm diversity. Candidates:

TF-VI.C.1	Identify capabilities and limitations of current and emerging technology resources that affirm diversity.	Assist teachers in selecting and applying appropriate technology resources to affirm diversity and address cultural and languages differences.	Recommend appropriate technology resources to affirm diversity and address cultural and language differences.

D. Promote safe and healthy use of technology resources. Candidates:

TF-VI.D.1	Enforce classroom procedures that guide students' safe and healthy use of technology and that comply with legal and professional responsibilities.	Assist teachers in selecting and applying appropriate technology resources to promote safe and healthy use of technology.	Recommend appropriate technology resources to promote safe and healthy use of technology.

E. Facilitate equitable access to technology resources for all students. Candidates:

TF-VI.E.1	Advocate equal access to technology for all students and teachers.	Develop a summary of effective school policies and classroom management strategies for achieving equitable access to technology resources for all students and teachers.	Conduct research to determine effective strategies for achieving equitable access to technology resources for all students and teachers.

Technology Facilitation Standard VII. (TF-VII)

Procedures, Policies, Planning, and Budgeting for Technology Environments. Educational technology facilitators promote the development and implementation of technology infrastructure, procedures, policies, plans, and budgets for P–12 schools. Educational technology facilitators:

Performance Indicator	Approaches Standard	Meets Standard	Exceeds Standard
A. Use the school technology facilities and resources to implement classroom instruction. Candidates:			
TF-VII.A.1	Identify plans to configure computer/technology systems and related peripherals in laboratory, classroom cluster, and other appropriate instructional arrangements.	Use plans to configure software/computer/technology systems and related peripherals in laboratory, classroom cluster, and other appropriate instructional arrangements.	Stay abreast of current developments to configure computer/technology systems and related peripherals in laboratory, classroom cluster, and other appropriate instructional arrangements.
TF-VII.A.2	Identify local mass storage devices and media to store and retrieve information and resources.	Use local mass storage devices and media to store and retrieve information and resources.	Stay abreast of local mass storage devices and media to store and retrieve information and resources.
TF-VII.A.3	Identify issues related to selecting, installing, and maintaining wide area networks (WAN) for school districts.	Discuss issues related to selecting, installing, and maintaining wide area networks (WAN) for school districts.	Differentiate among issues related to selecting, installing, and maintaining wide area networks (WAN) for school districts, and facilitate integration of technology infrastructure with the WAN.
TF-VII.A.4	Use software in classroom and administrative settings including productivity tools, information access/telecommunication tools, multimedia/hypermedia tools, school management tools, evaluation/portfolio tools, and computer-based instruction.	Model integration of software used in classroom and administrative settings including productivity tools, information access/telecommunication tools, multimedia/hypermedia tools, school management tools, evaluation/portfolio tools, and computer-based instruction.	Analyze software used in classroom and administrative settings including productivity tools, information access/telecommunication tools, multimedia/hypermedia tools, school management tools, evaluation/portfolio tools, and computer-based instruction.
TF-VII.A.5	Identify methods of installation, maintenance, inventory, and management of software libraries.	Utilize methods of installation, maintenance, inventory, and management of software libraries.	Analyze and critique methods of installation, maintenance, inventory, and management of software libraries.

TF-VII.A.6	Develop an awareness of strategies for troubleshooting and maintaining various hardware/software configurations found in school settings.	Use and apply strategies for troubleshooting and maintaining various hardware/software configurations found in school settings.	Stay abreast of current strategies for troubleshooting and maintaining various hardware/software configurations found in school settings.
TF-VII.A.7	Develop an awareness of network software packages used to operate a computer network system.	Utilize network software packages used to operate a computer network system.	Evaluate network software packages used to operate a computer network system and/or local area network (LAN).
TF-VII.A.8	Develop an awareness of the important roles for technology support personnel to assume to empower teachers and students to maximize technology resources to enhance student learning.	Work with technology support personnel to maximize the use of technology resources by administrators, teachers, and students to improve student learning.	Identify areas where support personnel are needed to manage and enhance use of technology resources in the school by administrators, teachers and students.

B. Follow procedures and guidelines used in planning and purchasing technology resources. Candidates:

TF-VII.B.1	Develop an awareness of instructional software to support and enhance the school curriculum and demonstrate recommendations for purchase.	Identify instructional software to support and enhance the school curriculum and develop recommendations for purchase.	Evaluate instructional software to support and enhance the school curriculum and demonstrate recommendations for purchase.
TF-VII.B.2	Develop an awareness of guidelines for budget planning and management procedures related to educational computing and technology facilities and resources.	Discuss and apply guidelines for budget planning and management procedures related to educational computing and technology facilities and resources.	Analyze guidelines for budget planning and management procedures related to educational computing and technology facilities and resources.
TF-VII.B.3	Develop an awareness of procedures related to troubleshooting and preventive maintenance on technology infrastructure.	Discuss and apply procedures related to troubleshooting and preventive maintenance on technology infrastructure.	Stay abreast of current procedures related to troubleshooting and preventive maintenance on technology infrastructure.

TF-VII.B.4	Develop an awareness of current information involving facilities planning issues and computer-related technologies.	Apply current information involving facilities planning issues and computer-related technologies.	Analyze and apply current information involving facilities planning issues and computer-related technologies.
TF-VII.B.5	Develop an awareness of policies and procedures concerning staging, scheduling, and security for managing computers/technology in a variety of school/laboratory/classroom settings.	Suggest policies and procedures concerning staging, scheduling, and security for managing computers/technology in a variety of school/laboratory/classroom settings.	Apply policies and procedures concerning staging, scheduling, and security for managing computers/technology in a variety of school/laboratory/classroom settings.
TF-VII.B.6	Develop an awareness of distance learning facilities.	Use distance and online learning facilities.	Use distance and online learning facilities routinely.
TF-VII.B.7	Develop an awareness of recommended specifications for purchasing technology systems in school settings.	Describe and identify recommended specifications for purchasing technology systems in school settings.	Research specifications for purchasing technology systems.

C. Participate in professional development opportunities related to management of school facilities, technology resources, and purchases. Candidates:

TF-VII.C.1	Identify opportunities for technology professional development at the building/school level utilizing adult learning theory.	Support technology professional development at the building/school level utilizing adult learning theory.	Design and plan technology professional development at the building/school level utilizing adult learning theory.

Technology Facilitation Standard VIII. (TF-VIII)

Leadership and Vision. Educational technology facilitators will contribute to the shared vision for campus integration of technology and foster an environment and culture conducive to the realization of the vision. Educational technology facilitators:

Performance Indicator	Approaches Standard	Meets Standard	Exceeds Standard
A. Utilize school technology facilities and resources to implement classroom instruction. Candidates:			
TF-VIII.A.1	Develop an awareness of current research in educational technology.	Discuss and evaluate current research in educational technology.	Locate and disseminate current research in educational technology.
B. Apply strategies for and knowledge of issues related to managing the change process in schools. Candidates:			
TF-VIII.B.1	Develop an awareness of the history of technology use in schools.	Discuss the history of technology use in schools.	Develop and implement activities that focus on the history of technology use in schools.
C. Apply effective group process skills. Candidates:			
TF-VIII.C.1	Develop an awareness of the importance of forming school partnerships to support technology integration and examine an existing partnership within a school setting.	Discuss the rationale for forming school partnerships to support technology integration and examine an existing partnership within a school setting.	Provide information on the benefits of forming school partnerships to support technology integration and locate an existing partnership within a school setting.
D. Lead in the development and evaluation of district technology planning and implementation. Candidates:			
TF-VIII.D.1	Develop an awareness of the importance of using cooperative group processes.	Participate in cooperative group processes and identify the processes that were effective.	Disseminate information on effective cooperative group processes.
TF-VIII.D.2	Develop an awareness of the importance of the school technology environment.	Conduct an evaluation of a school technology environment.	Create an evaluation instrument to use to conduct an evaluation of a school technology environment.
TF-VIII.D.3	Recognize the importance of national, state, and local standards for integrating technology in the school environment.	Identify and discuss national, state, and local standards for integrating technology in the school environment.	Examine the impact of national, state, and local standards for integrating technology in the school environment.

TF-VIII.D.4	Examine curriculum activities or performances that meet national, state, and local technology standards.	Describe curriculum activities or performances that meet national, state, and local technology standards.	Examine the impact of curriculum activities or performances that meet national, state, and local technology standards.
TF-VIII.D.5	Develop an awareness of the issues related to developing a school technology plan.	Discuss issues related to developing a school technology plan.	Determine essential components of a school technology plan.
TF-VIII.D.6	Develop an awareness of the issues related to hardware and software acquisition and management.	Examine issues related to hardware and software acquisition and management.	Determine strategies and procedures needed for resource acquisition and management of technology-based systems including hardware and software.

E. Engage in supervised field-based experiences with accomplished technology facilitators and/or directors. Candidates:

TF-VIII.E.1	Develop an awareness of the components needed for effective field-based experiences in instructional program development, professional development, facility and resource management, WAN/LAN/wireless systems, or managing change related to technology use in school-based settings.	Examine components needed for effective field-based experiences in instructional program development, professional development, facility and resource management, WAN/LAN/wireless systems, or managing change related to technology use in school-based settings.	Determine components needed for effective field-based experiences in instructional program development, professional development, facility and resource management, WAN/LAN/wireless systems, or managing change related to technology use in school-based settings.

Technology Leadership (TL) Standards and Rubrics

Supporting Explanation

Units preparing candidates for this program may collect artifacts demonstrating candidates' performances in addressing the program standards, assess performance by evaluating artifacts using the above ISTE/NCATE Technology Leadership (TL) rubrics and aggregate the performance data collected to provide program-level data. The standards and rubrics should help faculty to identify the kinds of experiences they provide in their courses and whether or not those experiences generate candidate performance that approaches, meets, or exceeds the standards. Each major assignment or experience should be planned to address the performance indicators at levels appropriate to prepare candidates for the essential benchmark assessments. Candidates should be aware of the level of expectations for their performance on each assignment and that their performances will be measured against the "meets standard" performance level of the rubric.

Rubrics, observation tools, self assessments, test scores, with quantifiable performance assessment ratings are often used to collect performance data that can be used to measure individual performance and be aggregated for program-level performance. When artifacts are collected in a portfolio, the portfolio may be available for online review, to substantiate the quality of work of your candidates. But, the performance artifacts used as evidence in the matrix should be selective. If you are indicating a website where student work is used to support the standard/indicator, provide performance data, the levels of your evaluation system, and an example of candidate work that was rated at each level.

Technology Leadership Scoring Rubrics

Technology Leadership Standard I. (TL-I)

Technology Operations and Concepts. Educational technology leaders demonstrate an in-depth understanding of technology operations and concepts. Educational technology leaders:

Performance Indicator	Approaches Standard	Meets Standard	Exceeds Standard
A. Demonstrate knowledge, skills, and understanding of conepts related to technology (as described in the ISTE National Educational Technology Standards for Teachers). Candidates:			
TL-I.A.1	Conduct needs assessment to determine baseline data on teachers' knowledge, skills, and understanding of concepts related to technology.	Identify and evaluate components needed for the continual growth of knowledge, skills, and understanding of concepts related to technology.	Develop and implement a professional development model that ensures continual growth in knowledge, skills, and understanding of concepts related to technology.
TL-I.A.2	Evaluate the effectiveness of modeling used to develop teachers' knowledge, skills, and understanding of concepts related to technology.	Offer a variety of professional development opportunities that facilitate the ongoing development of knowledge, skills, and understanding of concepts related to technology.	Assess a variety of professional development opportunities that facilitate the ongoing development of knowledge, skills, and understanding of concepts related to technology.
B. Demonstrate continual growth in technology knowledge and skills to stay abreast of current and emerging technologies. Candidates:			
TL-I.B.1	Evaluate the effectiveness of the modeling of appropriate strategies essential to continued growth and development of the understanding of technology operations and concepts.	Offer a variety of professional development opportunities that facilitate the continued growth and development of the understanding of technology operations and concepts.	Develop and assess a variety of professional development opportunities that facilitate the continued growth and development of the understanding of technology operations and concepts.

Technology Leadership Standard II. (TL-II)

Planning and Designing Learning Environments and Experiences. Educational technology leaders plan, design, and model effective learning environments and multiple experiences supported by technology. Educational technology leaders:

Performance Indicator	Approaches Standard	Meets Standard	Exceeds Standard
A. Design developmentally appropriate learning opportunities that apply technology-enhanced instructional strategies to support the diverse needs of learners. Candidates:			
TL-II.A.1	Model the creation of developmentally appropriate curriculum units that use technology.	Research and disseminate project-based instructional units modeling appropriate uses of technology to support learning.	Build an online database of project-based instructional units modeling appropriate uses of technology to support learning.
TL-II.A.2	Model methods and strategies for teaching computer/technology concepts and skills within the context of classroom learning.	Identify and evaluate methods and strategies for teaching computer/technology concepts and skills within the context of classroom learning and coordinate dissemination of best practices at the district/state/regional level.	Identify and evaluate methods and strategies for teaching computer/technology concepts and skills within the context of classroom learning and coordinate dissemination of best practices at the national and international level.
TL-II.A.3	Model strategies to support the diverse needs of learners including adaptive and assistive technologies and disseminate information to teachers.	Stay abreast of current technology resources and strategies to support the diverse needs of learners including adaptive and assistive technologies and disseminate information to teachers.	Develop technology resources and strategies to support the diverse needs of learners including adaptive and assistive technologies and disseminate information to teachers.
B. Apply current research on teaching and learning with technology when planning learning environments and experiences. Candidates:			
TL-II.B.1	Model strategies reflecting current research on teaching and learning with technology when planning learning environments and experiences.	Locate and evaluate current research on teaching and learning with technology when planning learning environments and experiences.	Conduct research on teaching and learning with technology when planning learning environments and experiences.

C. Identify and locate technology resources and evaluate them for accuracy and suitability. Candidates:

TL-II.C.1	Model the use of technology resources reflecting district and state standards.	Identify technology resources and evaluate them for accuracy and suitability based on the content standards.	Develop technology resources based on the content standards.
TL-II.C.2	Create professional development activities that reflect content standards and integrate technology resources.	Provide ongoing appropriate professional development to disseminate the use of technology resources that reflect content standards.	Develop, implement, and assess a professional development model aligning technology resources and content standards.

D. Plan for the management of technology resources within the context of learning activities. Candidates:

TL-II.D.1	Model the use of technology resources within the context of learning activities.	Identify and evaluate options for the management of technology resources within the context of learning activities.	Research findings on the management of technology resources within the context of learning activities and create a professional development model.

E. Plan strategies to manage student learning in a technology-enhanced environment. Candidates:

TL-II.E.1	Model a variety of strategies to manage student learning in a technology-enhanced environment and support the teachers as they implement the strategies.	Continually evaluate a variety of strategies to manage student learning in a technology-enhanced environment and disseminate through professional development activities.	Conduct research on a variety of strategies to manage student learning in a technology-enhanced environment and disseminate results.

F. Identify and apply instructional design principles associated with the development of technology resources. Candidates:

TL-II.F.1	Model the use of appropriate instructional design principles associated with the development of technology resources.	Identify and evaluate instructional design principles associated with the development of technology resources.	Develop, implement and evaluate a professional development model for assisting teachers in the identification and application of instructional design principles associated with the development of technology resources.

Technology Leadership Standard III. (TL-III)

Teaching, Learning, and the Curriculum. Educational technology leaders apply and implement curriculum plans that include methods and strategies for applying technology to maximize student learning. Educational technology leaders:

Performance Indicator	Approaches Standard	Meets Standard	Exceeds Standard
A. Facilitate technology-enhanced experiences that address content standards and student technology standards. Candidates:			
TL-III.A.1	Analyze methods and facilitate strategies for teaching concepts and skills that support integration of technology productivity tools (refer to NETS for students).	Design methods and strategies for teaching concepts and skills that support integration of technology productivity tools (refer to NETS for students).	Model strategies for teaching concepts and skills that support integration of technology productivity tools (refer to NETS for students).
TL-III.A.2	Summarize major research findings and trends related to the use of technology in education to support integration throughout the curriculum.	Design methods for teaching concepts and skills that support integration of communication tools (refer to NETS for students).	Model strategies for teaching concepts and skills that support integration of communication tools (refer to NETS for students).
TL-III.A.3	Analyze methods and support teachers as they use strategies for teaching concepts and skills that support integration of research tools (refer to NETS for students).	Design methods and strategies for teaching concepts and skills that support integration of research tools (refer to NETS for students).	Model strategies for teaching concepts and skills that support integration of research tools (refer to NETS for students).
TL-III.A.4	Analyze methods and facilitate strategies for teaching concepts and skills that support integration of problem-solving/decision-making tools (refer to NETS for students).	Design methods and model strategies for teaching concepts and skills that support integration of problem-solving/decision-making tools (refer to NETS for students).	Implement methods and strategies for teaching concepts and skills that support integration of problem-solving/decision-making tools (refer to NETS for students).
TL-III.A.5	Analyze methods and facilitate strategies for teaching concepts and skills that support use of media-based tools such as television, audio, print media, and graphics.	Design methods and model strategies for teaching concepts and skills that support use of media-based tools such as television, audio, print media, and graphics.	Implement methods and model strategies for teaching concepts and skills that support use of media-based tools such as television, audio, print media, and graphics.

TL-III.A.6	Analyze methods and strategies for teaching concepts and skills that support use of distance learning systems appropriate in a school environment.	Evaluate methods and strategies for teaching concepts and skills that support use of distance learning systems appropriate in a school environment.	Implement methods and strategies for teaching concepts and skills that support use of distance learning systems appropriate in a school environment.
TL-III.A.7	Analyze methods for teaching concepts and skills that support use of Web-based and non Web-based authoring tools in a school environment.	Design methods and model strategies for teaching concepts and skills that support use of Web-based and non Web-based authoring tools in a school environment.	Implement methods and strategies for teaching concepts and skills that support use of Web-based and non Web-based authoring tools in a school environment.

B. Use technology to support learner-centered strategies that address the diverse needs of students. Candidates:

TL-III.B.1	Analyze methods and strategies for integrating technology resources that support the needs of diverse learners including adaptive and assistive technology.	Design methods and strategies for integrating technology resources that support the needs of diverse learners including adaptive and assistive technology.	Implement methods and strategies for integrating technology resources that support the needs of diverse learners including adaptive and assistive technology.

C. Apply technology to demonstrate students' higher-order skills and creativity. Candidates:

TL-III.C.1	Analyze methods and facilitate strategies for teaching problem-solving principles and skills using technology resources.	Design methods and model strategies for teaching hypermedia development, scripting, and/or computer programming, in a problem-solving context in the school environment.	Implement strategies for teaching hypermedia development, scripting, and/or computer programming, in a problem-solving context in the school environment.

D. Manage student learning activities in a technology-enhanced environment. Candidates:

TL-III.D.1	Analyze methods and classroom management strategies for teaching technology concepts and skills in individual, small group, classroom, and/or lab settings.	Design methods and model classroom management strategies for teaching technology concepts and skills used in P–12 environments.	Implement methods and classroom management strategies for teaching technology concepts and skills used in P–12 environments.

E. Use current research and district/region/state/national content and technology standards to build lessons and units of instruction. Candidates:

TL-III.E.1	Disseminate information regarding curricular methods and strategies that are aligned with district/region/state/national content and technology standards.	Disseminate curricular methods and strategies that are aligned with district/region/state/national content and technology standards.	Model curricular methods and strategies that are aligned with district/region/state/national content and technology standards.
TL-III.E.2	Summarize and disseminate major research findings and trends related to the use of technology in education to support integration throughout the curriculum.	Investigate major research findings and trends related to the use of technology in education to support integration throughout the curriculum.	Disseminate major research findings and trends related to the use of technology in education to support integration throughout the curriculum.

Technology Leadership Standard IV. (TL-IV)

Assessment and Evaluation. Educational technology leaders communicate research on the use of technology to implement effective assessment and evaluation strategies. Educational technology leaders:

Performance Indicator	Approaches Standard	Meets Standard	Exceeds Standard
A. Apply technology in assessing student learning of subject matter using a variety of assessment techniques. Candidates:			
TL-IV.A.1	Analyze methods and facilitate the use of strategies to assess student learning of subject matter using a variety of assessment techniques.	Facilitate the development of a variety of techniques to use technology to assess student learning of subject matter.	Develop, implement and assess innovative techniques, which include the use of technology for assessing student learning.
TL-IV.A.2	Analyze methods and facilitate the use of strategies to improve learning and instruction through the evaluation and assessment of artifacts and data.	Provide technology resources for assessment and evaluation of artifacts and data.	Develop, implement and assess innovative technology resources for assessment and evaluation of artifacts and data.
B. Use technology resources to collect and analyze data, interpret results, and communicate findings to improve instructional practice and maximize student learning. Candidates:			
TL-IV.B.1	Examine the validity and reliability of technology resources to collect and analyze data, interpret results, and communicate findings to improve instructional practice and maximize student learning.	Identify and procure technology resources to aid in analysis and interpretation of data.	Develop, implement and assess innovative technology resources to aid in analysis and interpretation of data.
C. Apply multiple methods of evaluation to determine students' appropriate use of technology resources for learning, communication, and productivity. Candidates:			
TL-IV.C.1	Recommend evaluation strategies for improving students' use of technology resources for learning, communication, and productivity.	Design strategies and methods for evaluating the effectiveness of technology resources for learning, communication, and productivity.	Research and disseminate findings on the effectiveness of technology resources for evaluating learning, communication, and productivity.

TL-IV.C.2	Analyze data from a research project that includes evaluating the use of a specific technology in a P–12 environment.	Conduct a research project that includes evaluating the use of a specific technology in a P–12 environment.	Design a research project that includes evaluating the use of several technology resources in a P–12 environment.

Technology Leadership Standard V. (TL-V)

Productivity and Professional Practice. Educational technology leaders design, develop, evaluate and model products created using technology resources to improve and enhance their productivity and professional practice. Educational technology leaders:

Performance Indicator	Approaches Standard	Meets Standard	Exceeds Standard
A. Use technology resources to engage in ongoing professional development and lifelong learning. Candidates:			
TL-V.A.1	Use resources and professional development activities available from professional technology organizations to support ongoing professional growth related to technology.	Design, prepare, and conduct professional development activities to present at the school/district level and at professional technology conferences to support ongoing professional growth related to technology.	Evaluate professional development activities presented at professional technology conferences to support ongoing professional growth related to technology.
TL-V.A.2	Implement policies that support district-wide professional growth opportunities for staff, faculty, and administrators.	Plan and implement policies that support district-wide professional growth opportunities for staff, faculty, and administrators.	Plan, implement, and revise policies that support district-wide professional growth opportunities for staff, faculty, and administrators.
B. Continually evaluate and reflect on professional practice to make informed decisions regarding the use of technology in support of student learning. Candidates:			
TL-V.B.1	Continually evaluate professional practice to make informed decisions regarding the use of technology in support of student learning and disseminate findings to district administrators.	Based on evaluations, make recommendations for changes in professional practices regarding the use of technology in support of student learning.	Implement changes based on recommendations for changes in professional practices regarding use of technology in support of student learning.
C. Apply technology to increase productivity. Candidates:			
TL-V.C.1	Model the integration of advanced features of word processing, desktop publishing, graphics programs, and utilities to develop professional products.	Model the integration of data from multiple software applications using advanced features of applications such as word processing, database, spreadsheet, communication, and other tools into a product.	Create multimedia presentations integrated with multiple types of data using advanced features of a presentation tool and model them to audiences inside and outside the district using computer projection systems.

TL-V.C.2	Facilitate activities to help others in locating, selecting, capturing, and integrating video and digital images, in varying formats for use in presentations, publications and/or other products.	Create multimedia presentations integrated with multiple types of data using advanced features of a presentation tool and model them to district staff using computer projection systems.	Create multimedia presentations integrated with multiple types of data using advanced features of a presentation tool and model them to audiences inside and outside the district using computer projection systems.
TL-V.C.3	Facilitate the use of specific-purpose electronic devices (such as graphing calculators, language translators, scientific probeware, or electronic thesaurus) in content areas.	Document and assess field-based experiences and observations using specific-purpose electronic devices.	Document and assess field-based experiences and observations using specific-purpose electronic devices and then collaborate with peers regarding results.
TL-V.C.4	Use a variety of distance learning systems to support personal/professional development.	Use distance learning delivery systems to conduct and provide professional development opportunities for students, teachers, administrators, and staff.	Use distance learning delivery systems to conduct and provide professional development opportunities for students, teachers, administrators, and staff and other schools in surrounding communities.
TL-V.C.5	Apply instructional design principles to develop hypermedia/multimedia products to support professional development.	Apply instructional design principles to develop and analyze substantive interactive multimedia computer-based instructional products.	Apply instructional design principles to develop, analyze, and then compare substantive interactive multimedia computer-based instructional products.
TL-V.C.6	Model the use of appropriate tools for communicating concepts, conducting research, and solving problems for an intended audience and purpose.	Design and practice strategies for testing functions and evaluating technology use effectiveness of instructional products that were developed using multiple technology tools.	Design and practice strategies for analyzing content accuracy, testing functions, and evaluating technology use effectiveness of instructional products that were developed using multiple technology tools.

TL-V.C.7	Use examples of emerging programming, authoring or problem-solving environments that support personal/professional development.	Analyze examples of emerging programming, authoring or problem-solving environments that support personal and professional development, and make recommendations for integration at school/district level.	Analyze and model examples of emerging programming, authoring or problem-solving environments that support personal/professional development, and make recommendations for integration at school/district level.
TL-V.C.8	Set and manipulate preferences and defaults of operating systems and productivity tool programs, and troubleshoot problems associated with their operation.	Analyze and modify the features and preferences of major operating systems and/or productivity tool programs when developing products to solve problems encountered with their operation and/or to enhance their capability.	Analyze, evaluate, and modify the features and preferences of major operating systems and/or productivity tool programs when developing products to solve problems encountered with their operation and/or to enhance their capability.
D. Use technology to communicate and collaborate with peers, parents, and the larger community in order to nurture student learning. Candidates:			
TL-V.D.1	Stay abreast of current telecommunications tools and resources for information sharing, remote information access, and multimedia/hypermedia publishing in order to nurture student learning.	Model and implement the use of telecommunications tools and resources to foster and support information sharing, remote information access, and communication between students, school staff, parents, and local community.	Model and analyze the use of telecommunications tools and resources to foster and support information sharing, remote information access, and communication between students, school staff, parents, and the local/state/national/international community.
TL-V.D.2	Communicate with colleagues and apply current research to support instruction, using applications including electronic mail, online conferencing and Web browsers.	Organize, coordinate, and participate in an online learning community related to the use of technology to support learning.	Organize, coordinate, and monitor an online learning community designed for students, staff and members of the community related to a predefined curricular subject.

TL-V.D.3	Investigate and disseminate online collaborative curricular projects and team activities to build bodies of knowledge around specific topics.	Organize and coordinate online collaborative curricular projects with corresponding team activities/responsibilities to build bodies of knowledge around specific topics.	Organize, coordinate, and monitor online collaborative curricular projects with corresponding team activities/responsibilities to build bodies of knowledge around specific topics.
TL-V.D.4	Design, maintain, and facilitate the development of Web pages and sites that support communication between teachers, school, and community.	Design, modify, maintain, and facilitate the development of Web pages and sites that support communication and information access between the entire school district and local/state/ national/international communities.	Develop, organize, and conduct professional development to enable site/department Web personnel to develop and modify school-based Web sites.

Technology Leadership Standard VI. (TL-VI)

Social, Ethical, Legal, and Human Issues. Educational technology leaders understand the social, ethical, legal, and human issues surrounding the use of technology in P–12 schools and develop programs facilitating application of that understanding in practice throughout their district/region/state. Educational technology leaders:

Performance Indicator	Approaches Standard	Meets Standard	Exceeds Standard
A. Model and teach legal and ethical practice related to technology use. Candidates:			
TL-VI.A.1	Analyze rules, policies, and procedures to support the legal and ethical use of technology.	Establish and communicate clear rules, policies, and procedures to support legal and ethical use of technologies at the district/region/state levels.	Advocate rules, policies, and procedures to support legal and ethical use of technologies at the national and international level.
TL-VI.A.2	Plan activities that focus on copyright laws related to use of images, music, video, and other digital resources in varying formats.	Implement a plan for documenting adherence to copyright laws.	Implement an evaluation system to determine adherence to copyright laws.
B. Apply technology resources to enable and empower learners with diverse backgrounds, characteristics, and abilities. Candidates:			
TL-VI.B.1	Analyze and recommend appropriate technology resources to enable and empower learners with diverse backgrounds, characteristics, and abilities.	Communicate research on best practices related to applying appropriate technology resources to enable and empower learners with diverse backgrounds, characteristics, and abilities.	Research best practices related to applying appropriate technology resources to enable and empower learners with diverse backgrounds, characteristics, and abilities.
TL-VI.B.2	Analyze and recommend appropriate adaptive/assistive hardware and software for students and teachers with special needs and assist in procurement and implementation.	Develop policies and provide professional development related to acquisition and use of appropriate adaptive/assistive hardware and software for students and teachers with special needs.	Research adaptive/assistive hardware and software for students and teachers with special needs and advocate appropriate use at the national and international level.

C. Identify and use technology resources that affirm diversity. Candidates:

TL-VI.C.1	Recommend appropriate technology resources to affirm diversity and address cultural and language differences.	Communicate research on best practices related to applying appropriate technology resources to affirm diversity and address cultural and language differences.	Conduct research to determine best practices for applying appropriate technology resources to affirm diversity and address cultural and language differences.

D. Promote safe and healthy use of technology resources. Candidates:

TL-VI.D.1	Recommend appropriate technology resources to promote safe and healthy use of technology.	Communicate research and establish policies to promote safe and healthy use of technology.	Conduct research and advocate safe and healthy use of technology.

E. Facilitate equitable access to technology resources for all students. Candidates:

TL-VI.E.1	Conduct research to determine effective strategies for achieving equitable access to technology resources for all students and teachers.	Use research findings in establishing policy and implementation strategies to promote equitable access to technology resources for students and teachers.	Advocate national and international policies that provide equitable access to technology resources for all students and teachers.

Technology Leadership Standard VII. (TL-VII)

Procedures, Policies, Planning, and Budgeting for Technology Environments. Educational technology leaders coordinate development and direct implementation of technology infrastructure procedures, policies, plans, and budgets for P-12 schools. Educational technology leaders:

Performance Indicator	Approaches Standard	Meets Standard	Exceeds Standard
A. Use the school technology facilities and resources to implement classroom instruction. Candidates:			
TL-VII.A.1	Stay abreast of current developments to configure computer/technology systems and related peripherals in laboratory, classroom cluster, and other appropriate instructional arrangements.	Develop plans to configure software/computer/technology systems and related peripherals in laboratory, classroom cluster, and other appropriate instructional arrangements.	Disseminate plans to configure computer/technology systems and related peripherals in laboratory, classroom cluster, and other appropriate instructional arrangements.
TL-VII.A.2	Stay abreast of local mass storage devices and media to store and retrieve information and resources.	Install local mass storage devices and media to store and retrieve information and resources.	Configure local mass storage devices and media to store and retrieve information and resources.
TL-VII.A.3	Differentiate among issues related to selecting, installing, and maintaining wide area networks (WAN) for school districts, and facilitate integration of technology infrastructure with the WAN.	Prioritize issues related to selecting, installing, and maintaining wide area networks (WAN) for school districts, and facilitate integration of technology infrastructure with the WAN.	Make modifications based upon prioritized issues related to selecting, installing, and maintaining wide area networks (WAN) for school districts, and facilitate integration of technology infrastructure with the WAN.
TL-VII.A.4	Analyze software used in classroom and administrative settings including productivity tools, information access/telecommunication tools, multimedia/hypermedia tools, school management tools, evaluation/portfolio tools, and computer-based instruction.	Manage software used in classroom and administrative settings including productivity tools, information access/telecommunication tools, multimedia/hypermedia tools, school management tools, evaluation/portfolio tools, and computer-based instruction.	Evaluate and recommend software used in classroom and administrative settings including productivity tools, information access/telecommunication tools, multimedia/hypermedia tools, school management tools, evaluation/portfolio tools, and computer-based instruction.

TL-VII.A.5	Analyze and critique methods of installation, maintenance, inventory, and management of software libraries.	Evaluate methods of installation, maintenance, inventory, and management of software libraries.	Implement methods of installation, maintenance, inventory, and management of software libraries.
TL-VII.A.6	Stay abreast of current strategies for troubleshooting and maintaining various hardware/software configurations found in school settings.	Develop and disseminate strategies for troubleshooting and maintaining various hardware/software configurations found in school settings.	Implement strategies for troubleshooting and maintaining various hardware/software configurations found in school settings.
TL-VII.A.7	Evaluate network software packages used to operate a computer network system and/or local area network (LAN).	Select network software packages used to operate a computer network system and/or local area network (LAN).	Install and maintain network software packages used to operate a computer network system and/or local area network (LAN).
TL-VII.A.8	Identify areas where support personnel are needed to manage and enhance use of technology resources in the school by administrators, teachers and students.	Analyze needs for technology support personnel to manage school/district technology resources and maximize use by administrators, teachers, and students to improve student learning.	Formulate a plan to acquire technology support personnel to manage school/district technology resources and maximize use by administrators, teachers, and students to improve student learning.

B. Follow procedures and guidelines used in planning and purchasing technology resources. Candidates:

TL-VII.B.1	Evaluate instructional software to support and enhance the school curriculum and develop recommendations for purchase.	Investigate purchasing strategies and procedures for acquiring administrative and instructional software for educational settings.	Recommend purchasing strategies and procedures for acquiring administrative and instructional software for educational settings.
TL-VII.B.2	Analyze guidelines for budget planning and management procedures related to educational computing and technology facilities and resources.	Develop and utilize guidelines for budget planning and management procedures related to educational computing and technology facilities and resources.	Implement guidelines for budget planning and management procedures related to educational computing and technology facilities and resources.

TL-VII.B.3	Stay abreast of current procedures related to troubleshooting and preventive maintenance on technology infrastructure.	Develop and disseminate a system for analyzing and implementing procedures related to troubleshooting and preventive maintenance on technology infrastructure.	Operate a system for analyzing and implementing procedures related to troubleshooting, and preventive maintenance on technology infrastructure.
TL-VII.B.4	Analyze and apply current information involving facilities planning issues and computer-related technologies.	Maintain and disseminate current information involving facilities planning issues and computer-related technologies.	Evaluate current information involving facilities planning issues and computer-related technologies.
TL-VII.B.5	Apply policies and procedures concerning staging, scheduling, and security for managing computers/technology in a variety of school/laboratory/classroom settings.	Design and develop policies and procedures concerning staging, scheduling, and security for managing hardware, software, and related technologies in a variety of instructional and administrative school settings.	Evaluate policies and procedures concerning staging, scheduling, and security for managing hardware, software, and related technologies in a variety of instructional and administrative school settings.
TL-VII.B.6	Select distance and online learning facilities and resources.	Research and recommend systems and processes for implementation of distance and online learning facilities and infrastructure.	Operate systems and processes for implementation of distance and online learning facilities and infrastructure.
TL-VII.B.7	Research specifications for purchasing technology systems.	Differentiate among specifications for purchasing technology systems in school settings.	Make recommendations regarding specifications for purchasing technology systems.
C. Participate in professional development opportunities related to management of school facilities, technology resources, and purchases. Candidates:			
TL-VII.C.1	Design and plan technology professional development at the building/school level utilizing adult learning theory.	Implement technology professional development at the school/district level utilizing adult learning theory.	Evaluate technology professional development at the school/district level utilizing adult learning theory.

Technology Leadership Standard VIII. (TL-VII)

Leadership and Vision. Educational technology leaders will facilitate development of a shared vision for comprehensive integration of technology and foster an environment and culture conducive to the realization of the vision. Educational technology leaders:

Performance Indicator	Approaches Standard	Meets Standard	Exceeds Standard
A. Identify and apply educational and technology-related research, the psychology of learning, and instructional design principles in guiding the use of computers and technology in education. Candidates:			
TL-VIII.A.1	Locate and disseminate current research in educational technology.	Communicate and apply principles and practices of educational research in educational technology.	Conduct research in educational technology.
B. Apply strategies for and knowledge of issues related to managing the change process in schools. Candidates:			
TL-VIII.B.1	Develop and implement activities that focus on the history of technology use in schools.	Describe social and historical foundations of education and how they relate to the use of technology in schools.	Research the social historical foundations of education and how they relate to the use of technology in schools.
C. Apply effective group process skills. Candidates:			
TL-VIII.C.1	Provide information on the benefits of forming school partnerships to support technology integration and locate an existing partnership within a school setting.	Discuss issues relating to building collaborations, alliances, and partnerships involving educational technology initiatives.	Build collaborations, alliances, and partnerships involving educational technology initiatives.
D. Lead in the development and evaluation of district technology planning and implementation. Candidates:			
TL-VIII.D.1	Disseminate information on effective cooperative group processes.	Design and lead in the implementation of an effective group process related to technology leadership or planning.	Use effective group process related to technology leadership or planning.
TL-VIII.D.2	Create an evaluation instrument to use to conduct an evaluation of a school technology environment.	Use evaluation findings to recommend modifications in technology implementations.	Conduct evaluations to determine needed modifications in technology implementations.

TL-VIII.D.3	Examine the impact of national, state, and local standards for integrating technology in the school environment.	Use national, state, and local standards to develop curriculum plans for integrating technology in the school environment.	Assist in the development of national, state, and local standards for the development of curriculum plans for integrating technology in the school environment.
TL-VIII.D.4	Examine the impact of curriculum activities or performances that meet national, state, and local technology standards.	Develop curriculum activities or performances that meet national, state, and local technology standards.	Assist in the development of national, state, and local standards for the development of curriculum activities or performances.
TL-VIII.D.5	Determine essential components of a school technology plan.	Compare and evaluate district-level technology plans.	Facilitate the development of technology plans.
TL-VIII.D.6	Determine essential elements and strategies for developing a technology strategic plan.	Use strategic planning principles to lead and assist in the acquisition, implementation, and maintenance of technology resources.	Develop strategic planning principles to lead and assist in the acquisition, implementation, and maintenance of technology resources.
TL-VIII.D.7	Determine strategies and procedures needed for resource acquisition and management of technology-based systems including hardware and software.	Plan, develop, and implement strategies and procedures for resource acquisition and management of technology-based systems including hardware and software.	Research to determine effectiveness of strategies and procedures for resource acquisition and management of technology-based systems including hardware and software.

E. Engage in supervised field-based experiences with accomplished technology facilitators and/or directors. Candidates:

TL-VIII.E.1	Determine components needed for effective field-based experiences in instructional program development, professional development, facility and resource management, WAN/LAN/wireless systems, or managing change related to technology use in school-based settings.	Participate in a significant field-based activity involving experiences in instructional program development, professional development, facility and resource management, WAN/LAN/wireless systems, or managing change related to technology use in school-based settings.	Mentor participants involved in a significant field-based activity involving experiences in instructional program development, professional development, facility and resource management, WAN/LAN/wireless systems, or managing change related to technology use in school-based settings.

DATE DUE

OCT 0 6 2009			
OCT 1 9 2009			
NOV 1 2 2009			
NOV 1 8 2009			